TV FAMILY VALUES

TV FAMILY VALUES

Gender, Domestic Labor,

and 1980s Sitcoms

A LICE L EPPERT

RUTGERS UNIVERSITY PRESS

NEW BRUNSWICK, CAMDEN, AND NEWARK,

NEW JERSEY, AND LONDON

Library of Congress Cataloging-in-Publication Data

Names: Leppert, Alice, author.
Title: TV family values : gender, domestic labor, and 1980s sitcoms / Alice Leppert.
Description: New Brunswick : Rutgers University Press, [2019] | Includes bibliographical
    references and index.
Identifiers: LCCN 2018025411| ISBN 9780813592688 (cloth) | ISBN 9780813592671 (pbk.)
Subjects: LCSH: Situation comedies (Television programs)—United States. |
    United States—Social conditions—1980- | Television broadcasting—Social aspects—
    United States.
Classification: LCC PN1992.8.C66 L465 2019 | DDC 791.45/617—dc23
LC record available at https://lccn.loc.gov/2018025411

A British Cataloging-in-Publication record for this book is available from the British Library.

♾ The paper used in this publication meets the requirements of the American National
Standard for Information Sciences—Permanence of Paper for Printed Library Materials,
ANSI Z39.48-1992.

www.rutgersuniversitypress.org

Manufactured in the United States of America

For my parents, who managed to raise a feminist in the 1980s
(with a little help from *Who's the Boss?*)

CONTENTS

TV FAMILY VALUES

INTRODUCTION

The image of the "career woman" circulated broadly throughout the media and political landscape of the 1980s. She was demonized in some of the decade's most popular, iconic films. In *Kramer vs. Kramer* (director Robert Benton, 1979), she selfishly abandoned her child; in *Fatal Attraction* (director Adrian Lyne, 1987), she was a psychotic bunny killer. President Ronald Reagan blamed her for a downturn in the U.S. economy.[1] Yet network television saw her in a different light—she became their prized demographic. In the wake of a popular women's movement, family dynamics were in flux and hotly contested in the 1980s. While we tend to think of the Reagan era as a period where traditional "family values" were celebrated and their attendant gender roles were reified, network television's imperative to attract upper middle-class professional women viewers led to a bevy of programming depicting liberal feminist fantasies of gender equality in the realms of marriage, parenting, and housework. This book examines popular family sitcoms that were conceptualized during the conservative wave ushered in by Ronald Reagan and George H. W. Bush. I argue that the largely fantasy scenarios of 1980s sitcoms offered pedagogical models for organizing family life at a time when familial ideals were up for debate. The sitcom as a genre has long revolved around neatly resolved one-episode problems: 1980s family sitcoms literalize these lessons—thus *The Cosby Show*'s (NBC, 1984–1992) Cliff Huxtable (Bill Cosby) doles out parenting advice, and *Mr. Belvedere*'s (ABC, 1985–1990) titular character records each lesson learned in his episode-ending diary entries. By 1985, at least one family sitcom aired each night, thus offering daily guide-lines for the organization of family life to viewers struggling with competing sociocultural ideals of parenting, gender, family, and domestic labor.

In the United States during the 1980s, these competing discourses permeated the cultural, social, and political landscape. The shift to a service economy and the disappearance of stable union jobs, coupled with falling wages and a rising cost of living, made it nearly impossible to maintain a middle-class lifestyle with one income.[2] Increasing numbers of women did not enter the labor force purely as a result of liberal feminism's critique of domesticity; rather, many went to work out of economic necessity. The Reagan administration's welfare spending cuts collided with its ideological calls to strengthen the nuclear family. Ideals of free-market capitalism and individualism further appeared incongruous with the rhetoric of "family values." Clashes over women in the workforce, childcare, domestic labor, and the changing composition of the nuclear family often played out in popular media, resulting in many critics labeling the Reagan era as rife with postfeminism or a backlash against feminism.

Narratives of postfeminism and backlash see popular media as a driving force of these reactions to liberal feminism. In the foremost account, Susan Faludi details backlash as a Reaganite neoconservative move that locates feminism as an evil that has made women unhappy, dissatisfied, and, apparently, *more* oppressed.[3] Postfeminism takes a version of feminism for granted, suggesting that the goals of liberal feminism have been achieved, and thus feminist activism and organizing are no longer necessary; feminism is considered to be outmoded or passé. Postfeminism is especially tricky and dangerous for feminist politics, as it incorporates some aspects of liberal feminism, such as a belief in workplace equality, while eschewing other aspects, such as collective action. Critics often point to the media portrayal of career women and "new traditionalism" as exemplifying a postfeminist ethos in the 1980s. Here "choice" becomes the key word—in a postfeminist culture, women can *choose* to be working professionals or they can *choose* to be wives and mothers. Films like *Three Men and a Baby* (director Leonard Nimoy, 1987) and *Baby Boom* (director Charles Shyer, 1987), and television dramas like *L.A. Law* (NBC, 1986–1994) and *thirtysomething* (ABC, 1987–1991) serve as common touchstones for analyses of postfeminist media culture in the Reagan era.[4]

Seemingly reinforcing claims of postfeminism, television programming retreated to the home in the 1980s, replacing the workplace sitcoms of the 1970s[5] with a fresh crop of domestic family sitcoms.[6] While at first glance the prominence of this subgenre during the 1980s seems to confirm the "new traditionalism" critics locate in *thirtysomething*, these sitcoms often trouble the career woman–mother "choice" binary, working through the contradictions of postfeminism rather than erasing them.[7] The family sitcoms of the 1980s also incorporate elements of the workplace sitcom, positioning the home as a place of work rather than simply as a place of leisure. Instead of signaling a neoconservative return to the domestic nuclear family, and thus a return to the classic family sitcoms of the 1950s and 1960s, sitcoms of the 1980s question the very definitions of the nuclear family and of the domestic sphere. Many of these programs deal explicitly with the changing face of the family, featuring divorced and nontraditional family units. Episodes revolve around negotiating these "new" family arrangements, especially when it comes to parenting and housekeeping. These sitcoms usually aired during the first hour of prime time, anticipating that their target audience of upscale women would be watching television together with their children.

This book looks at these domestic family sitcoms as pedagogical texts that offered guidelines to the families of the 1980s struggling with competing ideas about family, gender, parenting, and domestic labor. While providing lessons in family and household governance, these sitcoms simultaneously enact liberal feminist fantasies of family, work, and domesticity. The generic pleasures of the sitcom contribute to these fantasies—problems are introduced and harmoniously solved in each episode, maintaining familial love, stability, and domestic bliss. Sitcom families become familiar, reliable sources of amusement and pleasure at the same time that they impart domestic lessons. I show how network television's industrial imperatives during the 1980s link up with the broader political, cultural, and social landscape, a connection that helps explain the explosion of family sitcoms and the particular family governance guidelines they offer.

Throughout the 1980s, networks were under increasing pressure from their advertisers to deliver the prized demographic of women ages eighteen to forty-nine, a group that marketers perceived as newly fragmented and difficult to target as more and more women worked outside the home. Hoping to reach professional women viewers, family sitcoms addressed the typical challenges facing dual-earner nuclear families and nonnuclear families alike: shifting gender roles, childcare, and domestic labor. The programs offered women viewers fantasy solutions to these common, wide-ranging problems: supportive husbands who did their share of the second shift, children who were cared for by family, friends, or exquisitely trained, dependable in-home caretakers, and domestic spaces expertly managed by loyal laborers who were treated and behaved as though they were part of the family. By and large, these fantasies flattened (or ignored) class and racial differences—the majority of the sitcom families were comfortably middle class and white.

Scholarship on sitcoms often reads these programs as hegemonic—the arguments often suggest that through the sitcom's generic narrative development, problems and anxieties are introduced and ultimately resolved in each episode (thus the "situation," or the status quo, remains intact).[8] For example, Bonnie Dow's analysis of *The Mary Tyler Moore Show* (CBS, 1970–1977) considers how the program incorporates feminist themes into the character of "The New Woman" in Mary (Mary Tyler Moore), a romantically unattached professional, yet undercuts its own version of feminism through Mary's constant deference to her male co-workers and her maternal characteristics.[9] One drawback of this approach is the tendency toward foregone conclusions. This literature becomes quite predictable as many scholars conclude that sitcoms had progressive potential, but this potential was ultimately undercut by the narrative impulse toward resolution, often read as the renewal of hegemonic consent. The fact that the generic conventions of the sitcom lend themselves to this sort of reading only makes it more ubiquitous and suggests the need for scholarship that will go beyond this framework. This book approaches the sitcoms not only as texts that promote dominant ideologies about family and gender, or as hegemonic tools for securing consent to these ideals, but also as sets of guidelines for organizing gender roles and family relations, for effective parenting, and for delegating household labor. These lessons were especially tailored to appeal to professional middle-class women, usually assumed to be heterosexual wives and mothers, who were actively engaged in reorganizing their family and work lives. While these programs undoubtedly often worked to renew consent to the nuclear family (though usually in a slightly altered form), I am more concerned with how they put forth guidelines for family governance and what exactly those guidelines were at a time when the meaning of the family was widely thought to be in flux.

Inspired by Michel Foucault, who saw government as dispersed through-out culture and everyday life, I look at sitcoms as a cultural technology, part of a broader governing rationality where the conduct of families is shaped in part through their engagement with media. Foucault's theory of governmental-ity suggests a move toward "governing at a distance" in liberal democracies, where we learn to govern ourselves in part through culture.[10] Few Foucauld-ian scholars have considered the family in depth, though Nikolas Rose affords the family a prominent position in citizen-shaping,[11] and Thomas Lemke suggests that for Foucault, "guidance for the family and for children, management of the household" were central to governance.[12] Jacques Donzelot traces the emergence of the "psy" disciplines as family experts in the mid-twentieth century and argues that they "regulated images" of the family, thus encouraging families to emulate sanctioned examples.[13] These "regulated images" might translate to television families—as Stephanie Coontz argues, "Our most powerful visions of traditional families derive from images that are still delivered to our homes in countless reruns of 1950s television sit-coms."[14] By working through governmentality, I consider sitcoms as a cultural technology that guides the conduct of families, serving as templates for family and household organization and management.

As a genre, family sitcoms have long offered lessons and morals, as Mary Beth Haralovich, Nina Leibman, and George Lipsitz have pointed out in their analy-ses of 1950s programming.[15] 1980s sitcoms offer lessons in both their form and content. For instance, similar to *Mr. Belvedere*'s closing journal entries, *Full House* (ABC, 1987–1995) usually ends with a heart-to-heart chat between one of the three caretakers and the children. The children learn a moral lesson, often at the same time that the caretakers learn lessons in parenting and household management. While not all of the sitcoms conclude so didactically, the form of the sitcom dictates that the problems that have plagued the family over the course of the episode must be resolved in some way before its conclusion. Family harmony is restored, problems overcome, thus the sitcom instructs in conflict resolution. In the 1980s, sitcoms revolve around lessons that deal with family organization, parenting, and domestic labor at a time when the makeup of the nuclear family and the strict gendered division of labor are beginning to change.

In an ethnographic study of media consumption and family life, Lara Descartes and Conrad Kottak found that 1980s family sitcoms had a powerful role in shaping middle-class family organization. They suggest, "The TV programs available during the 1980s played a prominent role in the enculturation of many of our Dexter [Michigan] informants."[16] Descartes and Kottak argue that media provide "scripts" after which families organize and model their everyday lives, both at work and at home. Particularly relevant to the liberal feminist fantasies put forth in 1980s sitcoms, Descartes and Kottak claim, "The media offer material with which to think through one's own circumstances by contemplating alternatives, including some that are unavailable in the local setting."[17] Descartes and Kottak's respondents (largely white middle-class mothers) positively received the fantasies that 1980s sitcoms offered. They found that "Working mothers tended to enjoy fictional media that portrayed positive family situations involving dual-income families. One full-time working mother recalled the show *Growing Pains*, saying, 'I liked that show. That was a working family show in my opinion, and I liked the way they did it. She worked, he worked, everybody had a role, and they were all a family, no matter if they were working or not, they came home and it was a family.'"[18] Programs like *Growing Pains* (ABC, 1985–1992) provided reassurance that the nuclear family, despite shifts in gender roles and socioeconomic changes, remained intact and that despite having to juggle two careers and children, "they came home and it was a family."

Family sitcoms reached their two-decade peak of saturation and ratings success in the mid-1980s, making up nearly 80 percent of total sitcoms on the air in 1985 and boasting four spots in the Nielsen Top 10 in 1986. By the mid-to-late 1990s, despite the addition of Fox, UPN, and WB, ratings success largely eluded family sitcoms, with only *Home Improvement* (ABC, 1991–1999) cracking the Nielsen Top 10 between 1995 and 1997. The 1970s produced very few family sitcoms, with less than five on the air between 1973 and 1978. The explosion of family sitcoms in the 1980s, their longevity, and their success all testify to the broader cultural and political obsession with redefining or restoring family life. The sitcoms I examine in this book offer family governance templates and fantasies of household and work harmony to a generation of families grappling with dramatic socioeconomic changes and shifting expectations of gender, work, and domesticity.

The first chapter demonstrates how the networks used family sitcoms to woo an audience of professional women that television advertisers actively coveted. Through an analysis of television industry trade and marketing journals, this chapter shows how networks and marketers sought to reach the professional wife and mother. Networks conceptualized this ideal viewer as someone who came home from work and watched the first hour of prime time together with her children. Marketers scrambled during the 1970s and 1980s to define what they perceived as a newly fragmented women's demographic, in regard to which CBS, NBC, and ABC increasingly employed market researchers to help them deliver programming that would attract a particular segment of women ages eighteen to forty-nine: upscale professional women who were thought to influence their peers. Prominent marketing research suggested that even women who did not work outside the home preferred seeing women with professional careers on screen. Family sitcoms managed to appeal to their target market of "career women" while also providing a fantasy of the seamless combination of career and family for homemakers attracted to the popular media image of the "new woman."

The second chapter investigates how sitcoms produced models of the "career" woman and ways that men were encouraged to reorient themselves in relation to family and domesticity. It considers how the sitcoms provide a liberal feminist fantasy of "having it all," complete with husbands who assumed household and parenting duties, through analyzing *Family Ties* (NBC, 1982–1989), *Growing Pains*, *The Cosby Show*, and *Silver Spoons* (NBC, 1982–1986; first-run syndication, 1986–1987). *Family Ties* and *Growing Pains* deal extensively with the workplace struggles endured by architect Elyse Keaton (Meredith Baxter Birney) and newspaper reporter Maggie Seaver (Joanna Kerns), respectively, as they return to work after prolonged absences spent child-rearing. Both programs represent the husbands sacrificing their own career ambitions for the sake of their wives and children. *The Cosby Show* and *Silver Spoons* both represent caring, involved patriarchs who model emotionally expressive and connected masculinity for their children. This chapter examines the various scenarios by which the characters and narratives structure their appeal to upper middle-class women.

The third chapter argues that family sitcoms entered into debates over the "day care crisis" of the 1980s, enacting solutions that the popular press and politicians often proposed, and refuting any calls for state-sponsored childcare. The programs provide fantasy solutions to an ongoing struggle for most American families, modeling idealized private childcare arrangements that would have been highly improbable if not simply impossible to achieve in ordinary lived experience. *Full House, My Two Dads* (NBC, 1987–1990), *Mr. Belvedere*, and *Kate & Allie* (CBS, 1984–1989) each in turn suggest that "live-in" help is the ideal solution to child-rearing. An extended family network helps Danny Tanner (Bob Saget) raise his three daughters in *Full House*; the dads on *My Two Dads* utilize "flex-time" to ensure that daughter Nicole (Staci Keanan) is supervised after school; *Mr. Belvedere* features a live-in nanny, which the popular press often lauded as many upper middle-class families' preferred solution; and *Kate & Allie* features two divorced friends who move in together, brokering a childcare co-op. With each of these options for live-in childcare, the family remains intact in the home, maintaining the family as an autonomous unit, albeit with a few extra members.

The fourth chapter explores domestic labor and household management. *Benson* (ABC, 1979–1986), *Charles in Charge* (CBS, 1984–1985; first-run syndication, 1987–1990), and *Who's the Boss?* (ABC, 1984–1992) all feature men assuming the role of domestic laborer, a role they transform into household manager. The interrogative title of *Who's the Boss?* suggests Tony Micelli's (Tony Danza) role as domestic employee of Angela Bower (Judith Light) somehow still renders him "the boss" of the household. Similarly, *Charles in Charge* positions Charles (Scott Baio) as both an erstwhile babysitter and "in charge" of the family and domestic bliss. *Benson* takes the audience-popular butler (Robert Guillaume) from *Soap* (ABC, 1977–1981) and transforms him into the glue that keeps the governor's mansion—and the government itself—together. Market research suggested that images of men performing housework were well received among many different female demographic groups, which helps explain why networks chose to cast attractive "hunky" stars to perform domestic labor with good cheer and charm. This chapter also examines the perpetuation of racial, ethnic, and class hierarchies at the heart of domestic employment.

While the majority of 1980s family sitcoms ignored class and racial differences, preferring to stage fantasies of upper middle-class domestic harmony, *Roseanne* (ABC, 1988–1997) and *Gimme a Break!* (NBC, 1981–1987)—the subjects of chapter five—highlighted these differences and at least partially broke from the fantasy mold. In this regard, scholars and critics have noted *Roseanne*'s representation of white working-class family life, lauding its appeal to realism. Still, in many ways, the Conner family lives a pared down version of the feminist fantasy on offer in most other sitcoms—though Roseanne (Roseanne Barr) and husband, Dan (John Goodman), head a dual-earner family by economic necessity, Dan is sensitive and caring and performs domestic labor, and the family often relies on an extended family network for childcare. *Gimme a Break!* similarly represents a white working-class family, but it directly addresses the racialized history of domestic labor through the voice of African American housekeeper Nell (Nell Carter) who repeatedly refers to the legacy of slavery in her conversations with the white patriarch police captain for whom she works. At the same time, Nell is devoted to and emotionally invested in the family, just as the housekeepers on *Mr. Belvedere*, *Who's the Boss?*, *Charles in Charge*, and *Benson* are. Though these programs engaged more clearly with the socioeconomic realities of the Reagan era, they still functioned as liberal feminist fantasies of family life.

While networks sought an audience of upscale women, sitcoms have long addressed children as well in their typical 8 P.M. time slot, informally (and briefly, officially) labeled the "family viewing hour." As the conclusion shows, sitcom producers promoted these programs to children and teens more explicitly as their child actors aged and when they sold them into syndication for enormous sums of money. In addition to their prime time dominance, family sitcoms regularly ran in the after-school and early evening hours from the late 1980s and well into the 1990s (and many remain in syndication today). Not only did these programs provide their original target audience of adult women viewers with liberal feminist fantasies of "having it all" but they also provided fantasy models for these women's children. Judith Light, who played Angela Bower on *Who's the Boss?*, acknowledges the impact her character had on girls growing up in the 1980s. In a 2015 interview, she noted, "To this day, I have young women come up to me and say, 'It was Angela Bower that changed my life about what I could do in the world as a woman. One of the first, most powerful feminists.'"[19] It is hard to imagine that women who grew up in the 1980s don't say similar things about Clair Huxtable (Phylicia Rashad), Elyse Keaton, Maggie Seaver, or Roseanne Conner. 1980s family sitcoms provided lessons in child-rearing, household management, and daily navigation of home and work life at a time when families were coming to terms with the economic realities that made two-paycheck households the necessity for attaining and maintaining a middle-class standard of living. At the same time, children growing up with these sitcoms had powerful new models of femininity and masculinity that counteracted the evil career women and hypermasculine "hard bodies" of some of the decade's most popular films and the neoconservative, traditional gender roles on offer in political discourse.

CHAPTER 1

SELLING MS. CONSUMER

In the early 1980s, U.S. network television was in trouble. Following two con-secutive labor strikes and a football strike, compounded by sagging ratings, changing demographics, aging programs, and failed pilots, tides finally began to turn for the networks as they shifted their schedules toward family-oriented situation comedy. This shift was further precipitated by debates over the "family viewing hour" and pressure groups like the Coalition for Better Television, which decried a lack of morality on television. The networks' financial troubles and their advertisers' demands for desirable demographics led to an increase in cheaper, profit-driven programming that could attract young adults and children as well as a newly defined "working women" demographic—programming that had the potential to remain in prime time for many seasons while reaping more financial gains in syndication.[1]

Bob Knight, regular *Variety* television writer, sounded a whistle in Janu-ary 1980, claiming that the networks were having trouble figuring out why their previously popular series were losing viewers. He suggested, "The possibility does exist that the mass audience is going through one of those changes in taste that occurs about every five years—and that could put a chill in any programmer at any web as he [*sic*] tries to fathom where that audience wants to go next."[2] Throughout the early 1980s, networks tried to buoy their failing, long-running sitcoms (Knight lists *Happy Days* [ABC, 1974–1984], *Three's Company* [ABC, 1977–1984], *Soap* [ABC, 1977–1981], and *Taxi* [ABC, 1978–1982; NBC, 1982–1983], among others) by pairing them with new sitcoms and launching spin-offs like *Joanie Loves Chachi* (ABC, 1982–1983) and *Benson* (ABC, 1979–1986). *Variety* devoted countless columns to detailing the networks' ordering of new sitcom pilots;[3] in fact, NBC, running last place in the ratings for several consecutive sea-sons, saw a new emphasis on sitcoms as key to its comeback strategy.[4] At the same time, NBC Entertainment president Brandon Tartikoff was quick to note that his 1980–1981 schedule would steer clear of "the standard half-hour sitcom—the one without a big star or a novel concept," which he thought could be "heading into a declining phase, like the Western some years back."[5] A few critics debated the quality of the newer sitcoms, suggesting they were a far cry from the "edgy" sitcoms of the 1970s. Producer Norman Lear blamed obsession with the bottom line for this perceived "decline" in sitcom quality. Speaking at the Kansas City Chamber of Commerce in 1980, Lear complained that "the content of television comedy is in a state of regression, reminiscent of bland, mindless, unstimulating comedies of the 1950s."[6] Knight also admitted concern that prime-time programming was skewing toward "light-hearted" fare featuring "physically-fit hunks of manhood."[7]

These "hunks of manhood" represented one strategy for reaching an upscale women's audience, provided that they performed a particularly domestic form of masculinity. One marketing study suggested that commercials featuring "male models participating in household tasks" were well received among female consumers.[8] Marketers scrambled during the late 1970s and 1980s to define and understand what they perceived as a newly fragmented women's demographic. Rena Bartos became a prominent voice among advertisers and marketers with a series of articles and her book *The Moving Target: What Every Marketer Should Know about Women*,[9] which divided women into four discrete categories: career working women, just-a-job working women, plan-to-work housewives, and stay-at-home housewives. Bartos's research, which suggested that the intention or desire to be in the workforce was more important in establishing a woman's consumer behavior than whether or not she was actually employed outside the home, was taken up in multiple studies and articles in the 1980s.[10] In marketing journals, Bartos's work was mobilized in the hopes of figuring out how to reach the largest number of women. As a 1985 article in the *Journal of Advertising Research* laments, "No longer do marketers have the luxury of advertising solely to the housewife to reach the majority of the market. In fact, it is not clear today that the dichotomy of the housewife versus the career woman is an appropriate categorization of the changing woman."[11]

In 1981, *Variety* reported, "Housewives favor commercials of women in liberated roles more than commercials of femmes in the more traditional roles of wife and mother."[12] Julie D'Acci cites one advertising executive's proposed solution to the problem: "Target the 'professional woman.' According to [corporate vice president of Colgate-Palmolive Tina] Santi, although professional women were still a small percentage of total working women, they were 'the *conspicuous consumers* . . . the role models [who] have enormous influence on the 41,000,000 women who are wage earners today.'"[13]

Indeed, as Sut Jhally and Justin Lewis found in their audience study of *The Cosby Show* (NBC, 1984–1992), "Although middle class viewers enjoyed seeing themselves reflected on the screen, most working class or lower middle class viewers simply did not want to see a family that was, in a material sense, more like them."[14] In order to reach these "role model" professional women, television networks produced sitcoms featuring female characters these demographically desirable women could aspire to—successful career women who were *emotionally* supported by domesticated dads who picked up household chores and child-care without hesitation or complaint. The networks received positive feedback on this trend from the National Commission on Working Women, which praised "'the emergence of men as nurturers as one of the most encouraging signs' of the fall lineup. 'Instead of being locked into aggressive roles, some male tv characters on the new fall shows actually care for their children, love their children—and do so without being objects of ridicule,' the report said."[15] The report noted that 76 percent of female characters on television were working outside the home. Still, sitcom career women maintained many elements of the home-maker image, perhaps so as not to completely alienate a fragment of the women's market. Thus family sitcoms both managed to appeal to their target market of career women while providing a fantasy of seamless combination of career and family for women who may not have been career women themselves, but who were attracted to the popular media image of the "new woman." In order to dis-tance themselves from the iconic traditional family sitcoms of the 1950s that loom large in the cultural imagination, 1980s family sitcoms playfully and self-consciously engage with the changing television industry, its place in the Ameri-can home, and its address to the professional woman and her family.

Targeting the "Working Woman" of the 1980s

In the 1970s, marketers struggled to understand what they loosely defined as "working women," a supposedly new demographic group with enhanced spend-ing power that complicated earlier monolithic notions of the housewife, often known as "Mrs. Consumer."[16] Bartos urged her marketing colleagues to stop con-ceiving of the women's market under the common umbrella of "any housewife, eighteen to forty-nine."[17] As Ved Prakash narrates the development of this strand of marketing research, studies began by comparing working and nonworking women,[18] then compared women's political views,[19] and finally looked at differ-ent types of women's employment and their attitudes toward their work.[20] Many of Prakash's citations come from the *Journal of Marketing*'s July 1977 issue, which published eight articles about the importance of finding new ways of marketing to a diversified women's demographic.[21] Barbara Hackman Franklin, then com-missioner of the U.S. Consumer Product Safety Commission, opened the issue with an editorial that proclaimed, "Marketers, take heed: Consumerism and the women's movement are strong, active allies that reinforce each other."[22] (Bartos echoes this sentiment in her book, with the pithy aside, "This isn't women's lib, it's marketing lib.")[23] Franklin further suggested that marketers needed to drastically revise their strategies for reaching female consumers, warning that "women no longer find their hopes and dreams in a jar or behind a mop; they can be turned off if you try to tell them they should."[24]

In the same issue, Suzanne H. McCall introduced what she termed the "workwife," whose impact on marketing she deemed "revolutionary."[25] McCall furthered Franklin's claim, arguing that this vital demographic could not be reached through advertising images of women as housewives or sex symbols. She also warned marketers that the most desirable workwives, those under age fifty-five, rarely looked at newspaper advertisements; rather, two-thirds of them spent their free time watching television.[26] McCall sketched the workwife in great detail, describing her influence over family members, her increased purchasing power, and perhaps most importantly, her role as a "trendsetter" who inspires other women to follow in her consumer footsteps.[27] The working woman's spending power created much excitement in many accounts. While women had long been perceived as the primary household consumers, according to many market researchers, working women exercised more independence over big-ticket or luxury items, rather than waiting to consult their husbands.[28] These observations made their way into the popular press as well, with the *New York Times* labeling professional women "free-wheeling spenders"[29] and noting that they are "likeliest to have the most disposable income."[30]

Bartos suggested that the most important demographic shift that marketers should be aware of was not simply the increase in women with professional careers, but more specifically that the fastest growing segment of married women entering the workforce had young children. Bucking Bartos's expectations, many mothers opted against delaying their careers until their children started elementary school.[31] She considered this statistic to be "the most revolutionary one of all of the demographic facts reported in this chapter. It was so unexpected that it caught some of the pundits in the Bureau of Labor Statistics and other governmental groups by surprise."[32] Suzanne McCall likewise observed that "of the 36 million women in the labor force, some 22.4 million (62.3%) of them are married and wielding consumer power over 78.4 million family members," further underscoring the desirability of working women with children.[33] Of note to the television industry, Bartos found that career women without children watched very little television. In fact, the only television series they reliably watched was *Rhoda* (CBS, 1974–1978).[34] Career women who were married with children watched more television, including a wide range of sitcoms, but Bartos notes that plan-to-work housewives outpaced all other female demographics in television viewership, again suggesting that appealing to the fantasies of women who would *like* to be in the workforce would be a lucrative strategy for advertisers and television producers. Bartos also charted a significant attitude shift, reporting that in a study conducted by the National Commission on the Observance of International Woman's Year, "nine out of ten women under thirty-five years of age do not aspire to be 'mainly a homemaker' for life."[35] Especially given advertisers' preferences for younger consumers, this attitude shift would not go unnoticed, compounded by Bartos's findings that on average, women who worked were younger and more affluent than nonworking women.

In 1986, an article in *Current Issues and Research in Advertising* studied which representations of women were most appealing to particular segments of the women's market. Mary C. Gilly and Thomas E. Barry devised three sample magazine covers, one using homemaking themes, another using career themes, and a third using "generic," supposedly neutral themes, and surveyed women across Bartos's categories on their preferences. To Gilly and Barry's surprise, "The homemaker ad was not the most effective for the low [desire to work] segment. Rather, the generic ad was the preference for this group. One would expect women with low desire to work to find a homemaker message most appealing. However, it is possible that the attention given working women in recent years has discouraged these women from identifying with a homemaker theme."[36]

The suggestion that even homemakers did not respond positively to images of women as homemakers makes the so-called "moving target" of the women's demographic even more difficult to pin down. Bartos marshals a great deal of evidence that shows stay-at-home housewives respond just as favorably to images of professional women as women in the workforce do. She frames it as a major takeaway message of her book, writing in her conclusion, "*The news* is that women in traditional life styles really endorse the new values. Whether or not women are living in 'new values' life styles, they respond very positively to symbols of change."[37] Going even further, a bolded heading in one chapter warns, "All Groups of Women Responded Most Negatively to Traditional Approaches."[38]

Bartos is quite clear on the approaches that receive positive responses from all groups of women: men performing domestic tasks and childcare. She describes at length a commercial she screened for all four groups of women of a father changing a baby's diaper, finding that "somehow, there is universal appeal for women today in seeing a young father happily caring for his baby."[39] This commercial was the most popular among both stay-at-home housewives and career women in Bartos's sample. All groups of women also responded positively to a gender role reversal commercial where a woman picks a man up for a date and gives him flowers. Thus it is no surprise that television networks turned toward "hunks of manhood" who delighted in childcare and shared domestic tasks— in a time when the television industry was beginning to shift to a narrowcast strategy, family sitcoms allowed networks to keep broadcasting to women eighteen to forty-nine, many of whom watched television with their children.

The Sitcom Strategy

While advertisers were eager to capitalize on the professional woman's disposable income, the television networks struggled to put together programming that
they could afford which would appeal to advertisers and their target markets.
With cable and independent stations beginning to cut into the networks' viewing audience, CBS, NBC, and ABC had even more trouble guaranteeing demographics to their advertisers.[40] Advertising sales were slow and unpredictable in
the early 1980s, due to low ratings, various labor strikes, and threats of product
boycotts from social conservatives.[41] CBS refused to guarantee specific demographic groups for the 1982–83 season, resulting in many fewer advertisers buying
time up front than NBC or ABC.[42] An executive with advertising firm Young and
Rubicam complained, "CBS is not adjusting its programming to reach the audience the advertiser wants to reach."[43] Perhaps not coincidentally, CBS had passed
on *Family Ties* (NBC, 1982–1989), informing producer Gary David Goldberg,
"Families are dead on TV."[44] In a testament to the importance of desirable demographics to advertisers, the network acquiesced to agency demands and reversed
their decision for the 1983–84 season.[45]

Meanwhile, the networks began to employ more and more market researchers in their attempts to make good on their demographic promises.[46] Yet of the
three networks, CBS remained in last place for much of the decade, tellingly only
launching a single successful family sitcom (*Kate & Allie*), often choosing to air
hour-long dramas in the first hour of prime time. Moreover, Ken Auletta points
out that in 1988, "CBS's schedule was dominated by male-oriented programming
about mobsters (*Wiseguy*), soldiers in Vietnam (*Tour of Duty*), and private detec-
tives (*Jake and the Fatman*), plus two news magazine shows. Advertisers joined the
generally negative chorus."[47] CBS' continual reluctance to program sitcoms that
would appeal to professional women and their families may have cost them a
decade's worth of ratings battles. After all, as NBC was reminded in the same
year, "The affiliates wanted urban shows that young women shoppers could identify with."[48]

As it has been throughout television history, the most desirable demographic
was women ages eighteen to forty-nine. However, this demographic was splintered in the 1980s, when networks sought to reach the professional wife and
mother, thought to come home from work and watch the first hour of prime time
along with her children.[49] As Lauren Rabinovitz shows,

> Foreseeing a national economic shift in consumption stimulated by the baby
> boom generation coming of age, advertising agencies began earmarking
> two-thirds of their advertising budgets to address consumers under fifty, and
> television executives merely followed suit by catering their products to the
> "demographic" products (the audience) for which the advertisers were look-

ing. The extent to which such strategies became thoroughly internalized policies in the 1980s is best summarized by CBS broadcast vice president for research David Poltrack: "The affluent, upscale woman between twenty-five and fifty-four is [now] the primary target of advertisers."[50]

. Thus the prized demographic shifted slightly older, and networks showed more interest in programming that was attractive to (and appropriate for) these women's children.[51]

In the middle of the 1981–82 season, Marvin Mord, vice president of ABC marketing and research wrote in *Variety* that changes in family structure "have posed a twofold challenge to tv marketers and programmers: to provide advertisers with ways to reach their target audiences more effectively and develop tv programs which appeal to contemporary American tastes and lifestyles."[52] He further called on the television industry to feature working mothers in prime time, a call that was answered (though not by his own network) in the 1982–83 season with the debut of *Family Ties* on NBC. However, Mord's network did premiere *Webster* (ABC, 1983–1987, first-run syndication 1987–1989) the following season, and *Variety* implicitly declared the beginning of a new prime-time era when it announced that "ABC's 'Benson' and 'Webster' have come on to wrest the time period leadership away from CBS' 'The Dukes Of Hazzard.'"[53] The trend continued when ABC's Tuesday night lineup of *Who's the Boss?* (ABC, 1984–1992) and *Growing Pains* (ABC, 1985–1992) beat *The A-Team* (NBC, 1983–1987), a feat heralded in *Variety*'s cover story declaring 1985 "Year of the Sitcom."[54] Implicit in these ratings fights is a battle of masculinities—the rough-and-tumble, traditional masculinity of *The Dukes of Hazzard* (CBS, 1979–1985) and *The A-Team* versus the softer, affable, more domestic father figures of the new family sitcoms.

. These sitcoms positioned men in domestic roles, which market research suggested was universally attractive to women in the eighteen to forty-nine bracket, regardless of occupational status. They likewise hedged their bets in their representations of women, allowing them careers, but spending the bulk of their onscreen time in the home. The sitcoms' inclusion of children, both young and teen idol-age, made the shows even more attractive to the networks and advertisers, as children were a key demographic group in off-network syndication. The family sitcom glut of the 1980s worked through a standardized set of characters in order to keep costs low, attract the most desirable demographics, and make the highest profit. Indeed, the sitcoms of the 1980s made unprecedented syndication deals worth billions of dollars. Though the profits belonged to the production companies rather than the networks, ratings of prime-time sitcoms could only improve with audience exposure to reruns in the late afternoon and early evening hours. By the mid-1980s, production companies heavily promoted their popular sitcoms for syndication, and the pages of *Variety* were full of articles expounding upon the staggering prices independent stations were paying for network sitcoms.[55] The demand for syndicated sitcom product was so high that production companies began mass-producing original sitcoms for first-run syndication like *Small Wonder* (first-run syndication, 1985–1989) and continued to produce cancelled network sitcoms like *Charles in Charge* (CBS, 1984–1985, first-run syndication, 1987–1990) and *Silver Spoons* (NBC, 1982–1986, first-run syndication, 1986–1987) for first-runs on the highest bidding independent stations.[56] The demand for syndicated sitcoms was so strong that even popular hour-long series were pushed out of the market. As Ken Auletta notes, "Everyone in Hollywood noticed when local stations refused to buy the hour-long *Miami Vice* reruns, forcing Universal to make a bargain-basement syndication deal with cable."[57] Buoyed by their sitcoms, during the 1988 November sweeps period, "for the first time in the history of television the independent stations trounced a network—CBS—in the ratings."[58] Family sitcoms dominated U.S. television in the 1980s not only in prime-time network programming, but in the afternoons and early evening fringe on independent stations as well. Their omnipresence in the after-school hours ensured that children of the 1980s would be well acquainted with new family structures, including working mothers and sensitive, caring fathers.

The primacy of family sitcoms on independent stations as well as the networks provided both children and adults with models of family life quite different from those on offer during television's "golden age." Judith Stacey names programs like *Father Knows Best* (CBS, 1954–1955 and 1958–1960, NBC, 1955–1958) and *Leave It to Beaver* (CBS, 1957–1958, ABC, 1958–1963) as arbiters of nuclear family life and suggests that families in the 1980s sought new ideals which more closely approximated their daily lives. She proclaims, "No longer is there a single culturally dominant family pattern to which the majority of Americans conform and most of the rest aspire. Instead, Americans today have crafted a multiplicity of family and household arrangements that we inhabit uneasily and reconstitute frequently in response to changing personal and occupational circumstances."[59]

Families tuning in to 1980s family sitcoms saw "new" family formations that worked: mothers who had both fulfilling careers and happy home lives, husbands who did housework and cared for children, and even children who did regular chores. Not only were these programs attractive to networks and their advertisers as potential draws for upscale women viewers but they also provided women viewers with fantasies of well-functioning households. In fact, Prakash's research, which confirmed Bartos's findings, suggested that career women actually watched very little television and that the "plan-to-work" women watched the most prime-time programming. "Stay-at-home" women, he claimed, "may sometimes long to be in the working woman's shoes in order to achieve self-fulfillment, may envy the latter's wardrobe, stimulating life and independence."[60] Sitcoms featuring career women with families thus provided a range of women with pleasurable narratives about marriage, work, and family.

FAMILY SITCOMS AND TELEVISION HISTORY

The family sitcoms of the 1980s were produced by an anxious industry desperate to attract a demographic that had become difficult to understand. ABC had so much trouble deciding in what direction to steer their network that network president Fred Pierce "even secretly hired a Hollywood psychic. Beginning in 1978, Pierce had placed Beverlee Dean on the payroll at $24,000 a year, consulting her in strictest confidence about what programs ABC should schedule, what scripts or actors might catch fire."[61] In putting family sitcoms like *Family Ties*, *Growing Pains*, and *The Cosby Show* on the air, the networks sought to attract upscale women by promoting fantasies of the harmonious combination of work and family among the professional middle and upper class.

At this crucial juncture when cable threatened to erode the network audience and to fragment it further into niche markets, family sitcoms held tight to the ideal of the family audience and offered their viewers templates for dealing with work and home arrangements that strayed from the ideals fostered by family sitcoms of the past. At the same time, many 1980s sitcoms engaged self-reflexively with their position in television history to varying degrees. Michele Hilmes sums up this strategy in her discussion of the comedic address of *Cheers* (NBC, 1982–1993), noting that the "appeal to an 'upscale' audience had to be made without alienating TV's 'mass' audience; 'high culture' viewers had to be entertained, but not at the expense of 'low-culture' fans."[62] Embedding self-reflexive comedy and liberal feminist ideals in the familiar form of the family sitcom became a popular way of attracting a desirable audience segment without losing hope of mass appeal. Moreover, these moments of self-reflexivity often directly address the upscale female viewer, adopting a strategy Bartos suggested for reaching career women by using "cooler approaches—those that employed a light, humorous, almost ironic touch."[63] While *Silver Spoons* and *The Cosby Show* grapple with cable's threatening penetration rate, *Family Ties* and *Who's the Boss?* reference television marketing and the career woman demographic, and *Growing Pains* consistently makes references to contemporary and 1950s television. This tendency toward self-reflexivity points to both an attempt at more sophisticated comedy and to the general anxiety within the industry at the time about the future of network television and its audience.

Silver Spoons becomes a mouthpiece for network executives in "The X Team" episode, when Ricky (Ricky Schroder) and his friends are exposed to the evils of cable television.[64] Despite the inexplicable lock his father, Edward (Joel Higgins), has jerry-rigged on the cable boxes, Ricky and his friends manage to see "Naked Nurses from Outer Space." Edward grounds Ricky for two weeks and revokes his television privileges for a month. However, he has the difficult task of explaining why pornography is coming across the airwaves into the Stratton home in the first place. When Ricky asks, "Why do we get these movies on *our*

Figure 1. Ricky and his friends manage to access cable porn on *Silver Spoons*.

TV?" Edward struggles to piece together his answer, as the studio audience knowingly chuckles: "Well, well, it, it comes with the cable service . . . you see I ordered the cable service because I want to see . . . recent movies without commercials. And to my *surprise* . . . they—they also broadcast these . . . skin flicks. See, I, I have no choice! I want to watch a decent movie, then I, then I just have to order these sleazy movies at the same time. Are you buying this?"

Edward's awkward laughter and inability to explain why their cable service provides porn suggests that he himself indulges in naked nurses from time to time, a suggestion that seems obvious to the giddy studio audience. It also serves as a cautionary tale for viewers of broadcast television who might be considering making the leap to a cable subscription. While curiously enough Edward does not pledge to cancel his cable subscription, the episode makes it clear that his elaborate system of keeping "adult content" away from twelve-year-old boys is not enough and that perhaps families should stick to broadcast network family fare like *Silver Spoons* instead.

Similarly, Cliff (Bill Cosby) repeatedly tries to mitigate the corrupting influence MTV has on his five children in *The Cosby Show*. In a season one episode, Cliff enters the living room while teenage son, Theo (Malcolm Jamal Warner), and youngest daughter, Rudy (Keshia Knight Pulliam), are watching a music video (presumably on MTV), telling them, "I told you I don't want you looking at that trash. All it is is a nightmare put to music."[65] Cliff looks for a quiet space to relax in the season two episode "Full House" only to find teenage daughter Denise (Lisa Bonet) and a friend watching "the all-music channel" in the living room, catatonically singing along to reggae music.[66] The season five episode "How Do You Get to Carnegie Hall?" demonstrates the menace MTV poses to (female) youth.[67] Fifteen-year-old Vanessa (Tempestt Bledsoe) is bitten by the show-business bug when she and her friends make an amateur music video, singing a karaoke version of "The Locomotion." Clair (Phylicia Rashad) and Cliff suggest the girls take some singing lessons, but the girls decide they are going to focus more on image than singing (a clear reference to MTV). Armed with skimpy new outfits and provocative choreography, the girls perform for Clair, Cliff, and young, impressionable Rudy. Reacting in horror to the dance moves and costumes (Vanessa is clad in a miniskirt and midriff- and cleavage-baring bustier), Clair turns off their boom box and decries, "I don't know who you think you are, but you are not the people who just came down here in my living room, half-dressed, flinging parts from one end to the other." While Clair and Cliff are horrified by the performance, Rudy is entranced, telling Clair, "I thought they were hot!" Symbolically turning off the live version of MTV happening in their living room, Clair responds, "Maybe you should go up to your room and cool off." In a parallel to *Silver Spoons*'s warning about the dangers of cable pornography, here *The Cosby Show* warns of the corrupting potential of MTV, especially on young girls, and assures that network sitcoms will provide valuable guidelines for appropriate behavior.

Self-consciously engaging with the need to appeal to upscale women, the season five episode "Mrs. Huxtable Goes to Kindergarten" depicts Clair's foray into television as a talking head on a weekend public affairs program called "Retrospective."[68] When she announces to the family that she is going to be on television, Cliff excitedly calls out, "*Soul Train!*" earning a bemused glance from Clair, which suggests that her demographic is not interested in such programming. In explaining the scope of "Retrospective," Clair notes that it revolves around "intelligent people" discussing history, marking her as a sophisticated, intellectual viewer (and thus deriding *Soul Train*, once again another dig at MTV-like programming). The episode sets Clair up as a female crusader breaking down the door to the old boys' club from the beginning, when Theo asks, "They have the same three guys every week, how'd you get on it?" When Cliff and Clair arrive on the set, Cliff refers to the regular panelists (one Republican, one Democrat, and the host) as the "three wise men." In a joke referencing the audience erosion networks were continuing to experience, Clair tells the panelists that she watches the show every week, and the host replies, "You must be the one person who shows up in our ratings."

The episode positions the bipartisan panelists as ridiculous caricatures, especially the Republican who insults everyone and is overly sure of himself,

Figure 2. Vanessa and her friends perform a provocative, MTV-inspired routine on
The Cosby Show.

refusing to back down even when Clair proves him wrong. None of the three
men is thrilled with the insights Clair provides, clearly viewing her as an inter-
loper, with the Republican complaining that she "was disrupting the flow."
When Clair explains, "I was trying to become part of the conversation," the
host interjects, "There she goes again!" in an exasperated tone. Letting slip the
producers' rationale for bringing Clair onto the program, the host suggests
they should "let her speak when we get to the black topics" and clarifies that she
is "also here to speak for women." This scene underscores the television industry's understanding that it needed to appeal to narrowcast demographics, those
not necessarily always served through a broadcasting model. Yet, the fact that Clair
is there to represent both her race and her gender suggests that the industry was
still trying to cobble together different narrowcast groups to produce broadcast
appeal. In the end, the episode concludes by insisting this strategy of token
change will not work to bring in a sophisticated female viewer like Clair. She
refuses the offer to join the show as a permanent panelist, and rather than
watch the show at its regularly scheduled time, she announces her intention to
time-shift it, videotaping it to watch later. Even then, her tone suggests a dis-
missiveness that indicates she may not watch it at all. This episode points to the
imperative that networks adjust their programming to appeal to upscale, pro-

fessional women or else risk a ratings disaster when these women turn their sets off in disgust.

Family Ties is also self-conscious about network television's target audience in the season two episode "This Year's Model," where Elyse (Meredith Baxter Birney) is cast as a harried career woman in a commercial for Proper Penguin frozen foods, much to the dismay of her daughter Mallory (Justine Bateman), an aspiring model.[69] While casting agents appear uninterested in Mallory primarily because she lacks poise in front of the camera, her lack of commercial appeal also suggests that middle-aged, successful Elyse is more marketable to television audiences than a teenage girl. The commercial shoots in the Keaton kitchen and features Elyse coming in wearing a business suit and carrying a briefcase, lamenting, "I was held up at work. Traffic was awful. How am I supposed to cook an impressive dinner for eight important friends in twenty minutes?" Her costuming and dialogue mark her as an upscale professional woman, while the product she pushes brings her more in line with working and middle-class women, emphasizing the aspirational nature of the career woman on television. Elyse's modeling career is cut short, however, when she realizes Mallory's jealousy and tells her, "I'm a mother first and a Penguin lady second." This resolution points to broader trends in 1980s sitcoms, which tried to appeal to what networks perceived as a fragmented female audience—Elyse needed to be a career woman to appeal to the ideal upscale working woman, but she also needed to remain relatable to nonworking women and their families.

Featuring an attractive man working as a housekeeper for a high-powered female advertising executive, *Who's the Boss?* is tailor-made for reaching the career woman demographic. Angela Bower's (Judith Light) job also allows for comedic engagement with the very industry on which the networks depended. In the season two episode "Educating Tony," Angela teaches a night class on advertising at a local college. To her surprise, her housekeeper Tony (Tony Danza) enrolls in the class in the hopes of becoming her star pupil. Angela assigns her students to produce a television commercial for laundry detergent and offers to give Tony advice, which he refuses, telling her he wants her to be surprised. When the students screen their commercials for the class, Tony's rival, Bradley (Larry Cedar), who took Angela up on her offer of advice, wins her praise with an ad where he impersonates Princess Diana to push "Buckingham Soap." Unimpressed, Tony beams as he slips his videotape into the VCR. His ad opens with a close-up on a young woman's face as she directly addresses the viewer with a seductive tone, purring, "In my line of work, the right detergent is very important." This close-up then cuts to a long shot of two women in bikinis mud wrestling, surrounded by a cheering crowd. This image cuts to a medium close-up of Angela, mouth agape and clearly displeased. Proud and anxious to hear Angela's feedback, Tony goads her into revealing his grade on the spot in front of the class. To his astonishment, she tells him, "It's the most offensive television commercial

Figure 3. Elyse portrays a "career woman" for a frozen foods ad on *Family Ties*.

I've ever seen!" When she and Tony return home, Angela explains to her mother, Mona (Katherine Helmond), "It deserves lower than an F. It deserves a G!"

Tony remains convinced of his commercial's merits, and when Angela brings a special guest speaker to class, it appears as though she may be overruled in her disgust. She introduces the class to "Jeremy Eichen, vice president in charge of advertising for Sunshine Laundry Detergent," promising that he will provide feedback on their ads. To Angela's surprise and Tony's delight, Jeremy (Brad O'Hare) begins by praising Tony, telling the class, "One of you had the audacity to put a couple of half-naked women in mud—and it is that kind of audacity that sells soap!" Angela explains that Tony's commercial had one "very serious flaw" and asks Tony if the ad will make him buy soap. He responds, "By the truck-load." Angela then asks Jeremy, who shrugs and says, "Well, actually, I don't buy the soap in my family, my wife does." With this admission, Angela paces the classroom, preparing to complete the day's lesson and win the argument:

> ANGELA: That's very interesting. Because in my household, the pig-headed
>   male housekeeper buys the laundry detergent.
> JEREMY: You have a male housekeeper? That's certainly—
> TONY (INTERRUPTING): Watch it, pal.
> JEREMY: Interesting, unusual, very . . . today.

ANGELA: So, if women are the ones buying the soap, what would that mean, Mr. Micelli?

TONY: That would mean my commercial stank. I mean, I forgot rule number five.

BRADLEY: Know your target audience.

ANGELA: Thank you, your highness.

TONY: And if women are my target audience, they probably wouldn't like the mud wrestling as much as I do.

With this exchange, Angela recognizes that her own household is atypical when it comes to its consumer habits. Angela's position of power within the advertising industry allows her to teach her students (and remind her colleague) that women are not going to be persuaded to buy a product that uses sexist imagery in its advertising. Here she acts as a stand-in for Rena Bartos, who warned that among all four demographic groups of women, "intense negative responses were elicited by advertising that showed women as sex objects."[70]

Growing Pains marks itself as similarly progressive and gives a nod toward its place in television history in the first season episode, "The Seavers vs. The Cleavers."[71] When daughter Carol (Tracey Gold) brings home a letter from the Parents' Association requesting chaperones for the school dance, Maggie (Joanna Kerns) and Jason (Alan Thicke) volunteer. As Carol is decorating the gym, she overhears the president of the Parents' Association, June Hinckley (Annette Funicello), bad-mouthing her parents to the principal, Ward (Drew Snyder), in an extended allusion to *Leave It to Beaver*. Telling him, "Ward, I'm worried about the Seavers," she says, "I don't know, maybe it's okay for a man to run a psychiatric practice out of the home, and maybe it's all right for a woman to go back to work *just* when her children need her most, and maybe letting our offspring run wild is hunky dory. And maybe I'm just old-fashioned . . ." *Growing Pains* plays up June's "old-fashioned" values by casting former Mickey Mouse Club mouseketeer Annette Funicello in the role. By pitting her against Maggie, the episode further points to changing ideals of femininity on television. That evening, Jason sets the dinner table as Maggie comes home from work, and they receive a call from Mrs. Hinckley, who explains that the school no longer requires their chaperoning services. However, Carol lets them in on what she overheard: "She said I have a mother who abandoned me, a brother who's a delinquent, a father who runs a mental ward at home, she made my life sound like a movie of the week!" Maggie and Jason are outraged, pay the Hinckleys a visit, and realize that Jimbo (Bill Cort) and June are from a different world, where their son is simultaneously coddled and strictly disciplined, and where all the furniture is covered with plastic slipcovers. Unable to reason with Mrs. Hinckley (or Mrs. Hitler, as Jason calls her), Maggie and Jason decide to attend the dance anyway. When the DJ plays "Land of a Thousand Dances" and announces that he's playing "fogey rock" so the chaperones would dance, The Hinckleys and Maggie and Jason undertake an impromptu dance-off, which unsurprisingly, Maggie and Jason win. Their victory serves as a narrative resolution for the episode—they have proved the Hinckleys (and thus the Cleavers) to be squares and have come out on top as a new generation of parents. While this resolution is ridiculous, and hardly levels a satisfying comeuppance for the Hinckleys, it shows that *Growing Pains* takes itself less seriously than 50s sitcoms and signals to women viewers that the series is in tune with liberal feminist fantasies of progress.

Growing Pains was often self-reflexive about its position on television in the 1980s and within television history. The season two episode "Jason's Rib" opens with teenage son, Mike (Kirk Cameron), watching a crime series titled "Undercover Mother," which appears to be a sensationalized version of *Cagney and Lacey*.[72] Carol takes the remote, saying, "I wanna watch something good!" and turns on *Growing Pains*, and as she, Mike, and youngest son, Ben (Jeremy Miller), sit down to watch, the opening theme starts. This comic device works to establish *Growing Pains* as a show that appeals to families, whereas "Undercover Mother" obviously (and perhaps paradoxically, considering that *Cagney and Lacey* was targeted toward older women, not teenage boys) had a narrow demographic. Indeed, *Growing Pains* landed in the Nielsen Top 10 among teens twelve to seventeen, women eighteen to forty-nine and twenty-five to fifty-four, and in the Top 15 among children two to eleven at the end of the 1985–1986 season.[73] Jason demonstrates that *Growing Pains* appeals to men as well in the episode "Thank God It's Friday."[74] When Ben claims that Friday is the best night for television, Jason disagrees, arguing for Tuesday, the night *Growing Pains* (and *Who's the Boss?*) aired on ABC. Regardless of their disagreement, the whole family (with the exception of Mike) enjoys TV dinners and watches television together that Friday night, which on ABC was billed as a night of family comedies featuring *Webster* and *Mr. Belvedere* (1985–1990).

In addition to its self-reflexive self-promotion, *Growing Pains* demonstrates the pedagogical potential of family sitcoms in general. In "Jason's Rib," the kids plot to resolve their parents' argument through a trick Mike saw on *The Cosby Show*, by ordering Maggie flowers with a false card from Jason.[75] The Seavers' enthusiasm for *The Cosby Show*, which Ben notes is "the number one show on TV," becomes the narrative frame for an entire episode where the family (with the exception of Mike, who predictably has a date) goes to a taping.[76] Ben is shocked that Mike would rather go on a date, but he quickly understands when he becomes transfixed by a girl sitting near him in the studio audience and misses much of the show. Suddenly interested in girls, Ben attempts to seduce his babysitter. Though she initially refuses his advances, when she learns he attended a taping of *The Cosby Show*, she is so smitten that her older sister has to drag her out of the Seaver home. Reflecting on his sitcom-induced sexual awakening, Ben sighs, "Everything was so simple before I went to *The Cosby Show*." Television's

Figure 4. The Seaver kids watch *Growing Pains* on *Growing Pains*.

hit sitcom serves not only to keep the family together (the kids use its practical advice to resolve their parents' argument and the family uses its taping as a family outing), it also sets the stage for rites of passage and provides Ben with the cultural capital he needs to avoid what was otherwise going to be painful romantic rejection.

1980s family sitcoms, caught between the broadcast and narrowcast eras, adopted narrowcast tactics in their targeting of upscale professional women while simultaneously promoting the well-worn broadcast genre as a newly invigorated family hearth. By bringing the production of television commercials into story lines on *Who's the Boss?* and *Family Ties*, these programs position their ideal viewer as too smart to fall for advertising. At the same time, network comedies self-consciously situated themselves within a rapidly changing television landscape, with programs like *Growing Pains* demonstrating the value of the broadcast sitcom that solicits a general family audience. *Silver Spoons* similarly played up cable television as a potential evil that could bring pornography into America's living rooms and before the eyes of children. In keeping with the 1980s' turn toward postmodern modes of storytelling and representation, network television self-reflexively addressed its ideal spectator, poking fun at the advertising messages designed to target the professional woman while suggesting that broadcast sitcoms would help keep her family together.

These winking story lines pitch the family sitcom to an upscale professional woman, suggesting that the networks value her intelligence while they simultaneously argue that the networks are still the safest bet for her children. After all, upscale professional women were very likely to be cable subscribers and thus to turn off the networks altogether. NBC Entertainment president Brandon Tartikoff noted that viewers who were cable subscribers but chose to watch network programming were particularly attractive to network affiliates. He explains, "We would renew several poorly rated new shows—including *St. Elsewhere*, *Family Ties*, and *Remington Steele*—strictly on the basis of their strength in key demographics and their pull in these cable-ready households."[77] The professional woman with children would be much more likely to watch *Family Ties* (and see a flattering image of herself) or *The Cosby Show* (and see how Cliff and Clair deal with their children's affinity for MTV) than to watch "Naughty Nurses from Outer Space." Even so, Tartikoff would learn that lesson the hard way, when he and his associates rationalized airing Aaron Spelling's *Nightingales* (NBC, 1989), a drama following scantily clad nursing students, by claiming, "We can present contemporary working women"—a gross miscalculation that only survived thirteen episodes.[78] The (successful) network formula for attracting contemporary working women provided fantasies of domestically-inclined husbands who supported their career-oriented wives, a pattern that market research of the 1980s strongly championed.

CHAPTER 2

"I CAN'T HELP FEELING MATERNAL—I'M A FATHER!"

DOMESTICATED DADS AND CAREER WOMEN

Family Ties (NBC, 1982–1989) producer Gary David Goldberg remembered NBC Entertainment president Brandon Tartikoff explaining to him the three-prong formula for a successful family sitcom: "First, the audience has to begin to watch because they recognize themselves in that TV family. Second, they continue to watch because, on some level, they want to be a part of that family. And third, and this is where you can really make your connection deep and lasting, they will watch because they believe they can learn how to be a better family."[1] This chapter shows how 1980s family sitcoms demonstrated how to be a "better family" through focusing on the two stock protagonists these programs overwhelmingly favored: the career woman and the "domesticated" dad.

Four popular iterations of these characters (Elyse and Steven Keaton on *Family Ties*, Maggie and Jason Seaver on *Growing Pains* [ABC, 1985–1992], Clair and Cliff Huxtable on *The Cosby Show* [NBC, 1984–1992], and Edward Stratton on *Silver Spoons* [NBC, 1982–1986; first-run syndication 1986–1987]) provided models of family life for a new generation coming to terms with the changing culture and economy of the 1980s. These models worked to shore up faith in the continued viability of the family unit at a time when the nuclear family was being simultaneously ideologically defended and socioeconomically undermined by the Reagan administration. With the exception of *Silver Spoons* (which never cracked the Nielsen Top 30), these programs were very popular. *The Cosby Show* debuted at number three in the Nielsen ratings and then held the number one spot for the next five years. *Family Ties* benefited from its *Cosby* lead-in, landing in the number two spot for 1985 and 1986. *Growing Pains* peaked at number five in 1987, but remained in the Top 30 from 1985–1990. All four sitcoms placed great faith in the survival of the nuclear family, while guiding families to readjust their expectations of gendered roles. These programs present pedagogies of masculinity that help renegotiate domestic life in order to maintain the family unit despite its slightly altered form.

As Nikolas Rose suggests, the family is governed "through the promotion of subjectivities, the construction of pleasures and ambitions, and the activation of guilt, anxiety, envy, and disappointment."[2] The sitcoms promote a masculine subjectivity that embraces domesticity and child-rearing, enabling successful and equitable dual-career couples who work to instill similar values in their children. Importantly, as Bridget Kies points out, viewers are not baited to laugh at the domesticated dad "for being engaged in matters of the home, and rarely does he express frustration that the wife-mother is unable to fulfill the domestic role."[3] Rather, these series represent the domesticated dad's masculinity as an ideal to be emulated, not only by their on-screen sons, but by viewers as well. On the side of the networks, the promotion of a domesticated masculinity was a calculated move to attract professional women as an upwardly mobile consumer group, as detailed in chapter one. Family sitcoms helped pull the networks out of a slump at the same time that they modeled revised gender and familial roles for millions of Americans, and provided fantasies of co-parenting and shared domestic chores for women viewers.

Appealing both to working and nonworking women, Elyse Keaton (Meredith Baxter Birney), the mother on *Family Ties*, manages to thrive as an architect by having her workspace in the kitchen of the family home. This allows her to pursue her own career while remaining a devoted "stay-at-home mom" and domestic manager, with the help of a supportive husband invested in "women's lib." Clair Huxtable (Phylicia Rashad) of *The Cosby Show* is a glamorous lawyer, who often comes home from work to find her obstetrician husband, Cliff (Bill Cosby), actively caring for their five children or preparing dinner. His office is in the basement of their house, allowing him flexibility to work around her hours. In *Growing Pains*, Maggie Seaver (Joanna Kerns) goes back to work as a newspaper reporter, and Jason Seaver (Alan Thicke) moves his psychiatric practice into their home. His profession makes him remarkably well-suited to dealing with the foibles of their three children in between seeing his patients. *Silver Spoons* revolves around Edward Stratton (Joel Higgins) learning how to be a father to the son he never knew he had. A textbook case of arrested development, Edward must learn to set aside his video games to parent son Ricky (Ricky Schroder). His growing aptitude for nurturance attracts the romantic attention of his maternal personal assistant, Kate (Erin Gray), resulting in the formation of a nuclear family where both parents manage to work at home.

These programs provided idealized models of career women managing to "have it all" with the support of husbands who performed a sensitive, emotionally invested, and domestically oriented masculinity. These domesticated dads functioned both as figures in a liberal feminist fantasy of heterosexual romance and family life, and as models for a new masculine ideal that privileged traditionally "feminine" characteristics such as nurturance and family care. In the 1980s, academic psychology journals buzzed with explorations of problems faced by "dual-career couples," especially the "role strain" faced by women balancing a professional career with motherhood.[4] One article points to the costs and benefits of life as a dual-career couple, claiming "it can provide them with new and rich sources of satisfaction as well as high levels of emotional stress, which is compounded by the relative absence of cultural models and normative guidelines for resolving their special problems."[5] However unrealistic family sitcom portrayals of dual-career couples may be, the genre has long provided models for idealized family life—thus it stands to reason that 1980s sitcoms produced the very cultural models for which dual-career couples may have been longing. However, the aims of network executives were less about shifting gender roles and more about creating content that would bring in advertising dollars at the lowest production cost, and advertising dollars were being spent on programs that attracted professional women.

Together, *Family Ties, Growing Pains, The Cosby Show,* and *Silver Spoons* present viewers with idealized visions of combining home and work—for Elyse, Jason, Cliff, and Edward, work is in the home, thus reducing the conflict between career and family. In order to appeal to a broad female audience, Elyse, Maggie, and Clair are both career-oriented and nurturing mothers, with most of their screen time taking place in the home. The programs also represent a sensitive, domestically oriented masculinity, a development that appears essential when women are working full-time. While the programs grapple with real, familiar problems encountered by dual-career couples, they also present fantasies of romantic partnership, shared domestic work, mutual sacrifice, and children happy to pitch in.

The Kitchen Architect and the Feminist Dad on *Family Ties*

Elyse Keaton is first introduced to television audiences through a slideshow she and husband, Steven (Michael Gross), present to their kids of the two of them participating in the March on Washington.[6] The opening credits for the first season duplicate these images, combined with images of their wedding and children, dutifully reminding viewers of the Keatons' strong political convictions as they relate to their ideals of marriage and child-rearing. Steven and Elyse were based on producer Gary David Goldberg and his wife, Diana Meehan, who were deeply dedicated to their progressive leftist ideals. In his memoir, Goldberg recounts the day care center he and his wife opened in Berkeley, California, in 1972, where "Diana and I scrupulously take turns sharing all the different roles equally. Driving, cooking, arts and crafts, sports. We want the kids to notice how none of these tasks is gender specific."[7] Those same lessons appear again and again throughout the seven-season run of *Family Ties*. The pilot episode establishes Elyse's dual roles as career woman and mother through mise-en-scène: the first scene following the credits opens with Elyse seated at her desk in the corner of the kitchen drawing up plans for an architecture project. Steven comes in and prepares breakfast while daughter Mallory (Justine Bateman) sets the table. When Elyse and the rest of the family sit down to eat, the remainder of the scene revolves around the kids fighting over the telephone, which hangs on the wall next to Elyse's desk—family members constantly appropriate her workspace.

Family Ties consistently deals with Elyse's difficulties maintaining both her career and her family, and her desk in the kitchen is a constant reminder of this problem. The season one episode "Margin of Error" opens with the whole family seated at the dinner table, but Elyse immediately gets up and sits at her desk while the rest of the family sit and chat.[8] Steven clears the table as Elyse explains that she's having trouble designing a multifaith chapel. As Steven and son Alex (Michael J. Fox) argue over the stock market, Elyse is effectively kicked out of her workspace. After she and Steven leave the room, Alex uses the phone by her desk as the scene closes. The beginning of the next scene finds Alex seated at Elyse's desk once again on the phone. She comes in and rather than ask Alex to vacate her makeshift office, she explains to him that her confidence has been shaken. By the end of the episode, Elyse has successfully completed the chapel and proudly shows off her plans to Steven and Mallory. These episodes never suggest that Elyse may be frustrated by the constant interruptions; instead she appears happy to share her workspace, as though it is all worth it for the sake of the time she gets to spend with her family. She can plan her work around her parenting and household duties, and she seems content with the arrangement.

Elyse takes it upon herself to mentor her housewife friend Suzanne (Brooke Alderson), who complains that she has "no identity of [her] own," by offering her clerical work in the Keaton kitchen.[9] As Elyse marvels at Suzanne's lack of typing skills, one of her clients comes in and proposes multiple changes to Elyse's plans for his summer house. When Elyse defends her vision, Suzanne jumps in and sides with the client, proposing changes of her own that delight him and horrify Elyse. Suzanne gets so chummy with Elyse's client that she sits down with him and requests that Elyse perform the secretarial work of making tea. As Elyse walks to the stove, the scene dissolves to Elyse working furiously in the living room two weeks later, surrounded by blueprints. She complains to Steven and the kids that Suzanne is sabotaging all of her work. Alex encourages her to fire Suzanne, arguing that she should not let their personal relationship interfere with business. Elyse agrees, but when Suzanne's husband leaves her, Elyse loses her nerve.

Figure 5. Elyse hires her newly divorced friend Suzanne to do secretarial work on *Family Ties*.

In the next scene, Steven leaves to take the kids to school as Suzanne arrives for work. Suzanne tells Elyse that seeing the Keatons so happy has made her depressed. When Elyse attempts to comfort her, Suzanne responds, "No, now is not the time nor the place to discuss my personal problems," while she unpacks a desk lamp and a name plate that reads "Ms. Suzanne Davis" onto the kitchen table, thus establishing her new role as single career woman. When Elyse refers to Suzanne's workspace as her "table," Suzanne interrupts, "desk, Elyse. You said you'd call it a desk." Elyse once again asks if Suzanne wants to talk about her impending divorce, and Suzanne refuses but quickly caves and complains, eliciting big laughs from the studio audience. Becoming increasingly agitated, Suzanne exclaims, "If one more person pussy-foots around me, and offers me comfort instead of respect, I'll scream, I just want to be treated like anybody else!" Inspired by this request, Elyse responds, "You're fired!" This episode contrasts Elyse and her successful career, marriage, and family, with Suzanne, a sad-sack former housewife and divorcée who has no work skills. Suzanne married and bore children at a young age—early in the episode she tells Elyse that her kids are all in college and she's forty—thus positioning her as exemplary of the failure of the traditional nuclear family.

The episode's B-plot expands on this theme, as Steven complains that he is somehow always in charge of the neighborhood carpool, and the kids explain that several divorces are to blame. Here the Keatons, with their progressive marriage and household arrangement, are held up as the ideal intact family. Still, youngest daughter, Jennifer (Tina Yothers), admits, framed in medium close-up for added emotional emphasis, that "it sure is hard to be a kid today. You never know when your family unit is gonna fall apart." The camera cuts to a medium long shot to include Alex and Steven as Steven replies, "Jennifer, you don't have to worry about that. This family unit isn't going to fall apart." When she asks him to promise, Steven glances at Elyse, offscreen, and the camera cuts to a medium close-up of her, her face expressing dismay at Jennifer's concern. Steven replies, "We can't promise, because nobody knows what the future is going to bring. But I can tell you we'll do our best to keep that from happening." Steven's hedging keeps the Keaton marriage from seeming overly traditional, despite the fact that they are apparently one of the only intact nuclear families that their kids know. Moreover, the episode suggests, Elyse and Steven's progressive gender politics has produced a stable marriage and family.

Still, the Keaton marriage does come up against many common problems experienced by families with two working parents. In the first season finale episode "Elyse D'Arc," Elyse's many commitments prevent her from celebrating Steven's work accomplishment with him.[10] Steven spends the first half of the episode attempting to accommodate her schedule, attempts that meet a dead end when he has cooked the two of them a celebratory dinner and she comes home too late to enjoy it. Even their attempts to make up are thwarted by both the weather and Elyse's women's group. At the end of the episode, Steven tells Elyse, "All of the things which have been taking up your time these past few days have been wonderful. Your career, spending time with the kids, helping distraught women. Even though part of me wants you around the house all the time, I love the fact that you're never here!" Though this line is met by an incredulous look from Elyse and is obviously intended to be comical, his meaning is clear: he respects her commitment to work and civic life outside the home. Elyse tells him that she appreciates that he lets her take him for granted, explaining, "I was brought up to think of a husband as the be-all and end-all of my existence, that a man should be the center of my life, and that I should learn to live in his shadow, and sublimate my ambitions to his, and wait on him hand and foot, and satisfy his every need, answer his every desire. You can see how ridiculous that is, can't you?"

Steven's dreamy look is met by audience laughter, but Elyse continues, telling him that she knows she has to make more time for him. As they go up to bed, they debate what commitments Elyse might be able to give up—they agree that clean air and Planned Parenthood are too important to abandon, finally settling on "Pets without Partners," though as they turn out the lights, Steven admits that he hates "to think of all those lonely pets." The first season ends with only a temporary solution to what promises to be a long-term problem, yet it also provides comic relief for viewers struggling with the same problem, as many undoubtedly were.

The second season finale works on similar themes, as Elyse lands a job at an architecture firm and is thus no longer working out of her kitchen.[11] Three earlier episodes make reference to Elyse having "gone back to work,"[12] suggesting that this episode may have been moved to the end of the season based on its compelling subject matter. On her first day on the job, Elyse is introduced to "the machines," an intimidating computer system that she doesn't know how to use. When she types a few words on the computer, paper shoots out rapid-fire. This chaos is mirrored at home, as the next scene finds Elyse desperately trying to finish plans for a health club that she has to pitch the next morning. Mallory has botched a dress she was trying to sew for Jennifer, and Jennifer begs Elyse to fix it, noting that Elyse has put it off all week. Elyse promises to do it later that night when she's finished working. As Steven tries to coax the kids to let her work, Alex comes up to her and says, "Mom, I sympathize with what you're going through. Today's woman is in a very difficult position. Tradition, and certainly biology, have put her in the home." This statement is met with a glare from Elyse and laughter from the audience. Alex continues, "Now there are these ridiculous new feminist pressures for her to do things outside of the home, like developing a career. Your anxiety's natural mom, you can't fool with mother nature." Elyse responds to Alex's overt sexism by exercising her maternal authority over him, telling him to go to bed, which he does. Steven encourages her to seek her boss's help, noting that she's overworked. Exhausted and exasperated, Elyse tells Steven that she could use help around the house too, as she manically straightens the living room. When he replies that he's happy to help, she exclaims, "That is exactly what I don't want!" She clarifies, "For the past two weeks, you've been doing more cooking than usual, you've been spending more time with the kids, you've been sweeter, kinder, more understanding than you have ever been in your life and I am sick of it!"

After her nonsensical tirade, she storms out of the room, and in the next scene she bombs her presentation, explaining to her client that she ran out of time because she had to make school lunches and sew Jennifer's dress. When she also has to admit that she doesn't know how to use the computer, she confesses, "I'm tired of pretending. Pretending that I know everything about architecture today, pretending that having a job and three kids is a piece of cake. The truth of the matter is, it's hard to design a building under this kind of pressure. It's hard using machines you've never even heard of before, and it is damn hard coming back to work after all these years." She runs out of the meeting, and the next scene opens with Steven comforting her at home. Elyse's boss, Karen (Rebecca Balding), pays her a visit and explains that everyone in the office has problems, and they all help each other. Elyse has managed to land in a woman-headed, noncompetitive, supportive workplace, a fantasy ideal for any woman returning to work after many years away. The episode (and season) resolves when Elyse calls the rest of the family into the living room, proclaiming that she's "still a working woman." After Elyse apologizes for taking her frustration out on the family, Steven and the kids make their own concessions:

> STEVEN: If you're going to work, we've got to make some adjustments too.
> JENNIFER: As a future working woman, I'm with you 100 percent.
> MALLORY: That goes double for me . . . not the bit about working.
> ALEX: I think what we're trying to say Mom is that we're willing to help out more.
> ELYSE: Thank you.
> ALEX: So Mom, what's for dinner?—what I mean is, what would you like us to make you for dinner? [applause, credits]

This resolution is perhaps the epitome of a working mother's fantasy, where children and husband all pitch in and everyone does their share of work around the house. While often these are empty promises, as studies in the 1980s suggested,[13] the fact that the kids perform household duties in most episodes, rarely with any complaint, makes this fantasy home all the more alluring.

Family Ties presents two opposing models of masculinity—husband and father Steven Keaton is the ideal domesticated dad, a product of liberal feminism and generalized "sixties activism," while son Alex P. Keaton is a reactionary ultraconservative Reagan supporter. Alex is held up as an Archie Bunker figure for the 1980s, consistently spouting off over-the-top antifeminist rhetoric. For example, in a season three episode, Alex tells his father, "You know, they may say things have changed, but basically [women are] happiest when they're barefoot and pregnant."[14] While Alex's digs against women's rights garner huge laughs from the audience, *Family Ties* carefully cuts him down through his parents' regular critiques of his politics. In an episode where Alex dates an older woman, she tells Elyse and Steven that Alex is very mature: "It's almost as if he's a throwback to another era." Steven replies, "Turn of the century."[15] Similarly, in an episode in which Alex becomes infatuated with a single, pregnant woman, he tries to mask his shock at her situation by proclaiming that he is "a contemporary guy," an obviously dubious claim met with audience laughter.[16] In the same episode, Alex himself endorses Steven's version of masculinity. After Alex has let go of his dream of being a surrogate father, he explains to Steven and Elyse, "You know, Dad, this whole thing is your fault. If you weren't such a great father, I wouldn't have been in such a hurry to become one." When Alex takes a job at Steven's station, he expresses his concern to Mallory: "Dad is a sensitive, caring man. I could pick up some bad habits from him."[17]

Many jokes revolve around Steven and Alex's discomfort when they *do* agree on things. When both Steven and Alex disapprove of Mallory's new boyfriend, Nick (Scott Valentine), Steven says, "Alex, I take no comfort from the fact that we are on the same side in this."[18] When Steven starts to doubt his decision to forbid Mallory from seeing Nick, Alex pleads, "Dad, I appeal to you, you have made a responsible and courageous decision. When I heard that you told Mallory that she couldn't see Nick anymore, I said to myself, 'What a dad!' Dad, I have never in my entire life been prouder of you than I am in this moment." Shaken, Steven turns to Mallory and says, "Mallory, let's invite Nick to dinner." Still, there are important moments when Steven and Alex's differences begin to fade. In "The Real Thing (Part 2)," Alex realizes he loves his new girlfriend's roommate, Ellen (Tracy Pollan).[19] He confesses to Elyse, and she replies, "It's so beautiful to hear you express those feelings. And this is the first time I have really seen your dad in you." Alex pauses briefly, then replies in the affirmative. Importantly, there is no punch line where Alex denies his father's influence. Instead, he walks over to the mirror and Elyse helps him tie his tie, as he gazes at his reflection as though he has come to some sort of epiphany about his masculinity.

Steven's role as domesticated dad became more prominent in the third season, when Meredith Baxter Birney gave birth to twins in October 1984.[20] Birney's pregnancy was written into the show, with Elyse giving birth in a two-part episode mid-season.[21] Steven was left to solve all familial dilemmas in several episodes in the first half of the season, as Elyse was out of town, on bed rest, or otherwise indisposed.[22] His nurturing ability is on full display in the episode "Auntie Up," where Mallory's favorite aunt dies and Steven must console her. He admits that grief counseling is not his forte, telling Mallory, "Funerals are usually your mother's area," and explaining, "when you've been together as long as your mother and I have, you tend to divide the big emotional responsibilities. Your mother handles funerals, first dates, and plumbing. I handle colds and flus, open school nights, and office supplies." He then fields Mallory's questions about what happens after death. As Mallory begins to cry, the camera positions move closer, such that Mallory is framed in a tight medium close-up, and when Steven pulls her into an embrace, the top of his head is cut off in medium close-up to emphasize the closeness of their emotional bond. The episode ends with Steven drying her tears and holding her close as he breathes a heavy sigh. The camera positions, along with Mallory and Steven's monochromatic black costuming, underscore Steven's ability to take on Elyse's nurturing role, as his and Mallory's bodies blend together and all emphasis is placed on Mallory's distraught expression and Steven's sympathetic reaction to her.

When baby Andrew (played in season four by Garrett and Tyler Merriman) is born, Steven and Elyse clash on parenting techniques, with Steven once again taking on a nurturing role. In "Cry Baby" they argue over whether or not to let Andrew "cry it out" at night.[23] Elyse admonishes Steven for picking up Andrew every time he cries; thus Steven has taken on the mother's typical role of dealing with overnight fussing. This story line was inspired by Goldberg's own approach to fatherhood. He recalls having "104 baby monitors" around his house, allowing him and his wife to respond "at the first hint of a cry."[24] A few episodes later, Steven worries about Andrew with Mallory and Alex, telling them, "I should go out for the evening, forget we even had a baby, and relax, but I can't help feeling maternal. I'm a father!"[25]

Steven's role as a "new," nurturing, domesticated dad is explored and put in historical context in the two-part season three finale, "Remembrance of Things Past," where the family goes to help Steven's mother (Anne Seymour) move out of her house following Steven's father's death.[26] While in Buffalo, Steven flashes back to his childhood with a gruff, emotionally distant father and a homemaker mother. When he questions his mother about her financial situation, she encapsulates her traditional marriage, telling him, "We made an arrangement. He'd take care of all the business, and I'd make pies!" Obviously, this arrangement does her no good now that her husband is dead, thus leaving her two sons to deal with her finances. In addition to his father (and Alex),[27] Steven has another foil in his brother Robert (Norman Parker), a fast-talking accountant who takes after his father. As soon as Steven describes his father to Elyse as a "very difficult man," Robert comes in and asks if he's talking about their father. He describes him as a "good man. Hard working, dependable. Salt of the earth. Like me!" Robert and Steven clash over whether or not to sell their mother's house and move her into a retirement home with her friends, or to hold out for more money. When Steven privileges his mother's happiness over money, Robert complains, "You haven't changed, Steve, Mr. Emotional." However, in the end, Steven's emotional caretaking wins out over Robert's financial caretaking, as he agrees that their mother is lonely and should move near her friends. Robert's masculinity proves to be outmoded—a throwback to the 1950s, while Steven's masculinity presents a preferable, modern alternative.

The season four episode "Nothing But a Man" displays Steven's devotion to his family when he gives up his promotion to spend more time at home.[28] The B-plot underscores the necessity of Steven's fathering, as Alex freaks out when his feminist girlfriend gives Andrew a doll and does everything he can to get it away from him.[29] Meanwhile, Alex manages Steven's "appointments" with Mallory and Jennifer, telling them "time is money" and that they don't get to see him anytime they want anymore. On a business trip in Washington, Steven's room service attendant's name is Andrew (Robert Costanzo), and as he sits down to eat dinner alone in his hotel room, he pulls photos out of his wallet and sets them up facing him to create a makeshift family dinner. He returns home at 3:30 A.M. and tells Elyse that he's giving up his promotion: "I don't want this job now, Elyse, it's not the right time in my life. What I do want is to be home to tuck Andrew in at night, to help Mallory with her homework, to fall asleep in your lap reading the paper. Have you carry me up to bed." The episode ends with Steven proclaiming, "I don't want to be number one at work, I want to be number one

Figure 6. Steven sets up family photos to keep him company during a business trip on *Family Ties*.

right here." While this could be understood to be Steven's assertion as "man of the house," in the context of the episode, it's clear that he means that he values achievement as a father over career achievement.[30] Though sacrificing career advancement for family was often cast in feminine terms (as in the controversial promotion of the "mommy track"[31]), according to Judith Stacey, this move was not all that unusual: "There are data, for example, indicating that increasing numbers of men would sacrifice occupational gains in order to have more time with their families, just as there are data documenting actual increases in male involvement in child care."[32] Here Steven Keaton provides a model of more involved, domestically oriented fatherhood that privileges the well-being of others over personal gratification.

Outside of the specific plots of *Family Ties* episodes, Steven Keaton is a domestic dad by virtue of mise-en-scène. Many of the scenes take place in the kitchen where he is regularly cooking,[33] and in episodes where he is not cooking, he performs other chores like setting and clearing the table,[34] doing dishes,[35] cleaning,[36] and grocery shopping.[37] On a quantitative level, Elyse still performs slightly more chores than Steven, but he is very rarely in the kitchen and *not* performing some sort of housework. Steven's commitment to undertaking a fair amount of domestic labor is not inconsequential in the 1980s, when dual-career couples were struggling to organize their home lives. *Family Ties'* equitable division of household labor may have been a fantasy for many working women, however, it still provided an ideal model of a well-functioning, happy couple who worked hard to maintain both successful careers and a fulfilling home life.

GENDERED CHOICES ON *GROWING PAINS*

Growing Pains is far less overtly engaged in politics than *Family Ties*, despite its similar formula of a humorously amorous dual-career couple with three children (increased to four after a few seasons), the eldest a son with teen idol potential. Indeed, *Variety's* review noted, "'Growing Pains' is a harmless sitcom series that reminds one vaguely of 'Family Ties,' with a much milder flavor than the NBC-TV hit series."[38] Although son Mike (Kirk Cameron) calls his father a "liberal humanist" in the pilot episode, neither the parents nor the kids readily engage in political discussion or action in the same way that the Keatons do. Still, it grapples with many of the same sort of home and work issues, with parents Maggie and Jason regularly struggling to balance their work commitments with their familial ones. Maggie struggles to let go of some of the control she once had over the house and the children, and Jason struggles to take on the role of primary disciplinarian and caretaker.

The first three episodes of *Growing Pains* clearly establish the premise of the show, with a voice-over introduction by Jason and Maggie. They explain:

> JASON: Hi, I'm Jason Seaver. I'm a psychiatrist, I've spent the last fifteen years helping people with their problems.
>
> MAGGIE: And I'm Maggie Seaver. I've spent the last fifteen years helping our kids with problems even Jason wouldn't believe.
>
> JASON: Now Maggie has gone back to work as a reporter for the local newspaper.
>
> MAGGIE: And Jason has moved his practice into the house so he can be there for the kids.[39]

The pilot episode begins with the family having breakfast. Maggie cooks and gives the kids their lunches, sending them off to school while Jason finishes paperwork before his first client arrives. Youngest child, Ben (Jeremy Miller), sneaks back in once Maggie is there alone and announces that his father didn't properly bandage his elbow. Upon inspection, Maggie correctly guesses that Jason failed to kiss it, and Ben complains, "It was all so clinical." When Ben quietly asks why she had to go back to work, Maggie explains that she wanted to and was bored staying home. She sits him on her lap as the camera slowly zooms in from medium long shot to medium close-up, and explains, "I worry about not being here for you, because, well, you're the youngest. And I worry about not being here for Carol, because she's a girl and she needs her mother. And I worry about not being here for Mike to keep him from accidentally blowing something up.

And *believe me*, I worry about leaving your father here to cope with all you monsters." Ben gives her an out, telling her she shouldn't worry so much and kissing her on the cheek. The camera zooms in slightly as they embrace, and she rocks him back and forth.

Despite Ben's soothing words, the rest of the episode proves that Maggie is right to worry, as Jason allows Mike to go to "The House of Sweat" with his friends, under the condition that if Mike is granted more freedom, he must assume more responsibility. Maggie is predictably furious, but Jason is even more incensed when his parenting strategy backfires and the police call to notify them that Mike has been arrested for driving without a license and hitting a police car. When Maggie wants to ground him for a month, Jason ups it to two, suggesting that he has made the move from good cop to bad cop and is settling into his new role as primary parent.

Maggie and Jason's work/home arrangement is threatened late in the first season when Jason is offered his dream job, head of psychiatry at Long Island General Hospital.[40] He is disturbed at the beginning of the episode when Carol (Tracey Gold) chooses to shadow Maggie rather than him for her career day project, telling him, "Dad, I need someone with a real job!" The morning routine showcases his domestic work, as he feeds Ben, takes Mike's temperature, and does laundry. As he fetches yeast to lend to a neighbor, his former boss shows up at his door, proceeds to make fun of his home office and private practice, and then offers to name Jason as his replacement. Jason explains that he cannot take the job because of his arrangement with Maggie. Meanwhile, Maggie gets in trouble at work when her editor finds out she failed to double-check the name of the man she accused of bribery in her front-page story. Jason makes a pros and cons list in the next scene, with a close-up revealing nine pros, including "increase in salary," "dream come true," "springboard to publishing," and "prestige," and a single con, "Maggie," written in capital letters, around which he draws a heart.

Maggie comes home and confesses to Jason that she is considering quitting her job. When she asks him what he thinks, he vaguely tells her that if she thinks she made a mistake going back to work, she should "do something about it." The next morning, Jason fears that Maggie has gone to quit and races to her office. However, before he arrives, Maggie and her (female) boss have mended fences, and Maggie admonishes Jason for giving her bad advice.[41] Jason admits, "I liked the idea of you coming back and taking over the house, Maggie. I've been feeling trapped." Maggie tells him she found his pros and cons list, and he says that when he made the list "it came out clearly against" taking the job, that the one con is more important than any of the pros, and acknowledges that it is his turn to stay home. Jason's willingness to stay home, sacrificing career advancement for his wife and family, particularly marks *Growing Pains* as a liberal feminist fantasy, where women and men sacrifice equally to combine full-time employment and family.

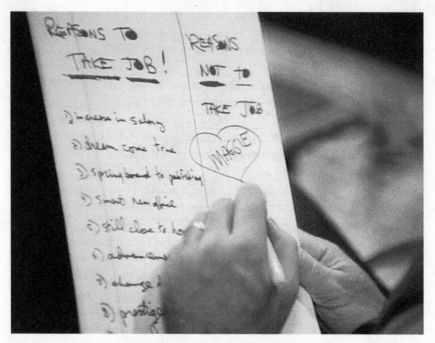

Figure 7. Jason prioritizes Maggie over his career on *Growing Pains*.

Yet Maggie's transition to full-time work is perhaps most difficult for Jason to deal with, as she does not have nearly as much time to spend with him. In "Jealousy," Maggie cannot come home to have lunch with Jason, so he goes to her office and meets Maggie's co-worker Fred (Thomas O'Rourke), who joins them for lunch and sparks Jason's jealousy. When Maggie repeatedly stays late at work, Jason comes up with an excuse to check up on her when Ben complains that Maggie is better at helping him with his science homework. Recognizing the real reason behind Jason's visit, Maggie suggests that he's going through the same thing she did for many years:

MAGGIE: I spent fifteen years in sweatpants cleaning toilets while you went to your office in your sexy psychiatrist sweater and your sexy psychiatrist jacket.

JASON: My jackets aren't sexy, Maggie, they're tweed!

MAGGIE: Women die for tweed and you know it.

JASON: I have no control over that!

MAGGIE: And how many nights did I spend watching your broccoli go limp while I waited for you to come home?

JASON: I was fighting traffic, Maggie!

MAGGIE: Yeah, with that brilliant young psychiatrist in your carpool!

Their argument resolves when Maggie explains that he will get used to wait-ing for her to come home, just as she did when she stayed at home. Yet clearly, this conflict is ongoing, as Maggie's work schedule interferes with their anni-versary plans in "The Anniversary That Never Was."[42] Maggie first makes them late for their lunch reservation by frantically cleaning the kitchen because "the cleaning woman's coming, I can't let her see this mess!" Just as Jason coaxes her out of the kitchen, she gets a call from her editor who is sending her to Wash-ington, D.C., to conduct an interview. She promises to fly there and back in time for a romantic dinner that evening, but just as Jason is putting the finishing touches on their meal, she calls to tell him the interview was postponed and she must stay in Washington overnight. In a classic sitcom plot formula, Maggie decides to fly home anyway and arrives just moments after Jason has left for the airport to fly to Washington. Luckily, Maggie is able to get on the same flight, and they celebrate their anniversary on the plane. Similar to the *Family Ties* episodes "Elyse D'Arc" and "Working at It," Maggie and Jason do not find an easy resolution to what promises to be an ongoing problem, yet their tempo-rary solution is romantic enough to provide satisfying closure to the episode, and to suggest to viewers that balancing two careers, marriage, and family can be done, even under extreme circumstances.

Though Maggie clearly enjoys escaping the confines of domesticity, Jason's transition to primary caretaker of the children upsets her, to the point where she accuses him of excluding her from the kids' lives.[43] Jason takes on the role of confidante for Carol, who is having boy trouble, and he encourages her not to believe all the secondhand gossip that has gotten her down. When Maggie comes home and tries to talk to Carol, she confirms that Jason already took care of it. Jason also pledges to be Carol's shopping partner, a move Maggie resents when she tries to plan a mother-daughter trip into the city. Recognizing Maggie's dismay, Jason attempts to involve her in Carol's next crisis; however, Carol goes back to Jason each time he tries to bring Maggie into the conver-sation. Carol sits on Jason's lap while he manages to rationalize the convoluted he said/she said story Carol is relaying, and as she calms down, Maggie slowly walks out of the room looking defeated. When Jason tries to catch Maggie, Carol cries, "Dad, it's just not fair!" and the camera cuts to a medium close-up of Maggie, gazing back at them longingly. After he comforts Carol, Jason goes to talk to Maggie, who accuses him of "pampering the children," for instance, baking Ben's favorite cookies. Jason tells her that she wants him to be good at taking care of the kids, but not as good as she is. In a reversal of their conversa-tion in "Jealousy," in this episode, Jason eases Maggie's jealousy of his new role in the home. He says, "I was at work when Ben took his first step. And when Carol spoke her first sentence. And when Mike committed his first illegal act. I missed out on all that. And now I have a chance to be closer to the kids, spend more time." She admits that she doesn't want to be the stay-at-home partner,

Figure 8. Maggie feels left out when Carol turns to Jason for advice on *Growing Pains*.

rather, she wants "to have it all . . . but you can't." After she and Jason quickly make up, the last scene of the episode features the entire family watching a sitcom together. Thus the episode suggests that, although working parents cannot truly "have it all," they can bond and spend time as a family watching primetime television.

Familial sacrifices come up again when Carol has the opportunity to skip a grade in the second season.[44] Jason expresses concern that Maggie has turned Carol into a manic overachiever who values academic success at the expense of her social life. His theory is confirmed when Maggie talks to Carol about her ambitions, and Carol reveals that she has no interest in getting married or having children, that she only wants a career:

CAROL: But for as long as I can remember you've told me to work hard, think about college and a career.
MAGGIE: Sure I did—
CAROL: So what's the point of doing that just to get married and give it up like you did?
MAGGIE: I haven't given up anything!
CAROL: Mom, you worked for *Newsweek* and quit to raise kids!
MAGGIE: Yes, but now I've gone back to work.
CAROL: For a *local* newspaper.

Carol's diminution of Maggie's career obviously hurts, as Maggie protests, touting the *Long Island Herald*'s circulation rate. Maggie tells Jason that Carol thinks she is "some kind of saint who gave up everything" for Jason and the kids. Jason asks, "Does she know that's the choice you made?" Maggie says Carol doesn't believe it, so Jason comes up with an idea to show Carol how Maggie felt about having children. While Carol studies, Jason brings out an audiotape recording of her birth. Carol listens to herself being born, with Maggie crying that it is "the happiest day of [her] life," and Maggie and Jason creep into the room. As the tape ends, Maggie asks, "Does that sound like a woman who regretted her choice?" Maggie tells Carol that she has "options," that she can have a family, a career, either or both. In the next scene, Carol decides not to skip the grade, noting her "choices," as though vicariously experiencing maternal joy has cured her of her intellectual ambitions.

Perhaps more disturbingly, in the next episode, Carol outperforms Jason in housework.[45] The episode begins with Carol cooking and Ben washing dishes while he laments to Mike, "Mom and Dad are sick and Carol's mad with power." Maggie is ecstatic with Carol's housekeeping, telling Jason, "I haven't seen the house this organized since I went back to—work." She recognizes the potential sting of her words too late, however, as Jason replies, "Oh good, no, that's, that's very good, you tell a dying man he's a bad housewife." He continues to mope throughout the rest of the episode as Carol excels at running the house, saying in self-pity that his patients are probably cured too. Once Maggie lets Carol know that Jason is upset, the episode resolves with Carol shirking her duties by letting Ben stay up past his bedtime and make a mess. When Jason has to take over, he exclaims, "Suddenly I'm feeling much better!"

Thus in two episodes, Carol first reduces her academic ambitions and then gives up her managerial position in the home. The rest of the season finds her dating a football player[46] and seeking a nose job,[47] a paradoxical trajectory that suggests that she has both transformed into a more socially adept teenager and that the "choices" that Maggie lauds have left her feeling more confused and lost than she was before. Carol's representation is a mark of sitcoms struggling to appeal to the amorphous women's demographic. So as not to alienate nonworking women, Carol's initial, adamant refusal to validate family life must be tempered through postfeminist choice rhetoric. At the same time, Carol's ensuing obsession over her appearance, which came to an extratextual head during actress Tracey Gold's well-publicized (and plainly visible) battle with anorexia, haunts her character, suggesting that in fact, Carol made the wrong "choice" in sublimating her academic and career ambitions.

Just as Maggie serves as a conflicted feminine model for Carol, Jason's masculinity, and the influence it has on his sons, is the subject of several episodes. In "Be a Man," he clashes with Maggie's police officer father, Ed (Gordon Jump), who doesn't respect Jason's profession.[48] In "First Blood," he clashes physically with Ben's hockey coach (Dan Lauria), who has taught the kids to play dirty.[49] When Jason questions his coaching methods, the coach calls him a wimp, prompting Jason to explain that the coach has "sublimated anger" that he takes out on the kids. The coach retorts that Jason sounds "like one of them wussy shrinks" and continues to egg him on until they get into a fistfight. Mike and Ben are incredibly impressed with Jason's black eye, and Jason revels in his sons' admiration, despite Maggie's objections. When Ben comes home with a black eye the next day, explaining that he did what "Jason 'The Animal' Seaver would do," Jason realizes he needs to reeducate his sons in masculinity. He and Ben return to hockey practice, and Jason takes a punch to the stomach and walks away. The last scene reveals Jason as the new coach of the hockey team. He leads the boys in a cheer before the game:

> JASON: What are we gonna do?
> KIDS: Try hard!
> JASON: How we gonna play?
> KIDS: In a sportsmanlike manner!
> JASON: And what if we don't win?
> KIDS: You'll kill us!
> JASON: How do I mean that?
> KIDS: Facetiously!

The camera cuts to Maggie, who gives Jason the "A-OK" sign, ending the episode. Here Jason's nonviolent, less competitive masculinity replaces the coach's homophobic, gruff, and abusive masculinity, leaving Jason as the role model for the next generation.

In a season two episode, Jason advises Mike to be "sensitive" to Carol.[50] When Mike protests "guys are supposed to be tough, not sensitive," Jason calls upon a history of more emotionally complex men on television, asking Mike to "explain Alan Alda."[51] Jason manages to speak Mike's language, suggesting that sensitivity attracts women and referencing Maggie and Carol swooning while watching *Casablanca*. Though Mike remains unconvinced, his romantic story line ends in disaster, and the episode resolves with Mike and Ben watching *Casablanca* for tips, suggesting that Jason has successfully swayed not only budding womanizer Mike but also his younger son into adopting a more "feminine" gender identity, an identity that is, importantly, adopted through modeling oneself after media images of men. By referencing not only Alda but a longer history of mediated masculinity, this episode teaches the Seaver boys to follow in their father's footsteps while simultaneously placing Jason Seaver in the same line of men who can model a different form of masculinity for viewers.

Feminist Lessons on *The Cosby Show*

In their audience study of *The Cosby Show*, Sut Jhally and Justin Lewis found that viewers simultaneously believed the series was a realistic depiction of family life and recognized it was a fantasy. They write, "In the course of the interview viewers would move from talking about the typicality of the Huxtables to commenting on their fairy-tale lives without any apparent sense of contradiction."[52] Labeling this contradiction "an easy realism that people desire," Jhally and Lewis argue that *The Cosby Show*'s depiction of an upper middle-class black family permits white viewers the "luxury of being both liberal and intolerant. They reject bigotry based upon skin color, yet they are wary of most (working class) black people. Color difference is okay, cultural difference is not."[53] Beretta Smith-Shomade refers to the Cosbys as "the ideal American Family that just happened to be Black,"[54] and John D. H. Downing calls *The Cosby Show* a "*realizable utopia,* with hints and suggestions, not for gardening or cooking, but for solving life's problems. The prescriptions offered are not conveyed like commandments, but emerge from the action like a contemporary morality play."[55]

Jhally and Lewis's interviewees note in particular the seemingly unlimited free time obstetrician Cliff seems to have, with one respondent noting, "Well, we've talked about this about a lot of shows—he's never busy. He's never working, it's not realistic . . . . The time factor of the parents is usually so unrealistic. They're working, but yet they're never really frenzied, and they have so much time and energy to put into each of their kids' problems."[56] Another respondent goes so far as to call Cliff a "house husband" since "you never see him in his office; he's home all of the time, and he's essentially home more than his wife is."[57] Shattering popular expectations for a doctor to have a hectic schedule with long hours, Cliff is almost always home in the afternoon when the children return from school. Conveniently, as he notes in a season two episode where he arrives home from the hospital in the morning just as Clair (a lawyer) is getting ready to leave for work, babies are often born in the overnight hours.[58] In the season five episode "Cliff Babysits," Clair is called to work to finish a sick co-worker's brief, leaving Cliff to babysit their daughter Sondra's (Sabrina Le Beauf) twins all by himself.[59] On her way out, Clair pauses and asks Cliff, "Can you handle this?" He replies, "Are you standin' there? I brought up five children by myself!" This joke, while obviously not intended to be accurate, still partially exemplifies Clair and Cliff's domestic arrangement, reassuring Clair as she leaves for a Saturday night at the office that her grandchildren will be well cared for.

Jhally and Lewis's respondents are correct in observing that Cliff and Clair live a charmed life, especially for a couple with two stressful, demanding professional careers and five children ranging from college age to preschool. Further adding to the fantasy, as Robin Means Coleman points out, both Clair and

Cliff have managed to "achieve professional success, in White male-dominated fields, completely unencumbered."[60] As a working mother with a demanding job, Clair certainly benefits from Cliff's domestic orientation, especially his dedication to child-rearing—*The Cosby Show* consistently reiterates Bill Cosby's credentials in this area, with the "created by" title that opens each episode reminding the viewer that he is not only Bill Cosby the actor or Dr. Cliff Huxtable the character but also William H. Cosby, Jr., EdD, doctor of education. Though by 2014, Cosby's public reputation was marred by a disturbing series of sexual assault allegations resulting in his conviction in 2018, in the 1980s, he was widely adored as "America's Dad," doling out weekly parenting tips not only as a TV dad but as an expert in education. Cliff regularly counsels the children in Clair's absence, as he is often napping on the couch when they come home from school. While Clair regularly prepares meals as soon as she returns home from work, Cliff cooks as well, especially taking up the slack on the occasions when Clair works late. Though Cliff's cooking is sometimes the butt of the children's jokes, as in the season one episode "Clair's Case" where he uses cow tongue to flavor a soup, they also acknowledge that his meals are delicious (as long as the ingredients remain a mystery).[61] In "Slumber Party," Cliff agrees to let Rudy (Keshia Knight Pulliam) have a sleepover, despite the fact that Clair is working late, and he enlists Theo's (Malcolm Jamal Warner) help in making dinner and Denise's (Lisa Bonet) help in entertaining the kids.[62] Clair and Cliff often delegate tasks between themselves and their children—in the season two premiere, Clair makes breakfast while Cliff gets the kids ready and makes their lunches.[63]

Just as Meredith Baxter Birney's pregnancy during the third season of *Family Ties* allowed Steven Keaton to fully display his abilities as a domesticated dad, Phylicia Rashad's pregnancy during the third season of *The Cosby Show* similarly allows Cliff's domestic aptitude to shine (though unlike Birney's pregnancy, Rashad's was not written into the narrative). Episodes in this season often include only a single, brief scene with Clair, and she is completely absent from a few episodes. While Clair is not present for a variety of reasons, including being bedridden with the flu,[64] in Washington, D.C., for a conference,[65] and visiting Denise at college,[66] Cliff handles everything at home with good cheer and effective delegation of tasks. Just as the Keaton children generously contribute to housework, the episode "Denise Gets a D" opens with Cliff, Vanessa (Tempestt Bledsoe), and Rudy preparing breakfast for Clair, who is bedridden, this time with a pinched nerve. After Cliff sends Vanessa and Rudy upstairs with Clair's tray, he turns to Theo, who is clearing the kitchen table.

CLIFF: What are you doing?
THEO: Cleaning the table.
CLIFF: Did I ask you to clear the table?
THEO: No.

CLIFF: Well, why are you clearing the table?

THEO: Well, with Mom laid up for a while, I think we all need to pitch in and do a little bit extra.

Cliff cannot believe what he hears, and follows up by making sure Theo still intends to do his regular chores, which he does, in addition to offering to take Rudy to her dance class. Theo continues his responsible streak in "A Girl and Her Dog," as he does the grocery shopping, and in "Calling Dr. Huxtable," as he cares for Rudy when Cliff is called to the hospital.[67] Theo's hard work pays off when Cliff proposes the inaugural meeting of the "Huxtable Men's Club," complete with hoagies, while Clair is at Hillman College planning a retirement celebration.[68] Given that the series usually frames Theo as the least responsible of the Huxtable children, these episodes are particularly notable in that they establish that Cliff's domestic masculinity has had at least some influence on Theo. Bambi Haggins calls *The Cosby Show* and *Family Ties* "mirror sitcoms," noting that both prioritize educating the eldest son in the familial value system, a feat made all the more difficult thanks to Theo's and Alex's hostility toward their parents' ideologies.[69]

Cliff often counsels other male characters in his form of domesticated masculinity. Downing suggests these messages could be equally as persuasive for male viewers, noting that Cliff's "condemnation of everyday sexism perhaps communicates itself all the more powerfully to male viewers precisely because he cannot be written off as a henpecked wimp."[70] Similarly, Jhally and Lewis point out that *The Cosby Show* seems much more invested in combating sexism than combating racism.[71] As Cliff tells a patient's overtly sexist husband in the season one episode "Father's Day," "You gotta understand that the days of being the boss, the barefoot and pregnant, I mean, that's thirty years ago, the old-fashioned man is out."[72] In a long-running joke, Cliff (and especially Clair) clash with Sondra's on-off boyfriend, Elvin (Geoffrey Owens). Elvin first appears in season two, when Sondra breaks up with him and he attempts to win her back, and the episode establishes the fact that they have broken up repeatedly, making everyone in the family miserable in the process thanks to Sondra's moping and short temper.[73] In an attempt to interrupt this pattern, Cliff encourages Sondra to go out with Daryl (Joseph C. Phillips), an Oberlin student her friends have been trying to set her up with, who turns out to be Cliff's ideal. The episode emphasizes the contrast between Elvin and Daryl through parallel conversations each man has with Cliff about familial gender roles. While Elvin complains about how his mother's career prevents her from serving the family a "hot meal" for dinner (to which Cliff replies, "Are your hands broken?"), Daryl explains how everyone in his family can cook and they all pitch in. Cliff expresses his admiration of Daryl to Clair, who informs Cliff that despite what he might like to think about himself, in fact, he used to be "an Elvin."

In spite of Cliff's attempts to push Sondra and Daryl together, however, Sondra goes back to Elvin and the two eventually marry in season four. Elvin's sexism and the conflict it produces within the Huxtable family is a running joke, as in the season three episode "Cliff in Charge," where Rudy and her friend Kenny (Deon Richmond) get in an argument about gender roles set off by Kenny's insisting that he open the door for Rudy. (Kenny's sexism also becomes a running joke, as he constantly parrots the chauvinistic ideas he hears from his brother.) Cliff intervenes, sitting between the two kids on the couch. He turns to Kenny and begins, "Now look, Elvin." Prior to marrying Sondra, Elvin appears to show interest in making a similar shift to Cliff, as in the opening scene of the season two episode "The Auction," where Elvin frosts a cake he baked in the hopes of getting in good with Clair.[74] Still, his gender politics have not made a full transition, as he calls cooking "woman's work," prompting Denise to protest, "This is not 'woman's work'—my dad cooks, a lot of men cook!" Judging his cake to be a failure, Cliff promises to take Elvin under his wing and help him cook a family dinner to impress Clair. However, Cliff's lesson is mainly in how to perform cooking, while jazzing up a store-bought pasta sauce with garlic and spices, and in the end, Clair reveals her knowledge of Cliff's counterfeit "famous" spaghetti sauce.

By season five, however, Elvin seems to have made a transition into the "Daryl" Cliff wanted him to be. When Cliff's father brings home eight tickets to

Figure 9. Cliff shows Elvin how to pretend he can cook on *The Cosby Show*.

see Michael Jackson, Sondra wants to take the opportunity to have a night out without their twin babies.[75] Clair agrees that she and Cliff can babysit, but Elvin has never left the twins alone and tries to come up with excuses for why they cannot attend the concert. He eventually brings over an absurd amount of baby paraphernalia for Cliff and Clair to babysit for a total of three hours, but even still, Clair has to drag him out of the house to get him to leave the babies. When Sondra and Elvin return from the concert, Elvin agrees that the night was a success, claiming, "We're definitely going to do that again—when they're three or four." In this episode, Elvin's approach to parenting mirrors Steven Keaton's—he is so devoted to his children that it pains him to leave them for a few hours.

In the season five episode "It Comes and It Goes," Sondra and Elvin are back to clashing over gender roles, as Sondra is staying home to care for their twins while Elvin attends medical school.[76] They plan to switch roles once he has set up his practice so that she can attend law school, but for the moment she feels burnt out and underappreciated. The episode largely revolves around a "battle of the sexes" with Sondra complaining to Clair, her mother-in-law, and her grandmother, and Elvin complaining to his father, Cliff, and Cliff's father. In the middle of the episode, a comedic exchange between Rudy and her sexist friend Kenny encapsulates *The Cosby Show*'s standard line on gender equality. As the two children look in on Sondra and Elvin's twins, they trade banter:

KENNY: My brother says that a baby is the greatest gift that a woman could give a man.
RUDY: Give a man? A woman does not *give* a man a baby. They share it.
KENNY: No they don't. She gives it to him. Then he lends it back to her to raise it.
RUDY: When I have my baby, I'm going out and getting a good job and my husband's staying home with the baby.
KENNY: Looks like you won't be having babies.
RUDY: Yes I will, and I'll have a good job, too.
KENNY: That's the problem with the world today. Too many women working. They mess things up.
RUDY: No we don't.
KENNY: Well, my brother works for a woman, and she's always on him. If he's a half hour late or he falls asleep at the desk, she's all over him. I'm never gonna work for a woman.
RUDY: You're never gonna work, because we're everywhere!
KENNY: I'll get a job building houses.
RUDY: Women do that.
KENNY: Then I'll dig ditches.
RUDY: Women do that.

KENNY: Then I'll join the army.

RUDY: We're in the army, too. We can do everything you can do, only better.

With that, Rudy leaves the room, emphatically marking her statement as the last word. Here, Rudy clearly articulates the gender politics of her parents, and she assumes Clair's position of exposing the faulty logic and assumptions under-pinning sexist opinions.

At the end of "Cliff in Love," the episode wherein Elvin and Sondra break up and reunite despite Cliff's best efforts, Clair offers Elvin and Cliff coffee, much to Elvin's surprise. He exclaims, "You mean, you're gonna get it?" and explains that he did not realize that Clair "served" Cliff. As Elvin digs himself further into a hole with Clair, Cliff slowly crosses in front of Elvin and sits down, and his bemused reaction shots interrupt the shot-reverse shot pattern as Clair and Elvin go back and forth. A medium close-up of Clair pointing her finger at Elvin and proclaiming, "Let me tell you something, Elvin" cuts to a shot of Cliff shak-ing his head and burying it in his hand. The camera then cuts to a medium close-up of Elvin, vaguely smiling as if woefully unprepared for Clair's impending remarks, as the studio audience's laughter guides the viewer to align herself with Clair. Once the laughter dies down, the camera cuts back to Clair, who continues, "You see, I am not serving Dr. Huxtable, okay?" The camera cuts back to Elvin, who quickly and nervously replies "okay" before she has finished. The camera cuts back to Clair, who again continues, "That's the kind of thing that goes on in a restaurant. Now I am going to bring him a cup of coffee, just like he brought me a cup of coffee this morning. And that, young man, is what marriage is made of, it is give and take, 50-50. And if you don't get it together, and drop these macho attitudes, you are never gonna have anybody bringing you anything, anywhere, anyplace, anytime, ever." As she finishes this statement, the studio audience whoops their agreement and the camera cuts to Cliff, wide-eyed and covering his mouth with his hand. A shell-shocked Elvin sheepishly offers, "Maybe I could get you some coffee."

In addition to clashing with Elvin, Clair regularly issues correctives to any sexist behavior that she witnesses. Here Clair acts a stand-in for the ideal pro-fessional woman viewer; as marketing guru Rena Bartos cautioned, "Advertis-ers should be warned that career women are particularly turned off by sexist tonality."[77] When Denise brings her seemingly intelligent, mature boyfriend David (Kristoff St. John) over for dinner, Clair is enchanted until he pointedly asks her, "What I really don't understand, Mrs. Huxtable, is why do you divide your time between pursuing your career and raising your family?"[78] After Clair incredulously asks him for his point, David replies, "Your husband makes a tre-mendous amount of money! Shouldn't you just stay at home with the kids?" Clearly incensed, Clair snaps, "That is a sexist statement, young man, why didn't

Figure 10. Clair takes Elvin to task for his sexism on *The Cosby Show*.

you ask Dr. Huxtable that same question?" Cliff swiftly shuffles Clair out of the dining room, and Denise rushes past them, dragging David behind her, explaining that they have to hurry off to a movie. The episode's resolution validates Clair's outrage, ending with Denise complaining that David took her to a documentary about polygamy, and she plans to break up with him, much to Clair and Cliff's delight.

Jhally and Lewis's respondents seem to idealize Clair, with one noting, "She's a very good representation of women. I think she carries off the whole scene . . . with humor and dignity and intelligence. And confidence . . . She dresses beautifully, yeah. And she always looks so beautifully groomed. Yeah, she's an inspiration."[79] Indeed, Jhally and Lewis discover that many of their respondents identified so strongly with the characters that "the Huxtables are frequently seen as behavioral models. Cosby, like a televisual version of Abigail Van Buren or Ann Landers, advises us on how to live our own lives."[80]

While Clair clearly spends more time at work than Cliff does (overnight births notwithstanding), her working life seems to be significantly less stressful than Elyse Keaton's or Maggie Seaver's. On the day she interviews to become a partner in her law firm, Rudy is sick, and Clair worries about leaving her with Cliff, since, despite his medical credentials, she does not believe he cares for sick children the way a mother would.[81] She wants to hire a babysitter, but Cliff protests (since he does not have any patients scheduled before 1 P.M.), and Clair agrees to let him take care of Rudy, though she leaves him with a list of instructions to ensure her proper care. At her office, Clair is interviewed by one of the partners she has never met, an older white man named Mr. Halifax (Clarke Gordon). While a viewer might expect that Clair would face at least some tough, skeptical questions, instead, Mr. Halifax talks about himself at a rapid-fire pace, barely allowing Clair to get a word in. Thanks to Mr. Halifax's verbosity, Clair is late getting home, and Cliff has to leave Rudy to see his first patient (luckily, he sets her up on the living room couch, just steps away from his basement office). When Clair tells Mr. Halifax that she needs to make a "personal call," he says "of course," then mutters, "I don't make many personal calls myself." This statement appears at face value to be in line with a masculine corporate culture that eschews any meaningful combination of work and family life; however, in the context of this particular character, the joke is clearly that he never stops talking about himself, thus making any "personal calls" unnecessary. Indeed, Clair is ultimately named partner, despite never actually interviewing for the position, when Mr. Halifax calls her at home and she leaves the phone off the hook as the episode ends while he continues talking without pausing for any response.

Clair only occasionally seems harried at home. When she does bring work home, it usually involves family, as in the season one episode "Clair's Case," where she represents Sondra in a lawsuit against a crooked mechanic who overcharged her. This episode revolves around Clair being unusually busy with work—Cliff teaches Theo to make a bed, and thanks him for pitching in; Rudy, Denise, and Vanessa clean the kitchen; and Cliff cooks, impersonating Julia Child. Meanwhile, Clair is up at 2 A.M. working in the bedroom, much to Cliff's delight when he comments, "I love when you practice law in your pajamas." This episode also provides a rare glimpse of Clair in the courtroom, flanked by Sondra (at the plaintiff's table) and Cliff (in the audience). Cliff is obviously attracted to Clair's courtroom demeanor, and while the episode makes clear that she has caught the mechanic in a lie, it ends with a kiss from Cliff as the defense asks for a recess, suggesting that her marriage and family are the true victory and that whether or not she wins the case is less important.

Clair also uses her legal expertise to her advantage in managing the family. In the season two episode "The Juicer," Clair playfully puts Cliff on trial after Rudy and her friend Peter (Peter Costa) have used his juicer and made a mess in the kitchen.[82] She gets him to admit that he left the juicer plugged in, thus "contributing to the delinquency of a six-year-old," but Cliff manages to weasel his way "out of contempt" by kissing her. She uses a similar, more formal tactic in the season four episode "Theogate," when she suspects Theo of lying about the reason he was late for Vanessa's school play.[83] When Theo begs to be treated as an adult, Clair agrees, serving him with a summons and his best friend, Cockroach (Carl Payne), with a subpoena. Clair rearranges the living room into a courtroom, complete with Cliff dressed as a bailiff and Vanessa dressed as a judge. Rudy and her friends Peter and Kenny serve as the jury, whom Cockroach (acting as Theo's attorney) tries to sway by prejudicing them against parental oversight and bribing them with a promise of ice cream. Once again, Clair's legal aptitude prevails when Theo admits that he was kicked off the cross-country team. Though the viewer rarely sees Clair in the courtroom or in her office, these episodes leave no doubt that she is a highly skilled attorney, as well as a highly respected authority in her home.

LEARNING TO CRY ON *SILVER SPOONS*

Silver Spoons debuted in 1982, the same year and on the same network as *Family Ties*, with a similar premise of parent-child discord. However, on *Silver Spoons*, the conflict between father and son is not political, but rather on the level of maturity—twelve-year-old Ricky is mature beyond his years, and his father Edward is ridiculously juvenile. Ricky had never met his father, having lived with his mother until she remarried and enrolled him in military school. Edward is a spoiled, wealthy man who owns a toy company and spends his days playing videogames in his toy-filled mansion. He was unaware that he had a son until Ricky showed up hoping to live with him. The series revolves around Ricky and Edward both learning to become sensitive, responsible men, as Ricky learns to loosen up a bit, and Edward learns to become a caring, responsible father. In the pilot episode, Edward's lawyer, Leonard (Leonard Lightfoot), accuses him of taking "no responsibility for [his] affairs," while Edward ignores him and plays Pac-man.[84] Shortly thereafter, Ricky appears at the door dressed in his military school uniform. The contrast between his costuming and Edward's (casual clothes and a baseball cap), suggests that while Edward is irresponsible, Ricky is responsible beyond his years. At the end of the pilot episode, when Edward goes to Ricky's school to bring him home, he tells Ricky, "I figured maybe I could help you be more of a kid, you could help me be less of one." As they leave for home, Edward replaces Ricky's military uniform hat with his own baseball cap, sealing their tradeoff. The program's theme song highlights this narrative thread, pledging that father and son will grow "together, taking the time each day / to learn all about those things you just can't buy." Clearly, the "things you just can't buy" are the emotional lessons that the two will learn over the course of the program.

Edward's career as head of a toy company makes him particularly well-suited to the role of domesticated dad. Not only does Ricky get to participate in testing out new toys, but Edward conducts all of his business in their home. His lawyer, assistant, and business managers all come to him—in fact during the first season of *Silver Spoons*, Edward never leaves the house unless he is with Ricky. He is home every day when Ricky comes home from school, as is Kate, Ricky's future stepmother, who also works in the Stratton home.[85] While Kate's nominal position is Edward's personal assistant, she takes on a motherly role for Ricky from the very beginning, making him a sandwich in the pilot episode and straightening his clothes in "A Little Magic."[86] Kate also plays the part of career woman. Though she turns down an executive-level job offer that Edward's father extended with the intention to sabotage her romantic relationship with Edward,[87] it is quite obvious that she performs just as many executive duties within the toy company as Edward does, and eventually, she becomes president.[88] Throughout the series, Ricky, Edward, and Kate live in familial, economic, and professional bliss. Their extreme wealth (the opening credits feature an exterior shot of their castle-like mansion) only adds to the fantasy of a dual-career stepfamily that manages to solve every argument with a hug, mutual understanding, and a healthy dose of tears.

The first lesson that Edward must learn is to discipline Ricky, which presents quite the challenge in the episode "Boys Will Be Boys."[89] When Edward doesn't have the nerve to punish Ricky, Ricky's friend Derek (Jason Bateman) tells him if his father doesn't punish him, it means he doesn't love him. Upset, Ricky continually acts out in the hopes of being punished and thus feeling secure in his father's love. Finally, after Ricky drops a balloon filled with whipped cream on Leonard's head, Edward realizes he has to punish him. Still, he is uncomfortable with the process, asking Ricky, "So, any thoughts on what I should do to you?" Clearly exasperated, Ricky replies, "Dad, it's not up to me! I did the messing up and now I'm supposed to think of my punishment too? I can't do everything, give me a break!" When Edward confesses that he feels bad about punishing Ricky, Ricky begins to cry, and asks, framed in medium close-up, "Why don't you like me?" Edward sits him down and explains his aversion to discipline. Like Steven Keaton, Edward strives to depart from the strict paternal authority he experienced as a child. As the camera zooms in from long shot to a medium two-shot for maximum emotional effect, he tells Ricky that when he was a kid he brought his father some orange juice, but tripped and spilled it. The camera cuts to medium close-up as Edward relays the consequences of his mistake. He begins to choke up as he recalls: "He called me a stupid, clumsy fool, and he sent me to my room, and I was never allowed in his study again." Midway through this sentence, the camera cuts to a tight close-up of Ricky wiping tears from his eyes. Ricky asks, "Well, did you cry?" The camera cuts to a close-up of Edward, who pauses, then admits, "Real hard." The episode ends as they exchange "I love yous" and Edward tells Ricky he has to stay in his room for two days.

Silver Spoons sets up Edward's masculinity and fathering style in opposition to his father's, Edward Stratton II (notably played by John Houseman, who receives applause from the studio audience every time he enters a scene). In the episode "Grandfather Stratton," Ricky seeks out his grandfather, since Edward refuses to have anything to do with him.[90] Broadcast the week following "Boys

Figure 11. Edward and Ricky share an emotional moment on *Silver Spoons*.

Will Be Boys," this episode finds Ricky trying to facilitate reconciliation between his father and grandfather. He successfully woos Edward II to their home, and just as Ricky tells him that "[Edward's] got me now, and that's made him a dependable, responsible, mature man," Edward III enters the living room via his toy train. Ricky manages to mediate a business dispute between them, then tries to initiate friendly conversation. Though he is unsuccessful in convincing them to tell each other that they love each other, he does manage to arrange a trip to a baseball game for the three of them. More progress is made in "Honor Thy Father," where Edward II orders Edward III to deliver a speech commemorating Edward II at an awards banquet.[91] Though he initially refuses and leaves Ricky to take on the task, Edward III has a change of heart. After further detailing his painful childhood to Kate, showing her a Father's Day card he made as a child that his father never received because he was on a business trip, Edward shows up at the banquet at the last minute, and gives his father the card. Following this symbolic moment of closure, Edward II admonishes him for being late, but then sincerely thanks him for coming. The episode ends with a father-son embrace, mirroring the majority of *Silver Spoons* episodes, which end with Ricky and Edward hugging. This emotional conclusion marks a new level of maturity for Edward III, who exhibits far less animosity toward his father in following episodes.[92]

Much of Edward III's sensitivity is displayed through his willingness to cry, a trait he encourages in Ricky as well.[93] When Ricky's mother, Evelyn (Christine Belford), challenges Edward for custody, Ricky and Edward's emotional openness takes center stage, and the episode revels in close-ups of their tear-drenched faces.[94] As Edward prepares for a court battle, Leonard details how the suit could turn nasty and ultimately hurt Ricky. Edward decides to sacrifice his parental rights in order to save Ricky any potential pain. As he tells Ricky that he has to live with his mother, the camera cuts between them in shot-reverse shot, each with tears in their eyes. Close-ups of Ricky reveal red eyes glistening with tears and tear-stained cheeks as he tells Edward how much he will miss him while sniffling. When he goes to pack Ricky's things, Edward asks if he can keep Ricky's *E.T.* shirt: "It's the one I cried on in the movie." As they say their goodbyes (Ricky makes Edward promise to "eat at least one green vegetable a day"), they both cry harder and sniffle more audibly, resulting in an extended embrace, with frequent cutaways to Evelyn, who looks increasingly touched. Their emotional display persuades her to allow Edward primary custody. Edward and Ricky's mutually caring relationship seems to have struck a chord with her as she tells them to "take care of each other" before she leaves.

Ricky tries to educate other men in the wonders of masculine sensitivity. In "Won't You Go Home, Bob Danish?," Kate's former suitor returns in an attempt to win her back.[95] Once Kate tells him to get lost, Bob (John Reilly) tries to put on a brave face, but Ricky encourages him to express his emotions. Bob explains to Ricky that his father taught him that "real men don't cry," once again underscoring generational differences, but Ricky counters that his father taught him that it is "okay for a man to cry," and that it makes a person feel better. Upon hearing this affirmation, Bob bursts into tears and clutches Ricky while he sobs. Ricky laughs nervously, but still strokes Bob's hair, kisses his head, and comforts him, offering him tissues. As he calms down, Bob admits that he feels better: "Son of gun! My first cry!" The episode ends with Bob putting the used tissues into his scrapbook, suggesting that this is a moment of conversion.

Ricky similarly deals a blow to tough masculinity in "Me and Mr. T" when he clashes with a school bully.[96] When Ricky comes home with a black eye, Edward panics and hires Mr. T to serve as his bodyguard. Mr. T terrifies not only Ox the bully (John P. Navin, Jr.), but also the rest of Ricky's classmates and his teacher. Ricky is mortified, and desperately wants to stand up to Ox himself. While Edward refuses to listen to Ricky, Mr. T steps in and suggests that he let Ricky handle the problem himself. Realizing he over-reacted, Edward apologizes to Ricky, telling him, "I'm kinda new at this father stuff, you know? I'm gonna make mistakes sometimes." They seal their agreement with the ever-present embrace, and the next day Ricky rallies his entire class to stand up to Ox and refuse to give him their lunch money. Despite Ox's attempt to appropriate Mr. T's masculine performance, the threat of the gang of his peers makes him back

Figure 12. Ricky encourages Bob Danish to get in touch with his emotions on *Silver Spoons*.

down, suggesting that Ricky's form of sensitive, communal masculinity, as modeled by his father, wins out over the individual tough guy persona.

CONCLUSION

Numerous feminist critics have taken issue with the continued impulse to maintain the nuclear family while encouraging a more domestically-oriented masculinity. Lynne Segal suggests that the figure of the domestic dad affords men even more power, "as it can be used to strengthen men's control over women and children, in a society where men are already dominant socially, economically and politically."[97] Similarly, Estella Tincknell argues that "rather than transforming or radicalizing masculinity, the new dad effectively extended the realm of male domination and patriarchal power, appropriating domestic space and expertise while resisting changes in the workplace."[98] Kies claims that the focus on domesticated dads marginalized women, removing them from "a television genre that had historically been dedicated to depicting feminine labor."[99]

Mary Vavrus argues that television news coverage of "Mr. Moms" in the 1990s does little to challenge the nuclear family, as they "naturalize the nuclear family and paternal dominance within it; they achieve, in essence, the domestication of patriarchy."[100] She further notes how the absence of gay fathers from this discourse shores up the nuclear family as staunchly heterosexual, regardless of who takes primary responsibility for child-rearing. At the same time, Vavrus points out that the stay-at-home fathers being profiled often point to the 1983 film *Mr. Mom* as providing "a parenting manual for them; it helps them to discern how fathers might do what has traditionally been expected of mothers."[101] Just as sitcoms like *Growing Pains* present templates for successful dual-career parenting, media iterations of the domesticated dad like *Mr. Mom* pedagogically orient fathers seeking models of masculinity that are commensurate with childcare and household responsibility.

While these critiques make valid and largely persuasive arguments about the limitations of the domesticated dad, most of the family sitcoms of the 1980s represent a rupture in the long-standing cultural preference for "mother care," a preference that, as Sonya Michel points out, "was reproduced, over and over again, as countless experts on childhood confronted the 'problem' of what to do with the children of working women."[102] Recognizing men as primary caretakers of children is an important step toward a more equitable workplace and more available childcare.[103] In addition to undermining cultural expectations of "mother care," *Family Ties, Growing Pains, The Cosby Show*, and *Silver Spoons* narratively solved many of the problems working women faced in the 1980s. By presenting new men and new workplaces, they erased many of the conflicts with which women dealt. Elyse and Maggie both go back to work under female bosses who understand their situations, and Steven, Jason, Cliff, and Edward are just as comfortable in domestic situations as they are at work.

Less than a year after *Growing Pains* and *The Cosby Show* went off the air, Nancy Marshall and Rosalind Barnett published an article in the *Journal of Community Psychology* that noted a potential solution to issues of work-family balance. They claim, "Two-earner couples in which the man encourages and supports his partner's employment, and both individuals hold less traditional attitudes about the roles of women and men, stand to reduce their experience of work-family strains and improve their sense of enhancement from combining work and family roles."[104] Marshall and Barnett assert, "Work-family strains are not inevitable." Perhaps the couples in their study who reported no work-family strains learned a few tips from family sitcoms. Recognizing the necessity of attracting professional women viewers, networks produced fantasies of domesticated dads who supported their wives' careers and took responsibility for the care of children and the home. The success of the programs translated into years of syndicated runs that presented domestic masculinity as a new ideal to a generation of children who watched the programs every day after school, all the while stirring anxieties about television serving as babysitter to unsupervised latchkey kids.

CHAPTER 3

SOLVING THE DAY-CARE
CRISIS, ONE EPISODE
AT A TIME

FAMILY SITCOMS AND PRIVATIZED
CHILDCARE IN THE 1980S

Throughout the 1980s, hand-wringing headlines cried out with questions like, "Who's Minding the Children?" "Who Will Care for the Children?" "Is Day Care Good for Kids?" and "Who's Watching the Kids?"[1] The *National Review* provided a clear response to these concerns, quoting a child development professor who suggested that infants placed in day-care centers were likely to experience adolescent problems with "drugs, alcohol, teen pregnancy, suicide."[2] These anxieties were heightened by several highly publicized abuse and injury cases at day-care centers.[3] Yet attempts to introduce legislation to help alleviate parents' struggles to obtain quality, affordable childcare were often met with conservative resistance, as critics labeled these moves socialist plots to undermine the strength and autonomy of the American family.[4] The need for day care in the United States in the 1980s, along with the Reagan administration's refusal to support comprehensive day-care policies, contributed to a media frenzy that proposed numerous solutions. Indeed, politicians often mobilized the phrase "family values" to cover over policies that did little to actually support families.

According to the Bureau of Labor Statistics, by the late 1980s, mothers of preschool-aged children were the fastest-growing segment of the labor force, and around 64 percent of mothers worked.[5] More than one hundred day-care-related bills were introduced into Congress in 1988, and none passed.[6] The Reagan administration continued to cut childcare funding throughout the decade, often appealing to a desire to keep government out of private life.[7] Instead, childcare took on an entrepreneurial cast, as day-care centers became lucrative business operations and as employment in childcare professions grew dramatically from the 1970s.[8] While Reagan slashed childcare aid for low-income families, he simultaneously introduced tax incentives for employers to provide day care and tax cuts for employees using employer-sponsored day care, a move "intended to facilitate parent choice and spur child care initiatives in the private sector."[9] Parents were duly encouraged to become conscientious day-care consumers, armed with all the information that magazines, newspapers, experts, and the government distributed. Reacting to calls for federal regulations pertaining to day-care centers, Jaclyn Fierman of *Fortune* wrote, "Parents are far better advocates for their children than bureaucrats. So are community health and fire officials. Consumers should decide whether providers are trustworthy, stimulating, and, above all, nurturing."[10] The U.S. Department of Health and Human Services equipped parents with the tools to discern appropriate day care, producing a pamphlet titled "A Parents' Guide to Day Care," which included a laundry list of things to check out before enrolling children.[11]

On the one hand, the news media and popular magazines offered tips for parents (especially mothers) seeking day care and implored corporations to offer some form of day-care or childcare benefits to their employees. On the other hand, family sitcoms modeled private, in-home forms of childcare that could accommodate working parents. These television family formations supplanted their 1950s counterparts, which had often been cited as exemplars of the "American family" in the popular press: in 1987, *Fortune* magazine noted that "the typical American family, with dad at work and mom taking care of the kids, is mainly the stuff of Ozzie and Harriet reruns. Less than 33 percent of families follow the Nelson family model, vs. 48 percent eleven years ago."[12] A few months later, *Time* substantiated this view, albeit with slightly different statistics: "Beaver's family, with Ward Cleaver off to work in his suit and June in her apron in the kitchen, is a vanishing breed. Less than a fifth of American families now fit that model, down from a third fifteen years ago."[13] These televisual images of the family loomed large in the national day-care debates as the premises of many sitcoms revolved around nonnuclear-family childcare arrangements. Conveniently, these invocations of golden-age family sitcoms ignore the programs that strayed from the nuclear-family form, such as *My Three Sons* (ABC, 1960–1965; CBS, 1965–1972) and *The Andy Griffith Show* (CBS, 1960–1968), as well as early programs that included extended families like *Mama* (CBS, 1949–1957) and *The Goldbergs* (CBS, 1949–1951; NBC, 1952–1953; DuMont, 1954; first-run syndication, 1955–1956).

Together, both nonfictional and fictional media operated as a governing strategy that instructed families of the 1980s to seek private solutions to their childcare needs. Michel Foucault saw government as "the way in which the conduct of individuals or of groups might be directed—the government of children, of souls, of communities, of families, of the sick . . . . To govern, in this sense, is to structure the possible field of action of others."[14] Sitcoms of the 1980s, alongside newspapers and magazines, direct the childcare choices of parent-citizens. These media structure the possibilities for childcare in such a way as to exclude the possibility of state intervention, guiding parents to make arrangements for the care of their children without any help from the state.

Mainstream newspapers and magazines overwhelmingly advocated workplace-provided day care, with the rationale that working parents would be more productive if they did not have to worry about their children's welfare.[15] Yet many articles also noted that parents considered live-in help to be preferable to day-care centers.[16] These solutions are buttressed by a variety of expert opinions that keep the focus off public-sector intervention. Dana E. Friedman, senior research fellow of the Conference Board's Work and Family Information Center and author of numerous books and studies, offered her opinion in a number of magazine and newspaper articles.[17] Friedman advocated corporate-sponsored day care for employees, aligning her with numerous corporate experts who cited loss of employee productivity in the absence of day care. For example, John P. Fernandez, manager of personnel services for AT&T, wrote *Child Care and Corporate Productivity*, in which he explained "that 77 percent of women and 73 percent of men he surveyed take time away from work attending to their children—making phone calls, ducking out for a long lunch to go to a school play. That alone translates into hundreds of millions of dollars in lost output for US corporations."[18] At the same time, child psychologists weighed in on the possible effects that day care (usually figured in the separation of the child from her or his mother—fathers are absolved of any responsibility for the most part) would have on children. Edward Zigler, a Yale University psychologist, offered the vague suggestion that children raised in day care might not be ready to take their appropriate place in society.[19] Even so, Zigler's solution is indebted to corporate logic; he suggested that elementary school buildings be used for day care, as "the schools in the United States represent a $1 trillion investment, and we ought to be using them more efficiently."[20] Many child psychologists and government officials argued for family care, in which children are cared for either by a parent or a member of extended family.[21] Family sitcoms offered a variety of in-home childcare solutions while ignoring the economic and logistical hurdles that made these models largely unattainable for the viewing public.

According to Foucault, the family is a primary instrument of government; thus, in the 1980s the issue of childcare was of great importance to neoliberal governance.[22] As Wendy Brown notes, "Neoliberalism normatively constructs and interpellates individuals as entrepreneurial actors in every sphere of life. It figures individuals as rational, calculating creatures whose moral autonomy is measured by their capacity for 'self-care'—the ability to provide for their own needs and service their own ambitions."[23] By arranging childcare without depending on the state, the family models self-responsibility for its children. Under a neoliberal governing rationality, parents act as entrepreneurial subjects in their pursuit of employment (at the expense of providing their own unwaged childcare) while at the same time childcare itself is entrepreneurialized as parents pay a wage to childcare providers and for-profit day-care centers crop up across the United States. In 1982, the *New York Times* detailed a day-care co-op that served two needs: "to provide day care in a home setting for children of working parents shut out of other facilities by income ceilings or waiting lists, and to offer employment for qualified women who want to work at home."[24] These models maximize individual productivity without state intervention such as public day-care centers.

In the mid- to late 1980s, many family sitcoms provided private, familial solutions to the day-care crisis that adhered to the same principles that the popular press advocated. These programs were scheduled in the first two hours of prime time with the hope of drawing a family audience of women and children. *Mr. Belvedere* (ABC, 1985–1990) offers the ideal situation: a British housekeeper with glowing references (Winston Churchill and the royal family) falls into the lap of a middle-class suburban family. Although *Mr. Belvedere* never cracked the top twenty in Nielsen ratings, its Friday-night time slot was intended to draw families with young children, and it was in the top twenty for children between the ages of two and eleven.[25] *Kate & Allie* (CBS, 1984–1989) presents an idealized image of the day-care co-op the *New York Times* described and remained in the top twenty Nielsen ratings for its first three seasons. Divorced friends Kate and Allie live together with their children. Allie stays home, performing domestic duties and looking after the children, while Kate works as a travel agent. This arrangement allows Allie to continue working as a homemaker and allows Kate reliable, in-home childcare. *My Two Dads* (NBC, 1987–1990) exemplifies one private solution the popular press had also offered: flexible work hours that accommodate childcare.[26] While one father works as a financial adviser, the other father works from home as an artist. In addition, the two men rely on an extended network to help them care for twelve-year-old Nicole, including the owner of the restaurant in their apartment building and the judge who arranged their family configuration. Despite falling out of the top twenty after its first season, *My Two Dads* managed to hold on to much of its lead-in *Family Ties* (NBC, 1982–1989) audience. *Full House* (ABC, 1987–1995) presents many conservatives' preferred model of childcare, with its elaborate extended network including widower Danny Tanner's brother-in-law Jesse and best friend Joey, and later Jesse's wife, Becky. *Full House* anchored ABC's "TGIF" Friday-night lineup, peaking in the top ten of Nielsen ratings in 1990 and 1991, despite its otherwise undesirable time slot.

It may be tempting to understand 1980s family sitcoms as toeing the line of conservative family values; however, they do not represent a simple return to the idealized traditional nuclear family. Although most of these programs do not come close to the more cynical, counternarrative sitcoms such as *Married . . .*

with Children (Fox, 1987–1997) and *Roseanne* (ABC, 1988–1997) that closed the decade, they do represent a negotiation wherein the idealized nuclear family must adjust to the socioeconomic and cultural pressures of the Reagan era. Most notably, many 1980s sitcoms featured men taking on more involved roles in parenting and housekeeping.[27] These more domestically oriented male characters suggest that for the family to remain an autonomous unit as the dual-income family became the norm, masculinity must be reformed so as to include more involvement in domestic life. Popular press coverage of day care and family sitcoms complement each other and work together under a neoliberal governing rationality that implores parent-citizens to take care of their own childcare needs without asking the state for assistance. Rather than presenting a united front for how the crisis should be solved, these media oblige parent-citizens to choose between many circumscribed options. Parent-citizens are free to choose whatever childcare arrangement works best for them, so long as that arrangement does not involve the state.

The Luck of the "Domestic Agency": *Mr. Belvedere* and Live-in Childcare

According to Dana Friedman in 1985, "Most working parents today are looking for live-in help for children under age three."[28] *Time* cites a woman who would prefer in-home care because "'that way there's a sense of security and family.' But she worries about the cost and reliability: 'People will quit, go away for the summer, get sick.'"[29] Indeed, turnover was of major concern to those seeking live-in childcare, especially as experts expounded the importance of consistency in caretakers.[30] *Mr. Belvedere* (along with *Charles in Charge* [CBS, 1984–1985; first-run syndication, 1987–1990] and *Who's the Boss?* [ABC, 1984–1992]) provided fantasy solutions to the problems that live-in housekeepers posed. Mr. Belvedere represents an ideal above and beyond his fellow television housekeepers. Whereas on *Charles in Charge* Charles (Scott Baio) is a full-time college student who regularly brings his buddies and dates to the house and on *Who's the Boss?* Tony (Tony Danza) requires an extra bedroom in the Bower home to accommodate his daughter, Mr. Belvedere (Christopher Hewett) seemingly has no family or friends and devotes his entire existence to the family. Mr. Belvedere remains faithful to the Owens family for the entire five-season run, never leaving the family in the lurch, even when he is ill, and managing to return to their home (legally) shortly after being deported. Although none of the Owens children is preschool age (the youngest, Wesley [Brice Beckham], is in elementary school), Mr. Belvedere gives vital advice and guidance to all of the children, beginning in the first episode.[31] The episode opens with the three children coming home from school and, as typical "latchkey" children, fending for themselves until their parents arrive. Trouble brews from the opening shot, where teenage Heather

(Tracy Wells) tries to talk her way out of a boy's sexual advances over the phone. Wesley interrupts her conversation by reminding her that she is supposed to start dinner. At this point teenage Kevin (Rob Stone) comes home, and Heather asks him to put a casserole in the oven. Mother Marsha (Ilene Graff) comes home from law school and mentions to the obviously harried children that she knows they need outside help. Kevin supports her claim by presenting her with his report card, littered with Ds. Fortuitously, the doorbell rings, yielding the help the Owens family so desperately needs in the form of a British housekeeper, Mr. Belvedere. Mr. Belvedere was ostensibly sent to the Owens residence by the "domestic agency" that Marsha had contacted.

Marsha and especially her husband, George (Bob Uecker), initially reject Mr. Belvedere for no apparent reason, other than perhaps his gender and his upper-crust sensibility. After Mr. Belvedere spends the night at the house, George explains to him over breakfast, "With the two of us gone so much, we need some-one to do more than just cook and clean," and Marsha interjects, "I mean, we need someone who can relate to the kids." Mr. Belvedere gets up to leave but then proves his worth, replying, "Oh, by the way, Kevin has changed his grades—downward. I'd ask him why. Heather doesn't want to go all the way—to Billy's house. And Wesley, I think Wesley would prefer a dog to this rather dusty, but durable creature," at which point Mr. Belvedere produces Wesley's lost hamster from his coat pocket and makes his exit. Wesley becomes the deciding vote, as he runs after Mr. Belvedere and whines, "You can't leave!" This episode positions Mr. Belvedere as a safeguard against the potential evils of a latchkey childhood, figured in Kevin's scholarly ineptitude (a recurring joke) and the threat to Heather's chastity.

Heather appears to be headed down the same road as a girl profiled in a sen-sationalized *Psychology Today* story, a latchkey child gone wild: "Doug and Lisa's thirteen-year-old daughter, who goes home to an empty house after school, often smokes dope with her friends before her parents get home. She recently announced that she is pregnant."[32] Mr. Belvedere prevents Heather from get-ting into sexual trouble again in the second season when her boyfriend Kyle (Rad Daly) pressures her for more intimacy.[33] When the whole family leaves Heather alone in the house with Kyle, Mr. Belvedere intuitively stays behind to chaperone, then pretends to leave them alone. After Heather runs away from Kyle, and Kyle pursues her, Mr. Belvedere appears from upstairs and tells him, "Maybe the young lady isn't ready yet." Not only does Mr. Belvedere serve as a moralizing protector of Heather's chastity but he also monitors Kevin's and George's sexual activities and polices their behavior. He reassures Kevin that he's still a man despite his failure to lose his virginity by his eighteenth birth-day,[34] and when George is tempted to cheat on Marsha with his high school crush, Mr. Belvedere places a framed family photograph on the bed to (success-fully) dissuade him.[35]

As an extension of his childcare duties, Mr. Belvedere is largely responsible for governing the family. As Foucault describes it, "Governing a household, a family, does not essentially mean safeguarding the family property; what it concerns is the individuals who compose the family, their wealth and prosperity. It means reckoning with all the possible events that may intervene, such as births and deaths, and with all the things that can be done, such as possible alliances with other families; it is this general form of management that is characteristic of government."[36] While Mr. Belvedere's childcare tasks are not as rigorous as they would be if he were dealing with younger children, he governs the family through his insistent life lessons, which he details for the viewer at the conclusion of every episode with his journal entries. At the end of the episode "Heather's Tutor," Mr. Belvedere describes the problems he has solved from both the A (Heather and Kyle) and B (dispute with the neighbors) plots: "Heather and Kyle are dating again, but they have an understanding: Kyle decides where they go, and Heather decides how far. Meanwhile, I've finally ironed out the details of the Owens-Hufnagel peace accord. They have agreed to keep their Doberman on a leash when near our property, and we have agreed to do the same with Wesley." In these sequences, Mr. Belvedere sits at his desk with his journal, facing the camera and framed in medium shot. He reads his insights in voice-over as an internal monologue. When he finishes, he closes his journal and the screen fades to black, suggesting a resolution to the household's problems. Through this staging, Mr. Belvedere not only recounts the lessons he has taught the Owens family; the episodes position him such that he also teaches the viewer.

Mr. Belvedere governs the Owens family as though he were a member of it, fulfilling a day-care fantasy in which the childcare provider comes to care for the children as a parent would (a common theme among television childcare providers, especially in *Who's the Boss?*, where Tony and Angela [Judith Light] pledge to look after each other's children in the event of catastrophe). The episode "Strike" from the second season displays Mr. Belvedere's devotion to the family when he forgoes his salary when George's union goes on strike and the family faces financial difficulty.[37] Mr. Belvedere suggests that he take on the role of a boarder, paying the Owenses what they regularly paid him. Mr. Belvedere begins to offer to "fix a meal or make a bed or two," but George refuses, telling him that he is not to do any housework. When Wesley unknowingly sells Mr. Belvedere's Fabergé egg at a garage sale, the family is shocked that Mr. Belvedere owns an item of such value yet works as their housekeeper. George asks, "So why you [*sic*] stickin' around here?" but his question is interrupted by Kevin, who comes in to tell George that he has returned the car George bought him before the strike. Moved, Mr. Belvedere says to Marsha, "There's the reason I'm sticking around." Mr. Belvedere not only sacrifices himself for the family but also holds the family together, mitigating family disputes and dispensing advice to the children. The credit sequence exemplifies Mr. Belvedere's position in the family, ending

Figure 13. Mr. Belvedere completes his journal entry on *Mr. Belvedere*.

with a series of two still family portraits. In the first, George and Heather sit together on the left side of the couch, Kevin and Wesley sit together in the middle, and Marsha sits alone on the right side. Mr. Belvedere stands upright behind the couch. This image dissolves to another family portrait, this time with all of the Owenses sitting close together on the couch, with Mr. Belvedere leaning over them with his arms around them. The dissolve between the two images produces the effect of Mr. Belvedere physically pushing the family together at a time when many socioeconomic factors were pulling the nuclear family apart.

Mr. Belvedere produces a fantasy solution to the day-care problem and the perceived collapse of the nuclear family. While many families were looking for live-in help or aspired to afford it, the kind of caretaking Mr. Belvedere provides was not easy to find or keep. In 1980, the *New York Times* featured an exposé of illegal aliens working as housekeepers for families who could not afford to hire a legal worker or could not find a legal worker willing and able to meet their needs. One woman explained: "'The other solutions that exist for working women, such as day-care centers, are not adequate,' [Mrs. Snyder] said. 'They are not for children who are in school. A housekeeper provides a stable, warm home environment for them.' When asked why she hired an undocumented alien, Mrs. Snyder replied: 'I've tried all kinds of arrangements. I advertised. I inter-

Figure 14. Mr. Belvedere produces family harmony on *Mr. Belvedere*.

viewed. I talked to people. But there was simply no one willing to come and live in my house to provide the flexibility I needed and take care of the children.'"[38]

The pseudonymous Mrs. Snyder continues, "Housekeeping is the kind of job where there is no labor pool in the United States other than illegal aliens."[39] Mr. Belvedere, though not an American citizen, is ostensibly a legal worker (through the first two seasons), as an agency provided him to the Owens family. He represents an ideal, cited by Claudia Wallis in *Time* magazine, that does not exist in the United States. She writes, "Most live-in sitters in the United States, unlike the licensed nannies of Britain, have no formal training."[40]

Mr. Belvedere nods toward the reality of live-in domestic laborers during the third season, in a two-part episode wherein Mr. Belvedere is deported.[41] After Mr. Belvedere tells George and Marsha that Wesley cheated on a test, Wesley calls the Immigration and Naturalization Service to report him. The INS shows up after Mr. Belvedere and Wesley have mended fences; however, Mr. Belvedere admits that he is not authorized to work in the United States. Unsurprisingly, the Owens house falls apart while Mr. Belvedere is in jail awaiting his hearing. They hire a replacement, an African American woman named Mrs. Lucas (Michelle Davison), but she lacks interest in the children and chain-smokes as she does chores. Kevin tries to talk to her about his girl problems, and she can respond only that they are having fish sticks for dinner. When Heather asks to bum a cigarette, Mrs. Lucas is quick to hand one over. Luckily, the Owenses have posted bail just in time for Mr. Belvedere to confiscate the cigarette. Mr. Belvedere confronts Mrs. Lucas, and she details her own family's problems, suggesting that she has no time to deal with the Owenses' predicaments. Her racial and class difference from Mr. Belvedere align her with the legal workers "Mrs. Snyder" found less satisfactorily self-sacrificing in the New York Times and further mark Mr. Belvedere as a fantasy ideal. The contrast between Mr. Belvedere and Mrs. Lucas is all the more pertinent when Mr. Belvedere goes before the judge and claims, "From the Immigration Code: an alien may be certified for employment if the job is deemed to require professional or unique abilities not possessed by any American." Although the judge incredulously replies, "I don't see where that's relevant; after all you are just a housekeeper," Wesley and Kevin proceed to detail Mr. Belvedere's "unique abilities"—he makes good French toast, he fixes electronics, and he prevented Kevin from going on an alcohol-fueled bender. While the judge is sympathetic, telling Mr. Belvedere that "there is no doubt that you're performing a unique service, possibly even a public one," she still rules against him, and he is sent back to England.

In his stead, the Owenses go through five housekeepers, thanks to Wesley's chronic misbehavior, pointing to the fact that Mr. Belvedere's ability to rein Wesley in is one of his most vital "unique abilities." Wesley has scared off the newest housekeeper with a snake and is on the phone with the domestic agency to replace her when Mr. Belvedere magically (and, he claims, legally) appears at the front door. In his journal that night, Mr. Belvedere writes, "To be honest, without the Owenses, there hasn't been much to write about." The fact that Mr. Belvedere proclaims his delight in devoting his entire life to the Owenses marks the major difference between him and Mrs. Lucas, and presumably all the other housekeepers the Owenses have gone through. At the same time, he has somehow managed to secure a green card in record time to return to care for them. Mr. Belvedere, with his impressive celebrity references, predilection for fine cooking, and childcare skills, is a dream come true for the Owens family and an unattainable dream for Mr. Belvedere's viewers.

KATE & ALLIE'S CHILDCARE CO-OP

Even during the height of the day-care crisis, much of the work of childcare remained informal and unpaid. As Fortune magazine put it, "The day care industry attracts a panoply of providers. The majority are family members and neighbors, who often babysit for free."[42] Day-care co-ops like the one profiled in the New York Times, which was organized by a local YMCA, supported calls for the government to stay out of childcare. Forbes lambasted the Act for Better Child Care, which proposed sliding-scale financial assistance for use in day-care centers, arguing, "Their bill would help drive out the relative-neighborhood-church approach; it favors creating a vast day-care bureaucracy, enormously increasing the cost of childcare. The bill punishes families in which the mother stays at home by having their tax dollars subsidize working couples."[43] *Kate & Allie*, perhaps unwittingly, supports this point of view, as best friends and divorced mothers Kate (Susan Saint James) and Allie (Jane Curtin) live together and help raise each other's children. Their co-op arrangement allows uptight, traditional domestic goddess Allie to continue homemaking and child-rearing while being supported financially and provides career woman Kate with childcare and meals.[44] Their parenting strengths complement each other—Kate relates well to Allie's son and deals with sensitive problems faced by both of their teenage daughters, whereas Allie excels as a disciplinarian and puts more emphasis on scholastic achievement.

In many ways, Kate and Allie's arrangement appears to be a conservative solution—as *BusinessWeek* put it in 1986, "Fewer than one in ten households now resemble the white-picket-fence world where father's income lets mother stay home with the kids. Yet parents seeking childcare must rely on the social policies and institutions of a simpler era and on the workings of the market. All have failed to meet the need."[45] Kate and Allie's household maintains the basic breadwinner model as Kate supports Allie and her children (presumably along with alimony payment from Allie's ex-husband, although Kate and Allie regularly face financial difficulty) and provides them with a place to live. According to *Newsweek*, "Some adults, not all of them old-fashioned, still maintain that child rearing should be a career—and that it belongs in the home."[46] Indeed, Kate and Allie solve their childcare problems merely by combining their households into a pseudo–nuclear family that still maintains a traditional division of labor with Allie as the housewife.[47]

Many episodes emphasize both the sameness and difference between Kate and Allie's family model and the traditional nuclear family. In "The Very Loud Family," the second episode of the series, Kate's daughter, Emma (Ari Meyers), decides to videotape the family for her school project on "our changing world" after Allie encourages Kate to push Emma toward a more difficult project than her already-completed dead-leaf display.[48] In an extended allusion to *An American Family* (PBS, 1973), Emma sets out to detail the day-to-day routines of her family, which she sees as representative of families dealing with divorce. She films Allie making dinner and her mother returning home from work and complaining about her boss, a typical representation of nuclear family life, albeit with Kate standing in for the breadwinner husband. When Emma's teacher selects her video to show on parents' night, Kate and Allie are horrified. The video turns out to be primarily a rehash of scenes Emma has shot earlier in the episode; however, the end of the video shows Emma's father calling Kate to cancel his plans with Emma. Kate reprimands him for letting Emma down, then tries to convince Emma to turn the camera off. Instead, Emma puts it down on the

Figure 15. Emma's camera captures Kate consoling her on *Kate & Allie*.

kitchen counter, and it captures her crying in her mother's arms. The video ends with the three kids sitting on the couch, with Kate and Allie leaning over behind them, similar to the posing of *Mr. Belvedere*'s credit sequence. Emma directly addresses the camera: "As you can see, divorce really causes changes. But in our case, it's not going too bad. The end." The main change the video captures is Emma's deteriorating relationship with her father. The rest of the video portrays conventional family scenes such as family dinners and sibling rivalries, suggesting that in Kate and Allie's household, traditional family life remains intact.

Kate and Allie's household is again the subject of media attention in the episode "High Anxiety," when Kate's television-producer friend Tom (Paul Gleason) is inspired to produce a segment on changing families.[49] Kate and Allie unwittingly display their familial roles when Kate makes a disparaging remark about the "jocks" Emma and Jennie (Allison Smith) want to call instead of clearing the table:

CHIP [TO KATE]: You're a jock!
KATE: Only part-time.
CHIP [TO TOM]: On Saturday Kate's giving me a basketball lesson.
KATE [TO TOM]: Yeah, through the legs, behind the back, fingertip roll!
TOM [LOOKING IMPRESSED]: Ooh!

ALLIE: To be followed by the famed Allie Lowell iodine and bandage roll.
TOM [LAUGHING]: You guys are really something. You know, you're just like a real family!
KATE: We are a real family.
TOM: Hmm, but not a typical one.

However, Tom just witnessed what he seems to think of as the "typical" family—Kate takes on the father's role of roughhousing with male children while Allie takes on the nurturing role of tending to the child's wounds. Tom gets an idea, telling Kate he wants to produce a program about "the new American family," suggesting that there are probably divorced fathers who live in similar arrangements. He continues: "A show about the traditional family unit and how people are trying to preserve it in new ways." Here, he articulates the fact that Kate and Allie's household is not all that new—instead, they are merely living out the nuclear family formation with a woman in the father's position.

On his show, Kate and Allie are joined by a pair of divorced dads and a man and woman who share a household in much the same way as Kate and Allie do. When the host asks why they have formed nontraditional family units, the woman answers, "For starters, simple economic necessity. I'm a housewife . . . but I can't get paid for what I do best. Daryl can, he's a lawyer. But he can't run a household too, so why not pool our talents?" The housewife is in the exact same position as Allie, who holds low-paying service jobs to earn extra income in addition to her unpaid labor in the home.[50] When the questions turn to Kate and Allie, the host inquires who takes out the garbage, an obvious nod to who takes on the masculine roles. Although Allie points at Kate, Kate protests that "in a family like ours, we don't really have any sexual stereotypes, so we share the jobs, only Allie is a *much* better cook than I am. But we're not locked into any roles." Indeed, the long-running joke throughout *Kate & Allie* is Kate's culinary ineptitude, but she also does very little housework and her child-rearing is mainly limited to playing "cool mom" to the teenage girls and indulging in masculine pursuits like sports and camping with Chip (Frederick Koehler).

In "Odd Boy Out," Kate takes on the father role for Chip, who got into a fight at school.[51] As Allie frets and makes an ice pack, Kate scoffs that "all boys fight" and enthusiastically asks Chip the trademark dad question, "Hey, sluggo, what'd the other guy look like?" When Chip runs upstairs, ashamed, Kate asks Allie if he knows how to fight. Allie replies, "I taught him everything I know. Not to walk down dark streets, not to talk to strangers, not to flash jewelry"—Kate interjects, "Keep his purse close to his body?" Kate's mocking of Allie's failure to properly educate her son in masculine decorum leads Allie to begrudgingly admit that she needs her ex-husband, Charles (Paul Hecht). Kate protests, "What do you need Charles for when you've got me?" When Jennie and Emma come home, they reveal that Chip gets picked on because the other kids perceive him as a sissy. Kate and Allie discuss whether or not their parenting of Chip is causing harm to his gender identity. Allie muses, "Maybe Chip *is* turning into a sissy, maybe we *are* instilling feminine values and don't even know it." Kate counters, "That would be great, he'd growing up to be a nurturing, thoughtful human being!" Still, Allie convinces Charles to take Chip and some of his friends to a hockey game to increase Chip's macho quotient. When Chip returns triumphantly with hockey stick in hand, he announces that he wants to live with his father, which Allie explains is impossible because of Charles's work schedule.

Charles further disappoints Chip when he cancels a camping trip he had planned for Chip and his friends. When Kate suggests that she and Allie take the boys camping, Allie protests that she is "not comfortable in the out of doors." Kate retorts, "Where *are* you comfortable?" and Allie reinforces her domestic identity, replying, "At home! In supermarkets, in department stores with wide aisles." Though Allie agrees to go camping, bad weather thwarts their plans, and Kate and Allie host a camping-themed sleepover instead. Kate impresses the boys with burping contests and stories of bear attacks, inspiring one boy to tell Chip, "You're really lucky, your mothers are even better than your dad." When Allie is jealous of Chip's admiration of Kate, Kate tells her, "Mothers aren't supposed to be fun. You cooked, you made each one of them brush their teeth, you fulfilled your function." The episode concludes with Kate teaching Allie to burp, and Allie telling Kate, "You make a great father." Kate, in other words, is not merely the "other mother" that the *New York Times* profiles in its article about day-care co-ops.[52] She is also the other father, and a hyperinvolved one at that, who provides childcare on a day-to-day basis, as opposed to Chip's biological father, who lives in another state and constantly lets him down. In this way, *Kate & Allie* presents an idealized model of co-parenting in which friends share childcare duties and re-create the nuclear family.

However, life with Kate and Allie is not always easy. In "Allie on Strike," Allie has started a part-time job at a movie theater and starts feeling the demands of a double shift when Kate and the kids constantly call her at work to request favors.[53] Fed up, Allie refuses to perform her household duties when she feels underappreciated. After a few days of pizza delivery and piled-up laundry, Kate decides to divvy up the chores. As the kids groan and Chip protests that he is just a kid, Kate delivers a motivational speech: "Self-reliance is what made this country what it is today. Self-reliance is what tamed the rivers, cleared the forests, built skyscrapers!" Allie comes home and finds Emma and Jennie preparing dinner, Kate doing laundry, and Chip vacuuming and is convinced that they are attempting to guilt-trip her, but by the end of the episode, everyone is at their breaking points. Emma complains that Chip is "getting away with murder" because everyone else is too busy to keep track of him, and she micromanages Jennie's cooking while Kate critiques Chip's vacuuming. Just as each of them is individually about to strike, Allie bursts through the door and exclaims that she can't take it anymore: "I don't like just taking care of myself. I like taking care of this house. I just want to be thanked for it every once in a while!" Thus Allie accepts, even desires, her domestic care duties in addition to her paid work. As the *New York Times* suggested in 1987, "Women's lives have changed in ways that require changes from men, from employers, from support services, from communities—all of which are very slow in coming. Women, it is said, must decide whether they want to change the world or have a bigger piece of the world as it is."[54] When the episode ends with Kate and Allie hashing out a contract, Kate clearly benefits—her only contractual obligation is to thank Allie when she does "favors," which are defined as above and beyond regular domestic chores and childcare duties. Neither Kate nor Allie are "changing the world"; in fact, their childcare arrangement merely mirrors what David Blankenhorn, director of the Institute for American Values, called the "1950s time warp" that employers still lived in, where "they are rooted in the quaint assumption that employees have 'someone at home' to attend to family matters."[55]

"This Parenting Thing's Like a Full-time Job": Flex Time and Childcare Networks on *My Two Dads*

Alongside corporate day-care centers, many corporate strategists also advocated flexible hours, or flex time. According to the *New York Times* in 1984, "Allowing employees a more fluid work schedule without jeopardizing career advancement may do more for childcare needs than the establishment of on-site care centers, according to a federally funded study on employer-supported day-care programs."[56] Two years later, the *New York Times* cited a study by Suzanne M. Bianchi and Daphne Spain that argued, "If we want a productive labor force of female and male workers, but also value the family, work hours must be flexible, day care available and affordable, and work within the home equitably divided."[57] Janice Castro's article in *Time* magazine details flex time as one of the many ways corporations were trying to meet their employees' childcare needs. She tells of one father who chose to "follow the 7:00 A.M.-to-3:15 P.M. schedule that he had chosen under Transamerica's flextime policy" and of employees at DuPont's corporate headquarters who "have trickled in between 7:00 and 9:30 A.M., chosen a half-hour or one-hour lunch, and left between 3:30 and 6:00 P.M.—as long as they have put in eight hours each day."[58] *My Two Dads* takes flex time to the extreme, with Joey (Greg Evigan) working from home, another popular sitcom scenario. As discussed in chapter two, Cliff Huxtable (Bill Cosby) on *The Cosby Show* (NBC, 1984–1992) and Jason Seaver (Alan Thicke) on *Growing Pains* (ABC, 1985–1992) both run medical practices out of their homes, and on *Family Ties*, Elyse Keaton (Meredith Baxter Birney) spends the first two seasons working as an architect out of the family kitchen. On *My Two Dads*, Joey's work as an artist allows him to provide after-school supervision for Nicole (Staci Keanan). At the same time, Joey's active dating life necessitates Joey and Michael (Paul Reiser) securing childcare with the Judge (Florence Stanley), Klawicki (Dick Butkus), the restaurant manager below their loft, and various babysitters.

In the first-season episode "Whose Night Is It Anyway?" Joey and Michael argue over who was scheduled to stay home with Nicole because they both have dates.[59] Neither Joey nor Michael feels comfortable leaving Nicole by herself, and the Judge is unavailable to sit with her. The Judge delivers a soliloquy supporting her hands-off approach to family governance, telling Joey and Michael, "Much as I'd like to be of assistance, there comes a time when I must withdraw to the care of my own affairs and allow you two gentlemen to settle your own domestic conflicts. It's the only way you'll grow as parents." Here the Judge adheres to a neoliberal governing rationality, in which "individuals are to become 'experts of themselves,' to adopt an educated and knowledgeable relation of self-care in respect to their bodies, their minds, their forms of conduct, and that of the members of their own families."[60] Thus, the Judge leaves Joey and Michael to master their identities as parents and to solve their conflict within the family unit. Nicole, for her part, points out that because she and her friends are of baby-sitting age themselves, perhaps they could simply babysit each other. Joey and Michael agree to this arrangement on the condition that they have their dates in Klawicki's downstairs. When they return from Klawicki's with their dates, they find Nicole hosting a slumber party with eight friends. As Joey's and Michael's dates join in the slumber party girl talk, Joey's date Madeline (Lise Hilboldt), a sexually adventurous botanist, tells the girls of her multiple conquests and teaches them how to be "sexy," at which point Michael throws her out of the loft.

Madeline's conversation with the girls underscores the importance of appropriate childcare providers. Michael tells an angered Joey, "She was teaching Lolita classes" and suggests that Joey needs to be more responsible with the women he brings home. Michael delivers this message by telling the girls a variation on "Goldilocks and Three Bears," where, now that they are "papa bears," their porridge must not be "too hot." Joey endorses this message, telling Michael in all sincerity, "That's probably one of the best stories you've ever told." This episode teaches lessons not only about responsible childcare—obviously, Nicole cannot be trusted to stay home alone, and the fathers cannot just depend on the state (in the form of the Judge)—but also about single parents' dating etiquette.

Michael grows resentful of Joey's flex time in the first-season episode "Quality Time."[61] The episode begins with Joey working on a sculpture as Nicole wakes up. Joey prepares breakfast for Nicole and has an in-depth conversation with her about her school gossip. Michael does not have time to partake in breakfast or conversation as he rushes out the door to get to the office. He pauses in the doorway and looks back enviously at Nicole discussing "wet willies" with Joey. This image dissolves to an establishing shot of Manhattan office buildings accompanied by forlorn saxophone music. The establishing shot cuts to a medium shot of Michael behind his desk, brow furrowed, seemingly distracted by thoughts of Nicole as his boss (Dakin Matthews) talks to him about "the numbers." As soon as his boss leaves the room, Michael calls Nicole to ask her about the gossip she was relaying to Joey: "How come I don't know about Amy and Rebecca? And what's a wet willie?" Michael makes a date with Nicole to go to a movie that night, only to have his plans thwarted when his boss returns demanding that he work late. When Michael explains that he has a "personal obligation," his boss says he will just get "the new guy, Hungry Sid" to take on the work instead: "I like him. Know why? No family, no friends, no personal obligations. All he's got is his unbelievable appetite to work his way up the ladder. He'd be only too glad to take on your work." Michael's boss's manipulation is in line with the corporate culture that flex time was designed to work against—allowing parents to adapt their schedules to accommodate childcare. By the end of the episode, Michael convinces his boss to allow him more flexibility in his schedule so that he can spend more time with Nicole. This conciliation inspires Michael's boss to go home and spend time with his own children, a gesture that concludes the episode and signals a desirable shift in corporate culture.

Figure 16. Michael's boss agrees to allow Michael to use flex time on *My Two Dads*.

Yet Michael's work continues to be a source of narrative conflict throughout the series, and Joey continues to flaunt his parental privilege, telling Michael in the second season's premiere, "I know what our daughter likes, okay? I'm the one who works at home, remember? I know where she goes, I know what she does, I know who she hangs out with."[62] A second season episode opens with Michael in his office saying good night to Nicole over the phone.[63] Despite the long hours he has put in, his boss tells him he is selling the company and that Michael is being replaced. Luckily, by the end of the episode, Michael's boss hires him to start a magazine as a tax shelter and hires Joey to do design. This new work arrangement provides Michael with more flexibility, although it does involve Joey spending some work hours in an office. At the same time, subsequent episodes feature Michael working in his new home office, conveniently tucked into the alcove below Nicole's bedroom, allowing for maximum parental supervision.[64] Michael and Joey also share an open office space, with desks positioned only a foot apart and facing each other, allowing them to co-parent Nicole when she visits after school.[65]

As Nicole gets older, Michael and Joey's care strategies become more complex, as does the Judge's hands-off approach. When Joey and Michael catch Nicole coming home drunk during the second season, they confiscate the drunk driver's car keys and have a talk with her, which she clearly brushes off.[66] As they lament their failure, the Judge tells them that "words don't work," prompting Michael and Joey to hatch a scheme to get excessively drunk in front of Nicole to teach her the evils of alcohol. The Judge appears to serve as supervisor, asking them to "sign in" with every shot of whiskey they take and explaining their rapidly deteriorating behavior to an increasingly concerned Nicole. When Nicole pleads for them to stop, the Judge denies her request, instead turning on a car-racing video game to further prove their point. As Joey and Michael pick up their joysticks, the camera cuts to a full-screen shot of the video game, thus also teaching the viewer the consequences of drunk driving as each of them quickly crashes and their vehicles burst into flames. When Michael suggests that they all "get out and push," Nicole's driver from her drunken evening returns seeking his keys. Joey and Michael gleefully remember that they have access to a real car and prepare to leave the apartment. The Judge jumps up and exclaims, "Party's over boys!" but Joey pushes her aside on his way out the door. She and Nicole chase after Joey and Michael, who are quickly apprehended by Klawicki in the hallway. Nicole tearfully thanks him after the Judge admits that his action was not part of the plan. Nicole then angrily turns to the Judge, telling her, "You should never have let them do this!" The Judge insists upon her lack of involvement, replying, "They were going to do what they were gonna do no matter what I said. Just the way you are, no matter what they say." As slow, mournful piano music comes on the soundtrack, Nicole sits on the couch with her passed-out fathers. The Judge pauses to gently touch Joey and Michael's heads and exits the

Figure 17. The Judge leaves the family alone after the drunk-driving experiment on *My Two Dads*.

frame as the episode concludes, leaving the family to deal with the ramifications of the evening's lesson on their own.

My Two Dads solves childcare problems on a micro level. Joey works primarily from home, Michael utilizes flex time, and they depend on neighborhood friends for help from time to time, including the Judge, who becomes a maternal figure for Nicole. However, the Judge avoids getting too involved in family disputes, encouraging Joey and Michael to make their own parenting decisions and thus to "grow as parents." Here the Judge, as representative of the state, adheres to a neoliberal governing rationality, where "by stressing 'self-care,' the neoliberal state divulges paternalistic responsibility for its subjects but simultaneously holds its subjects responsible for self-government."[67] In this way, *My Two Dads* encourages an ethic of self-responsibility to oneself and one's family. In an episode in which a newspaper challenges the Judge's decision to award custody of Nicole to Joey and Michael, a television news-magazine program seeks the advice of Dr. Joyce Brothers, who concurs with the Judge's approach to governing the family from a distance.[68] Responding to accusations that Joey and Michael are too inexperienced to be proper parents, Dr. Brothers suggests that the problems they might face are not life-or-death situations, that if "she breaks a leg, they take her to the doctor"; thus, social services need not intervene. The news magazine also interviews New York City mayor Edward Koch, who agrees

that the family arrangement should be left intact, that the state should not intervene any further. *My Two Dads* solves all parenting and childcare problems
within the family, never relying on the Judge or any other authority for more
than a few pearls of wisdom here and there. And even those pearls of wisdom
only encourage self-reliance.

"I Wanted to Make Sure You Had a Babysitter. Need One?": *Full House* and the Extended Family Network

Many who denied the need for day care in the 1980s cited the existence of and
parental preference for extended family, friend, and neighborhood childcare
networks. Ignoring the family migration that became commonplace in the 1950s,
many who opposed funding for day care suggested that parents in need of childcare could turn toward their relatives. However, as *BusinessWeek* noted in 1981,
"Women workers are finding that the old family-support networks of relatives
and neighbors are dissolving as families move and even middle-aged women
enter the work force."[69] Jo Ann Gasper, assistant secretary of the U.S. Department of Health and Human Services, "scoffed at the notion of a day-care short-
age in the United States. She insisted that the growth of 'informal' arrangements
involving help from 'a relative or a friend' was providing an adequate supply of
day care for children."[70] According to *Forbes* magazine, in an article positioning itself against governmental intervention into day care, "most parents prefer
to leave their youngsters with relatives, neighborhood baby-sitters, or with day-
care services provided by local churches or synagogues."[71] Harking back to early
extended-family sitcoms like *The Goldbergs*, *Full House* creates this "preferred,"
yet elusive, family network model when widower Danny Tanner (Bob Saget)
acquires the live-in (and ostensibly free) childcare services of his brother-in-law,
Jesse (John Stamos), and his best friend, Joey (Dave Coulier). With this arrangement, Danny's three daughters get constant and consistent care. The preexist-
ing familial bonds linking Jesse to his nieces ensures his lasting dedication to
the family, so much so that when Jesse gets married and has children of his own,
he and his family remain in the Tanner house, living in a renovated attic space.[72]
When Jesse considers moving out during the first season, a fantasized montage
of images of him caring for baby Michelle (Mary-Kate and Ashley Olsen) draws
him back home, and she rewards his loyalty by calling him "Dad."[73] At the beginning of the series, both Jesse and Joey have part-time or unstable jobs (Jesse as
a part-time exterminator and aspiring rock star, Joey as a struggling stand-up
comedian), allowing them to work their schedules around caring for the girls
and making them grateful for the room and board Danny provides.

Joey and Jesse begin working together writing commercial jingles at home
during the second season.[74] At the beginning of the episode "Working Mothers,"
Joey and Jesse try to squeeze in some work before the girls come home from

school—Joey notes that "at the stroke of three we turn back into housewives."[75] Although they have been selling jingles freelance, an advertising agency expresses interest in hiring them full-time, resulting in middle child Stephanie (Jodie Sweetin) asking oldest daughter DJ (Candace Cameron), "If Uncle Jesse, Joey, and Daddy are all working, who's gonna take care of us?" DJ can only shrug at the question, and the scene ominously fades to black. The next scene underscores this tension, beginning with an exterior aerial shot of downtown office buildings and cutting to Jesse and Joey preparing for their presentation at the agency. Jesse says to Joey, "Any moment, our future's gonna come walking right through that door." A sound bridge of Michelle's voice complicates their notions of their future, and the camera cuts to a medium shot of her walking into the office, her entrance serving to embody the day-care crisis. Jesse's mother (Yvonne Wilder) follows Michelle into the office, explaining that she has to go to work herself and is dropping Michelle off as they had planned. Despite the fact that the client is running late, Jesse's mother cannot watch Michelle any longer. Joey and Jesse bribe Michelle to hide under the desk with a cookie and a promise of playing hide and seek, but of course she trots out midway through their presentation. Still, they manage to land full-time positions. As they celebrate, Danny comes home with DJ, who just became a green belt in karate, and Stephanie, who won her talent show. When Jesse and Joey share their news, DJ and Stephanie appear crestfallen. Stephanie lays on a guilt-trip, suggesting that they will "miss the whole rest of our lives." As they all hug, the scene dissolves to Jesse and Joey making a pros and cons list for accepting full-time employment, and Jesse admits that he "dig[s] being Mr. Mom."[76] The next day, they ask their boss (James Hampton) if they can work from home, and he agrees, thus allowing Joey and Jesse to continue being "Mr. Moms" while remaining gainfully employed. Upon learning the good news, Stephanie turns to Danny and asks if he can work from home too. Danny acknowledges the reality, telling her, "Unfortunately, most parents' jobs aren't that flexible." Yet all three men hold jobs that are flexible enough to allow them to arrange for consistent childcare.

When Joey and Jesse leave town to shoot a commercial in the episode "Danny in Charge," Danny manages to play "superdad," albeit with a few hitches.[77] The biggest dilemma he faces is a conflict of after-school activities—Stephanie's science fair and DJ's drama festival fall on the same day. To make matters worse, he accidentally cooks Stephanie's science project as part of dinner, mistaking it as a prepared dish left by Joey. He stays up all night redoing her project and vows to leave the science fair in time to make it to the second act of DJ's play. However, he is so exhausted that upon coming home from work, he takes a nap with Michelle and misses both functions. The girls come home worried about him, and when they wake him up, he apologizes profusely, telling them, "I am so sorry, I wanted to be there so badly, I let you both down. You know, this single parent stuff is not as easy as I thought it would be." DJ and Stephanie apologize for

Figure 18. Joey and Jesse land jobs despite Michelle's surprise appearance on *Full House*.

pressuring him to attend their events, and when Danny says he'll start making dinner, DJ protests sincerely, "Dad, wait. You do so much for us. Let us cook dinner for you." Stephanie agrees, and they enlist Michelle to help them, leaving Danny alone to finish his nap. While the episode makes it clear that Danny needs help to fulfill his parental obligations, in the end his daughters end up caring for him and themselves in a parents' fantasy world where children are eager to do substantial chores to make life easier for their parents. At the same time, the girls learn self-reliance and the importance of family care.

Even with two live-in babysitters and one daughter of babysitting age, the Tanner household still experiences myriad childcare hurdles. In the second episode of the series, the arrangement already appears strained on their first night as a newly constituted family, when both Jesse and Joey want to go out after the girls are asleep, and Danny has to go to work.[78] Danny explains the particulars of their agreement as all three men stand by the door: "The only way that three adults can leave the house at the same time is if three children are with them. Two adults can leave, one adult can leave, three, two, or one child can leave with one to three adults. But three adults can never leave with less than three children. Got it?" Another first-season episode demonstrates an even more complex childcare problem, when Stephanie, Joey, and Jesse all come down with chicken pox.[79] This predicament leaves Danny and DJ the only ones in the house able to care

Figure 19. Danny's daughters offer to cook him dinner while he resumes his nap on *Full House.*

for Michelle. Unfortunately, Danny has an important sporting event to cover, and DJ has her first slumber party to attend. Danny must scramble to find a babysitter in less than an hour in order to make it to work on time. His frantic search mirrors those of the many parents profiled in newspapers and magazines who lose hours and days of work to care for sick children.[80] Between calls to babysitters, Danny calls his boss and begs him not to reassign the segment to another sportscaster. When he reaches the end of his list of babysitters with no luck, Danny contemplates calling DJ home from her slumber party but decides that that would be cruel. Just as Danny laments missing his game, DJ flies through the door, and exclaims, "I wanted to make sure you had a babysitter. Need one?" Danny is overcome with pride when he learns of DJ's sacrifice, and she utters a line that would fulfill any parents' fantasy: "You do so much for me, this is my chance to do something nice for you. Isn't that what being part of a family is all about?" Danny exclaims that he is "so honored to be a part of this family" and tells Joey and Jesse that the three of them must be "doing something right" in the way they are raising the children.

The Tanners weather the storm of a chicken pox outbreak without interrupting Danny's productivity at work. Even as a fifth grader, DJ shows an initiative toward personal responsibility in her decision to return from her slumber party to take care of her family and ensure their well-being and productivity. The goal of the episode is to prevent Michelle from contracting chicken pox. In their practice of quarantine, DJ's self-sacrifice works not only to preserve the well-being of the family, both in terms of its health and its economic prosperity, but also to preserve its autonomy by eliminating both the need for an outside babysitter and a broader call for more available day-care options.

This episode of *Full House* provides a perfect example for how television sitcoms of the 1980s present models of family governance. As Rose describes, "The modern private family remains intensively governed, it is linked in so many ways with social, economic, and political objectives. But the government here acts not through mechanisms of social control and subordination of the will, but through the promotion of subjectivities, the construction of pleasures and ambitions, and the activation of guilt, anxiety, envy, and disappointment."[81]

Danny, Jesse, and Joey have molded DJ into a familial subject who feels a great sense of responsibility to her family, such that she takes pleasure in taking care of them and in helping her father make it to work on time. She bounds into the room where Danny is in despair with no small amount of enthusiasm, even though she has given up her first slumber party, about which she spends the entire first half of the episode raving. However, through Danny's commitment to raising his family as an autonomous unit, with help only from an extended family network, DJ feels a need to participate in and further this ethic of family self-care.

DJ regularly cares for her sisters, and often her father, as she did in "Danny in Charge." She frequently wrangles Michelle and imparts older-sister wisdom to emotionally fragile Stephanie.[82] In "Slumber Party," Stephanie must deal with the absence of her mother in the face of the Honeybees' (a variation of Girl Scouts) mother-daughter sleepover. Jesse's fiancée, Becky (Lori Loughlin), initially offers to take her but ends up stranded with car trouble, so Joey takes her. All goes well until one girl demands mother-daughter makeovers, and all the girls except for Stephanie gather excitedly on the couch. Despite Joey's willingness to participate, one of the mothers suggests another activity. When one girl whines, "Why can't we do the makeovers?" the camera cuts to a medium shot of Stephanie, who stands alone with Joey on the opposite side of the room. She cries out, "Because of me, that's why!" and runs out of the room as the camera cuts to a long shot showing all of the girls and their mothers grouped on one side of the frame and Stephanie and Joey alone by the door and separated from the rest of the group by a vast swath of white carpeting. Joey chases after Stephanie, and the camera zooms in on the door as he closes it behind them, emphasizing Stephanie's isolation and longing for a maternal figure.

When Stephanie returns home, DJ truncates her own sleepover, sending her best friend, Kimmy (Andrea Barber), home so that she can counsel Stephanie. When Danny enters the room to talk to Stephanie, DJ sends him away, pledging to take care of it. As Stephanie cries on her shoulder, DJ tells her that they are the only ones with "a Dad, an Uncle Jesse, and a Joey" and that they also have each other. They embrace, with Stephanie framed in medium close-up with tears streaming down her cheeks. This image dissolves to Danny, Joey, and Jesse lamenting Stephanie's pain until Stephanie and DJ enter the room, and Stephanie thanks Joey for taking her to the party and announces she is going back to do makeovers with DJ. Once again, DJ has sacrificed her own leisure time to help nurture her family members and provide the maternal care (in the form of feminine self-fashioning) that their adult caregivers cannot. Through *Full House*'s insistence on the "lessons" the family learns by the end of each episode, the viewer is likewise addressed to adopt these family governance strategies, which the program reinforces with every episode as the viewer witnesses the family grow and prosper over nine seasons.

CONCLUSION

While television sitcoms promoted private solutions to the national day-care crisis and corporate and administrative leaders advocated workplace-based day care, both approaches worked to govern parent-citizens such that they would not ask for state assistance. The many guidelines and solutions 1980s media posed to ameliorate the day-care crisis provided the sense of a multitude of options for working parents to choose between. As Rose writes about neoliberalism, "It does not seek to govern through 'society,' but through the regulated choices of individual citizens, now construed as subjects of choices and aspirations to self-actualization and self-fulfillment. Individuals are to be governed through their freedom."[83] At the same time, the delegation of childcare to the market provoked anxiety for parents and nonparents alike. Condominium associations debated whether in-home day care constituted a business and thus a nonresidential use of residential property, and parents worried about leaving their children in the hands of "strangers."[84] Sitcoms like *Mr. Belvedere*, *Kate & Allie*, *My Two Dads*, and *Full House* modeled ideal private solutions for viewers and showed happy, self-reliant families who did not need the public sector's help to solve their childcare dilemmas. With their long runs in syndication, especially in the after-school hours of the late 1980s and 1990s, these programs duly ensured that the children of the day-care crisis would learn from characters like DJ and would be well poised to understand and model the neoliberal rationalities that mainstream politics and popular culture offered as they entered adulthood.

CHAPTER 4

"YOU COULD CALL ME THE MAID—BUT I WOULDN'T"

LESSONS IN MASCULINE DOMESTIC LABOR

Arlie Hochschild locates a "stalled revolution" in the 1980s, where women's lives had changed, but men's and the workplace had not. The *New York Times* labeled this problem the "working woman's unworkable world."[1] During this period, middle-class family life was increasingly in flux as parents struggled to work, care for children, and keep up with domestic chores. In an article titled "The Superwoman Squeeze," *Newsweek* profiled middle-school teacher Sue Greenwell and observed of her husband, Jim, "Occasionally, he helps clean up or puts the boys to bed. But for the most part, Jim reads in the living room while Sue vacuums, does late-night grocery shopping, grades papers from 9 P.M. to 11 P.M.— and collapses."[2] Hochschild found that although the majority of the women she studied were performing most of the household chores, "Most couples *wanted* to share and imagined that they did."[3] These fantasies of equitable childcare and domestic labor divisions among couples found their expression on television screens, as sitcoms presented models of domestic management and of masculinity that complete the revolution.

As chapters two and three have shown, sitcoms habitually represented the struggles that dual-income and nonnuclear families faced when combining work and family, and offered up solutions for viewers dealing with similar problems. One of the principal ways women could "have it all" in this televised world was to employ household help and, in the process, shift gendered expectations of domestic labor. As chapter one shows, advertisers believed that images of men performing domestic labor were particularly attractive to the upscale female viewers who made up the most desirable audience segment. To this end, family sitcoms often constructed images of masculine domestic citizens, workers who transformed the labor of the private sphere so as to preserve some of the privileges of public citizenship.

The number of male domestic laborers and caregivers exploded on Reagan-era film and television screens in films like *Mr. Mom* (director Stan Dragoti, 1983), *Three Men and a Baby* (director Leonard Nimoy, 1987), and *Look Who's Talking* (director Amy Heckerling, 1989) and on television programs such as *Benson* (ABC, 1979–1986), *Full House* (ABC, 1987–1995), *My Two Dads* (NBC, 1987–1990), *Silver Spoons* (NBC 1982–1986), *Mr. Belvedere* (ABC, 1985–1990), *Charles in Charge* (CBS, 1984–1985; first-run syndication, 1987–1990) and *Who's the Boss?* (ABC, 1984–1992). Numerous critics caution against seeing this development as feminist or progressive, arguing that these films and television programs do not challenge the structure of the nuclear family.[4] However, by masculinizing the work of childcare and other domestic duties, these mediated family labor constructions also legitimate the oft-unpaid and undervalued work of the domestic sphere—what is typically considered "women's work."

Wendy Brown discusses the gendered division of labor under liberalism, paying special attention to the ways in which the public and private spheres are separately constructed for distinctly gendered subjects. She notes that the liberated, male, public citizen depends for his very being and independence on the invisible labor and confinement of the female private dependent.[5] Thus a "crisis" emerges when women move into a professional-class workforce that is structured for men who are assumed to have a wife at home. For Brown, this division of labor is part of liberalism's subject formation, where "one group surrenders selfhood so that another group can have it."[6] Brown is careful to point out, however, that these subject positions are not essentially gendered and that class plays a vital role in reconfiguring the gendered separation of spheres: "the emancipation of particular women can be 'purchased' through the subordination of substitutes."[7] She continues, "Gender and class converge here, as every middle- and upper-class woman knows who has purchased her liberty, personhood, and equality through child care and 'household help' by *women* earning a fraction of their boss's wage."[8] While upper- and middle-class white women have long employed working-class women of color, in many family sitcoms of the 1980s, men are employed to manage households, and the programs focus on the home as a place of masculine labor rather than simply as a place of masculine leisure.

The home is the primary setting for *Who's the Boss?*, *Benson*, and *Charles in Charge*. Ella Taylor notes a shift from the workplace sitcoms of the 1970s, claiming, "By the middle of the 1980s the sphere of the domestic had reasserted its supremacy in the Nielsen ratings."[9] However, these programs crucially combine both the domestic and the workplace sitcom forms, through presenting the home as workplace. Rather than functioning as a haven for family leisure, the home is the place of employment for protagonists Tony (Tony Danza), Benson (Robert Guillaume), and Charles (Scott Baio). That domestic labor is recognized as labor when men perform it is significant. As Brown argues, "If men become too self-less, even in the household, their masculinity is called into question."[10] In other words, women are expected to be selfless and to not ask for monetary compensation for their work in the home, but in order for Tony, Benson, and Charles to maintain their status as civil subjects, their work in the home must be in some respects for their own (financial) self-interest. Thus, it is fitting that even when Tony and his boss, Angela (Judith Light), begin dating and finally get engaged, she continues to pay him for his housework. This tendency is manifest in Tony's insistence on the label "housekeeper," going so far as to threaten Angela's client who seems incredulous about the moniker by saying, "You could call me the maid—but I wouldn't." Through this semantic shift, Tony claims a managerial role ("housekeeper" implying some sort of ownership), rather than a title steeped in servitude (and femininity) like "maid." For his part, Benson is considered "management" in the governor's mansion, and though his previous position was as a butler (in *Soap*, ABC, 1977–1981), he solves not only household but also governmental problems from his desk in the kitchen. Charles is "in charge" of two different families over the series' five seasons, and he performs vital emotional labor that the children's parents are not able to provide in exchange for room and board. Still, *Who's the Boss?*, *Benson*, and *Charles in Charge* suggest that domestic work is not only financially but also personally fulfilling for these men, just as it is supposed to be for women. All three remain in the home even when they are offered more lucrative positions outside of it, and the programs imply that they stay with their surrogate families due to their emotional ties.

The centrality of domestic labor in these shows, and the value the characters place on it, provides an important lesson to viewers of the 1980s familiar with the media image of the "superwoman." According to Barbara Ehrenreich and Arlie Hochschild, the ideal of the career woman who can "do it all" often masks professional women's reliance on domestic laborers, who "make the house hotel-room perfect, feed and bathe the children, cook and clean up—and then magically fade from sight."[11] *Who's the Boss?*, *Benson*, and *Charles in Charge* raise the literal and figurative value of household labor. As Rosie Cox points out, domestic work comes with low pay and low status and "is considered to be unskilled and the knowledge and qualities needed to do it go unrecognized."[12] By transposing the workplace onto the domestic sitcom, these programs argue that domestic labor should be paid and valued. However, because the protagonists maintain much of their status as civil subjects, the programs suggest that this work is only legitimate as work because those who perform it are still in some ways liberated, rights-governed citizens, even though they have taken positions within the needs-based economy of the private sphere.

These programs offer models for masculine domestic subjectivity, as well as lessons in domestic labor and household governance, providing different models of masculine household management: *Benson* provides a model of scientific efficiency, delegating tasks and running the governor's mansion and the state simultaneously; *Who's the Boss?* showcases familial sacrifice and compromise as essential management tools; *Charles in Charge* presents a model of family governance primarily through emotional labor that leads family members to care for themselves. At the same time, Tony, Benson, and Charles act as comic figures that allow for the expression (and/or repression) of cultural anxieties around the nexus of class, race, gender, and domestic labor. Finally, *Who's the Boss?*, *Benson*, and *Charles in Charge* provide female viewers with idyllic pictures of households that function particularly well thanks to the (paid) domestic work performed by men. As Patricia Mellencamp argues about *Who's the Boss?* "In many ways, this series, not taken seriously by anyone, might indeed be a middle-class female fantasy rather than contradiction. Angela has the best of both worlds without being trapped in either."[13] *Who's the Boss?* was also by far the most popular of these three programs—it was in the Nielsen Top 10 for four seasons. By contrast, *Benson* only cracked the Top 30 in its first season, and *Charles in Charge* only ran one season in prime time, though it found success in first-run syndication with an additional four seasons.

These sitcoms also provide more conventional fantasies. Sexual tension structures *Who's the Boss?*, which sees Angela and Tony's employer-employee relationship shift toward romance. The program frequently represents Tony as eye candy, often shirtless, dressed in tight pants, or wearing shirts that expose his muscular arms. Similarly, Scott Baio was a teen idol mainstay of the late 1970s and 1980s, thanks in part to his role as Chachi on *Happy Days* (ABC, 1974–1984) and its spin-off *Joanie Loves Chachi* (ABC, 1982–1983). *Charles in Charge* delights in showcasing an attractive younger generation of men who would contribute more to domestic chores and childcare. Jennifer Fuller suggests that Benson's sexuality is pushed to margins, and indeed, *Benson* relies less on its star's physical appearance and more on Robert Guillaume's talent and reputation as a comedic actor.[14] However, *Benson*'s plots often position him as an object of female desire—in a season two episode, a woman finds him so irresistible that she follows him home from vacation, and in a season five episode, a local magazine names him "Bachelor of the Month."[15] Moreover, the program holds much appeal for women struggling to manage home, work, and family, as he runs the governor's mansion with impeccable precision, going above and beyond the call of duty to make sure the house and the lives of its occupants run as smoothly and efficiently as possible.

BENSON'S DOMESTIC AND GOVERNMENTAL EFFICIENCY

While Tony insists on the title "housekeeper," Benson ups the ante. As boss to head housekeeper, Gretchen Kraus (Inga Swenson), and the rest of the governor's mansion staff, his title is "manager of household affairs."[16] Much of the humor in *Benson* comes from Benson's relationship with the bumbling governor, Gene Gatling (James Noble). The governor is, for the most part, completely incompetent, and his jokes are reminiscent of Gracie Allen's—heavily dependent on overly literal interpretations of the words of others. The running joke is that Benson is more fit to be governor than Gatling, encapsulated in the episode "The Layoff" where, after one of their regular late-night chats, the governor heads toward the servants' quarters, and Benson heads toward the governor's. Just after walking offscreen, they catch themselves and reverse course. This joke comes to its logical conclusion during the final season, when Benson runs against Gatling for the governorship. Throughout the series, Benson not only must teach the governor how to be a good father to Katie (Missy Gold),[17] he regularly takes over for the governor in policy decisions (usually giving the governor full credit). In the pilot episode, "Change," Benson makes it very clear that his duties will extend beyond household management.[18] His first day on the job, Benson meets Katie, who explains to him that she is very upset with her father because a new development plan he is backing will necessitate the removal (and therefore death) of beavers native to the area. When the governor lets Benson know that he is in a tough spot, caught between the need to create industrial jobs and the environmental cause of preserving wildlife, Benson stays up all night to devise a plan that will allow the development project to move forward without removing the beavers. He interrupts the governor's press conference to deliver the plan, which he bills as belonging to the governor, to the delight of both environmentalists and businesspeople alike. He thus gets the governor out of a potential jam with voters, special interest groups, and, perhaps most importantly, his daughter, thus solving personal, familial problems as he simultaneously solves public, political problems.

Benson's household role harks back to the ideals of domestic science in the early twentieth century. As Taylorist efficiency rose to prominence in industrial culture, the national obsession with efficient production made its way into the domestic sphere through advocates of "domestic science" like Ellen Richards and Christine Frederick. Efficiency became even more of an obsessive mantra for time-starved dual-career couples in the 1980s and 1990s, as Arlie Hochschild shows.[19] Domestic efficiency is a primary focal point in *Benson*. In the pilot episode, the governor's secretary, Marcy (Caroline McWilliams), tells Benson his job is to run the governor's mansion efficiently, organize things, and "eliminate waste." Another season one episode, "Kraus Affair," finds Benson negotiating with the laundry service and inspecting the meat delivery, as the B-plot revolves around cutting costs at the mansion to set an example for the Taxpayers' Association.[20] According to Barbara Ehrenreich and Deirdre English, "The new 'scientific management' meshed immediately with the domestic scientists' goals of eliminating (or redefining) drudgery and elevating housekeeping to a challenging activity."[21] To this end, Frederick and other domestic scientists suggested, "Housewives, who spent family funds, must similarly learn about market conditions (when to buy and what to pay) and make their decisions according to their particular needs, family incomes, and express goals. 'In other words, every woman running the business of homemaking must *train herself* to become an efficient "purchasing agent" for her particular firm or family, by study, watchfulness, and practice.' This new role offered housewives a truly managerial position in the modern household that stood at the intersection of the previously separate spheres."[22]

From the very first episode, Benson takes on the role of "purchasing agent," auditing Kraus's grocery bill. He admonishes her for not saving leftovers, which she dismisses as a disgrace, a practice below the class standards of the governor's mansion. Though initially Benson seems to back off, allowing Kraus to maintain her protocol, Kraus later finds leftovers in the fridge, evidence that Benson has taken charge of the household economy.

The first season episode "The Layoff" opens with Benson once again going over Kraus's grocery expenditures, decrying the amount of money she spent on candied yams. He spends the rest of the episode finding ways to cut costs, starting with cancelling the weekly changing of all the light bulbs in the mansion. When he balks at the prospect of firing five mansion employees, the governor's political advisor, Taylor (Lewis J. Stadlen), reminds him, "Aren't you the manager of household affairs?" This scene cuts to Benson sitting at his desk in the kitchen reviewing employee files. He considers the assistant groundskeeper, whose only job is to turn the sprinklers on and off, and the seamstress, who is

Figure 20. Benson goes over Kraus's grocery bill on *Benson*.

currently engaged in monogramming cocktail napkins. However, Marcy provides him with a sob story for each, convincing him to keep them. She is less convincing in her attempt to save Miss Ellie (Meg Wyllie), the elderly pastry chef. Benson explains that Miss Ellie does not perform an essential task, that rather, she's a "luxury." However, Benson is so distraught over the firings, the next scene opens with him on the phone, attempting to secure new jobs for those he's letting go. He has yet to break the news to Miss Ellie, and to make his job all the more difficult, she enters the kitchen carrying homemade fudge which she gives to Taylor, and a rose for Marcy, which she thought would "brighten up" Marcy's desk. She informs Kraus that she is making strawberry tarts. Miss Ellie reveals herself to be a model homemaker, selflessly producing joy for those around her. When Benson asks how she has time to make so many people happy, she replies, framed in close-up, that her "whole life [is] doing little things for people. This is my home, Benson, and everyone here is very dear to me. Everyone here is my family." After this heartfelt speech, Benson loses his nerve to fire her. Still, Miss Ellie's old-fashioned ideals of homemaking are incompatible with Benson's new plan of housekeeping efficiency. He regains his nerve the next day and fires Miss Ellie as she performs another "luxury" task, carefully arranging flowers in the parlor. Though Miss Ellie tells Benson she understands and that it is his job to fire her, she still leaves the mansion in tears. Here *Benson* presents homemakers as a dying breed, their labor frivolous, and instead positions efficient management as the preferable mode of household governance.

As Benson excises the last vestiges of homemaking from the governor's mansion in favor of Taylorist efficiency, he achieves the logical conclusion of and the anxiety provoked by the domestic science advocates, where the "scientific home—swept clean of the cobwebs of sentiment, windows opened wide to the light of science—was simply a workplace like any other. No sticky dependencies held the scientific housekeeper to her home, only a clear sense of professional commitment."[23] Kraus is a perfect example of this kind of detached housekeeper, as many jokes revolve around her being a cold-hearted automaton.

Benson, despite his obsession with efficiency, still does not allow the mansion to be completely given over to science. In the episode "Conflict of Interest," he plays surrogate father to Katie when she feels neglected by her father. As Benson tries to convince the governor not to attend a function at the White House in favor of attending Katie's school play, he delivers an emotionally charged speech that indicates his dedication to maintaining the mansion as a loving family home. He tells the governor, "Katie's a part of this job that I didn't bargain for. I didn't come here to be a nanny for an eight-year-old orphan. Just the same, I can't help caring about her. There's a lot that I don't mind doing for Katie, but one thing I can't do is be her father." Similarly, in "Trust Me," when Katie sneaks out to see a Kiss concert after her father has grounded her, Benson disciplines her, laying on an elaborate guilt-trip that quickly teaches her a lesson.[24]

Benson becomes Katie's confidante, a status that allows him to nurture her while simultaneously solving political snafus. In "Checkmate," Benson figures out that Katie is hiding a homesick Russian child chess prodigy and comes up with an elaborate plan to reunite him with his family while maintaining diplomatic relations with his handlers, and by extension, the Soviet Union.[25] Benson is also able to deduce that Katie is responsible for an embarrassing leak to the press, when he picks up on the fact that she wanted to impress her peers at school.[26] The resolution of the episode "Conflict of Interest" makes clear Benson's fatherly dedication to Katie, as he and the governor bicker over who knows Katie's bedtime routine better. Katie resolves their dispute over whether or not she likes to sleep with the window open by telling them to simply leave it half open, a resolution that tellingly does not reveal which one of them is right (and thus, which one of them is a better "father").

While ensuring efficiency appears to be Benson's main household task, the domestic science model was not so successful in most U.S. households. The Taylorist model did not work out so well for housewives, who were not able to delegate tasks. Instead, "For the homemaker, household scientific management turned out to mean *new* work—the new managerial tasks of analyzing one's chores in detail, planning, record-keeping, etc. . . . . Then there was the massive clerical work of maintaining a family filing system."[27] Benson takes on this "new" work, leaving the "old" work to the rest of the household staff. He does this new work in the very place the domestic scientist-housewife was supposed to do it—from a desk in the kitchen. Frederick suggested that "like the busy executive who needs a place to keep his papers, the homemaker 'needs an "office" corner, no matter how humble, where she can go to plan her menus, write out her orders and make up her accounts.'"[28] Most episodes of *Benson* open and close with Benson at his desk, going over paperwork of one kind or another. This task is symbolic of his position as "management," as, unlike Tony in *Who's the Boss?*, he rarely engages in tasks that could be considered "drudgery." He and Kraus bicker over the arrangement of a banquet table in "Old Man Gatling," and he regularly serves the governor coffee during the day and warm milk at night.[29] Yet more demanding and "demeaning tasks" like heavy cleaning are never part of Benson's daily work, with the exception of the labor he assumes during a staff strike. In the pilot, before Benson knows what his duties will be, he walks into the parlor and exclaims, "Well, I ain't cleanin' this. No way am I gonna clean this, this is a career!" And indeed, the cleaning is left up to staff members dressed in traditional black and white maid's uniforms. While Benson has achieved an air of professionalism in his managerial role, the labor of those under him remains less so. According to Ehrenreich and English, one of the failures of the domestic science movement is the professionalization of domestic labor. They note, "In one central way the reformers would have had to admit defeat: their promise to feminism—the upgrading of housekeeping to professional status—had been broken along the way. Instead of becoming an elite corps of professionals, homemakers were as surely as ever a vast corps of menial workers."[30]

Herman Gray suggests that Benson represents "the culmination of all of the servant and helping roles that blacks have historically played in television and the movies." Gray contends that there is one significant difference between Benson and these earlier roles, though, and that is he is "sophisticated, competent and arrogant when necessary," seemingly middle class.[31] Yet despite Benson's management title, his stint as the governor's cousin Jessica Tate's (Katherine Helmond) butler in Soap leaves a stain on his class position. In the episode "Benson in Love," Benson falls unknowingly for state senator Francine (Beverly Todd).[32] After they have gone on several dates, the governor's staff begins to gossip. Taylor expresses concern about the budding romance to Marcy, suggesting that Francine's political party is worried about potential ramifications to her career. Taylor exclaims, "Do you know what the papers can make of her running around with a butler!?" While Marcy tries to interject that Benson is not "just" a butler, Taylor retorts, "Benson may be a climber, but he's out of his class." This comment clearly refers to Benson's new management position, but it also expresses Taylor's resentment of Benson's consistent influence on the governor and Benson's disdain for Taylor. Throughout the episode, Benson continually expresses his anxiety over his cross-class relationship, and when Francine rejects his marriage proposal, he explains that he understands, pointing to his hands while he says, "The callouses are here," then pointing to his head, "not here, senator!" Yet Francine dismisses his class critique, arguing that she is an independent, career-driven woman who does not see marriage in her future. While Francine wants to continue their relationship as is, Benson leaves her apartment, and the episode concludes with him fixing Katie's roller skate. This is one of the only episodes in the first season that portrays Benson's life outside of work. The majority of the program's action takes place within the governor's mansion, and when Benson travels outside of the home, it is usually for governmental purposes. "Benson in Love" provides the viewer with a rare glimpse into Benson's private life, only to have that door slammed when he is rejected and reminded of his place as a domestic laborer.

Later seasons allow Benson more latitude; in season two, he rents an apartment for use on his days off.[33] When Kraus demands to know why he needs what he gleefully refers to as his "bachelor pad," he notes the ways his domestic duties creep into his time off, telling her, "Somebody is always coming to my door. 'The mail's not here? Check with Benson.' 'The chauffeur's drunk? Check with Benson.' 'The airport's fogged in? Check with Benson.'" His first night in the apartment begins promisingly when an attractive woman, Rhonda (Fay Hauser), introduces herself as his neighbor. Their attempt to get to know each other, however, is foiled when the governor and his staff descend on the apartment for a surprise housewarming party, proving that even when Benson maintains a private resi-

Figure 21. Benson's work life invades his home life when his co-worker needs a place
to stay on *Benson*.

dence, the workplace finds its way in. Literalizing this problem, the governor's
press secretary, Clayton (Ethan Phillips), having been thrown out by his ex-
wife, displaces Rhonda and sleeps in Benson's pajamas, in Benson's bed, with
Benson. When Rhonda knocks on the door the next morning, Benson suggests they go someplace "more private"—the governor's mansion. This slippage
between private life and paid domestic work mirrors the work conditions for
many live-in domestic laborers, who often find themselves perpetually on the
clock, and harks back to earlier sitcoms featuring black domestics like *Beulah*
(ABC, 1950–1952), which, as L. S. Kim has pointed out, represented none of its
title character's private life.[34]

Benson's race and class come in handy for the governor, paradoxically elevating Benson above household help to a vital member of the governor's political staff. In "The President's Double," which Guillaume named as his favorite
episode, Benson impersonates an African leader who is under threat of attack
when he is the only available black man who fits the leader's general description.[35]
In the process, he helps prevent a violent fringe group from taking over the fictional African country, while the reception he planned to coordinate himself
goes off without a hitch. In "Takin' It to the Streets," Benson helps the governor
understand the working class when Taylor's elitist sensibility proves inadequate.[36]
He escorts the governor to a dive bar, and they take a seat next to a black

construction worker, who is in "no rush to get home" because his "wife went back to work." The bartender commiserates, noting that the only way to keep up with the cost of living is with two incomes. The governor is eager to participate in their conversation, but Benson must coach him on working-class decorum and he is forced to diffuse tense situations when the governor fumbles his performance.

Benson is consistently sympathetic to working-class politics, and he supports the governor's mansion staff in their bid for higher wages, emphasizing the value of domestic work. In the season one episode "One Strike, You're Out," Benson walks the line between worker and management.[37] Benson sympathizes with the striking workers, though he is nominally management, and promises that the governor will give them a raise. In the meantime, he, Marcy, and Katie pick up the slack of household chores like folding towels, polishing silver, and vacuuming. Unfortunately, Benson and his impromptu household staff do the work a bit too well, resulting in the workers pressuring Benson to strike and in Katie calling Benson a "sore," which Marcy corrects as "scab." Rather than further harm the staff's strike, Benson tells the governor he is resigning, only to be told that as management, it is his duty to fill in. Benson replies, "Telling myself I'm management doesn't change how I feel. I've been a worker all my life. I still am." However, instead of resigning, Benson and Marcy come up with a scheme to convince both the governor and the state finance committee to raise wages as they sabotage a dinner party. Benson, dressed as a butler in a white jacket and bow tie, serves dinner by tossing rolls across the table and sloppily and carelessly serving a poorly executed meal. Thanks to Benson's heroic act (and his willingness to periodically engage in servitude and drudgery), the governor informs the staff that the finance committee has granted them a raise. Benson plays a hand in increasing the value of domestic labor by showing the governor and the finance committee both its importance and the skill required to execute it well.

"Tony Is More Than Just a Housekeeper": *Who's the Boss?* and Exceptional Homemaking

Tony's approach to household management is similar to Benson's in terms of attention to detail and efficiency; however, Tony also preserves much of the emotional labor of homemaking. The fifth season episode "Working Girls" provides overt training for Tony's style of domestic work when Tony's daughter Samantha's (Alyssa Milano) high school class does a project where the students shadow different careers.[38] Tony and Angela promote their jobs to Samantha and her friend Bonnie (Shana Lane-Block), who are the last to choose careers, after Tony overhears a boy complaining about his assignment working at a mortuary, then conceding, "It could have been worse. I could have been stuck cleaning house with Mr. Micelli." Tony's pitches are "who wants to learn how to balance a household budget?" and "who wants to make their own hours?" countered by Angela offering a backstage glimpse at a jeans commercial shoot. Samantha picks Tony to shadow, thinking it will be a cushy job, but of course, he immediately proves her wrong and along the way offers household management guidelines for the viewer. Tony refers to his position as that of "domestic engineer," thus masculinizing traditionally feminized housework and aligning himself with the domestic science movement like Benson. Tony provides Samantha with a list of chores to do for the day, then offers his "philosophy of household management": "A household is an intricate ecosystem where man and house coexist in harmonic symbiosis." When Samantha interjects her dismay at being told to make Angela's son Jonathan's (Danny Pintauro) bed, Tony attempts to shift her perspective, retorting, "We don't make beds. We create a peaceful sleeping environment." While the episode plays Tony's zen approach to housekeeping for laughs, his earnest delivery of these lines suggests that he truly believes this mantra and that it contributes to his contentment working in the home. Samantha, however, does not buy into his philosophy and feels miserable and underappreciated. When Tony returns home and asks what she has prepared for dinner, she is outraged at his expectation. When Tony tells her that dinner preparation is twenty-third on her list, Samantha replies, "I'm on four." Tony tries to calm her down, relaying some expert wisdom: "I've had my days were I feel underappreciated, undervalued, and underpaid, but then Sam, I step back and I take a look at the bigger picture and I realize, wow, it's all worthwhile." Once again here, Tony emphasizes the self-fulfillment of domestic labor, and he references the fact that she is making the home more comfortable for the rest of the family, implying that making others happy should, in turn, make her happy.

While Samantha's disparagement of domestic labor occupies much of the first part of the episode, the rest focuses on Samantha's jealousy of Bonnie's close relationship with Angela. Samantha rebuffs domestic work not just because she hates it but also to be closer to Angela. She convinces Bonnie to switch positions with her momentarily, and Bonnie develops a close relationship with Tony, too, but the episode ends with both girls going to work with Angela. As Samantha says early in the episode, she and Bonnie are "women of the nineties" and they "want it all." At the same time that *Who's the Boss?* offers lessons in household management, it also offers a liberal feminist fantasy wherein a woman can maintain a successful career and have a happy and well-managed home life. Indeed, according to Tania Modleski, "Despite the notorious problems inherent in claims for the subversiveness of comedy as a genre, feminists themselves have found the realm of comedy and carnival to be an important arena both for the working out of utopian desire and for ideological and psychical subversions of the dominant regime."[39]

E. Ann Kaplan also notes the prevalence of comedy in cultural images of domestic and nurturing men, suggesting that this subject matter could not be taken seriously in dramatic programming.[40] While Susan Faludi disdains the character of Angela, who she dismisses as "so selfishly self-absorbed by her professional ambitions that her muscular male housekeeper has to take charge of her kids [sic],"[41] Faludi herself shows a paradoxical attitude toward professional women in assuming that Angela's focus on her career makes her selfish or self-absorbed. Rather, Who's the Boss? presents a liberal middle-class (white) feminist fantasy where a man enjoys performing domestic duties and is happy to support his female partner in a successful career.

The Who's the Boss? series finale epitomizes the feminized theme of self-sacrifice for love and family. Who's the Boss? ended its eight-season run with a three-part episode story arc where Tony takes a job teaching and coaching baseball at a small college in Iowa (an especially unrealistic storyline, given that Tony only holds a bachelor's degree). By this point in the series, Tony and Angela are engaged, and the two of them carry on an especially difficult long-distance relationship. Earlier episodes in the final season focus on Tony's quest for self-betterment and career development. He began attending college at the beginning of the fifth season, and he decides to become a teacher in the sixth season. In the final episode, Angela moves to Iowa to be with Tony, momentarily making the feminine sacrifice of career for love.[42] Angela's avowed reasons for temporarily leaving her career in Connecticut resemble the "choice" discourses of new traditionalism that Elspeth Probyn details in thirtysomething (ABC, 1987–1991).[43] Angela tells Tony that she wants to "lead the simple life. Do all the things I've always wanted to do—painting, gardening." While she speaks this line in a dreamy voice, framed in a soft focus medium close-up for ultimate feminine effect, the episode immediately undercuts this supposed contentment in a flash-forward to one month later where Angela sits in the same place in the kitchen, clipping coupons and talking on the phone. As she mentions a sale at Piggly Wiggly, her joy in her career resurfaces as she says, "Boy, if they were my client, the first thing I'd do is change the—" and she trails off, catching herself. Tony comes home from teaching, and Angela is thrust into the supportive role, listening to the accomplishments of his day. When Tony inquires as to her own day, Angela replies, "Another day, another afghan," and the camera pans right to reveal two couches littered with knitted throw blankets, apparently her new hobby. Along with her transformation into a housewife, Angela also adopts a lower-class lifestyle, commensurate with her rural Iowa surroundings. When the rest of the family comes for a visit, Angela is clad in a bowling shirt, shocking the family. When she goes to hug her mother Mona (Katherine Helmond), Mona exclaims, "Attention K-Mart shoppers!" and asks whether or not the tractor pull was rained out. In order for Angela to become Tony's subordinate, she must sacrifice her class privilege, finally allowing for the articulation of Tony's male privilege.

Mona outs Angela's performance of both class and gender identities by tricking her into admitting her lust for her career. One minute Angela says she does not care what happens at the advertising agency, but when Mona lies and tells her that an important client wants out, Angela immediately comes up with a plan to woo him back. Mona tells Angela that she cannot fool her, and Angela admits, "It's beginning to wear a little thin here" but tells Mona that she can "grin and bear it." As she speaks that line, Tony bursts into the kitchen, demanding dinner, at which point Angela says, "Dinner's almost ready, sweetheart," and Mona counters sarcastically, "Well, you've got the grin down." As Angela puts meatloaf on a serving platter, Tony exclaims proudly to Mona, "Isn't this a switch? The woman cooking and the *man* bringing home the bacon. I've come a long way baby!" Tony's invocation of the "feminist"-inspired Virginia Slims campaign aligns his move from the private sphere to the public sphere with 1970s liberal middle-class feminism, a move which, as Brown shows, inevitably subordinates another, in this case, Angela. However, when Tony's one-year contract is extended for three more years, Angela breaks up with him in order to return to her job in Connecticut.

This episode briefly reverses the gender role reversal on which the entire series is based—thus by reversing the reversal, the conventional gender roles appear strange and unnatural, as the logic of the series was from the beginning completely different. As Jeffrey Sconce argues, "What television lacks in spectacle and narrative constraints, it makes up for in depth and duration of character relations, diegetic expansion, and audience investment."[44] These aspects of television programming work to denaturalize the gendered spheres, at least within the diegesis of *Who's the Boss?*. To see Tony as the "breadwinner" and Angela as the "housewife" is jarring to the invested viewer, who longs for the equilibrium to which the sitcom generically returns. Indeed, *Who's the Boss?* as a series concludes by returning to the equilibrium of the gender role reversal. The final episode ends as the series began—Tony arrives at Angela's door, and asks to be her housekeeper. While he claims that he will look for jobs "in the area," he already failed in a Connecticut-based job search two episodes prior, so it seems likely that he would remain Angela's housekeeper, a decision he makes as a career sacrifice for love. Tony's work in the home is valued (and monetarily compensated), and this episode especially emphasizes Tony's value for the household, as Angela has gone through several housekeepers in search of one who approaches Tony's level of distinction. Domestic labor is valued and compensated, but it also maintains its associations with familial needs and the feminine personal fulfillment that supposedly goes along with caring for the home and family.

While Tony's career is the main narrative force of *Who's the Boss?*, Angela's career is not only present onscreen, but it is also firmly feminist. Angela's dealings with sexual harassment and discrimination work against Bonnie Dow's model of the postfeminist family sitcom—in no way does *Who's the Boss?* suggest that because Angela has an upper middle-class job, feminism has done its work. The first season episode, "Protecting the President," deals specifically with gender discrimination at Angela's advertising agency.[45] Vice president Jim Peterson (Earl Boen), a recurring character, attempts to usurp Angela's position as president when a new chairman of the board is appointed. The very beginning of the episode emphasizes Angela's position in the company as a marginalized one, as Jim shows up to tell her the news of the personnel shake-up. When Jim refuses to disclose his source, Angela deduces that he heard it "in the executive men's room" and then tells him that the news is just "a washroom rumor." However, as she dismisses his claim, the phone rings to confirm the new chairman. Here the narrative explicitly positions Angela as an outsider in the company of which she is the president, all on account of her lack of access to the men's bathroom. Angela expresses anxiety over Jim's potential to convince the new chairman to appoint him president, telling Tony that "he's real good at being one of the boys. He drinks scotch, talks sports. He knows all the dirty jokes." When Angela throws a party to welcome the new chairman, Jim shows his true colors, making the sexism of the workplace perfectly clear. Jim tells Tony that Angela has had a "free ride" to the top, implying she used sex to secure her powerful position. While Angela wavers on how to handle the situation—both how to quiet Jim and maintain her position as president—she finally confronts Jim, telling him that if he spreads more "smutty innuendo" that she will fire him. As in any sitcom, this conflict is nominally "resolved" at the end of the episode: Jim seems to understand his job is at stake if he continues to discriminate against Angela. However, Jim does not disappear nor does his overt sexism.[46] Angela continually has to deal with him and the other men she works with until she opens her own advertising agency, which she staffs solely with women.[47] These situations would have been especially familiar to many white, middle-class working women viewers, and Angela's ability to reinvent the workplace when she opens the Bower Agency represents a particular triumph in the context of the "stalled revolution." In the world of Who's the Boss?, Angela has managed to revolutionize both home and work, completing one version of the feminist revolution.

Who's the Boss? also regularly grapples with issues of class and Tony's role in the home, making it an exceptional television engagement with liberal feminism. As Lauren Rabinovitz notes in her analysis of Designing Women (CBS, 1986–1993) and Murphy Brown (CBS, 1988–1998), "Although television consistently articulates feminism as reformist, liberal, and progressive, it simultaneously disavows any racial or class determinants."[48] As Patricia Mellencamp puts it, "The equality between [Tony and Angela] might be the result of this monetary inequality: his low economic and professional status and her executive achievements and economic power."[49] In addition to class, the program makes frequent references to Tony's ethnic background, and he returns periodically to his working-class Italian American neighborhood in Brooklyn. He and Angela acknowledge these differences quite often, he referring to her as a WASP,[50] and her calling his familial

Figure 22. Angela feels marginalized by her male co-workers on *Who's the Boss?*

ideals "ethnic."[51] While in general Angela is sensitive to Tony's class position, so much so that her neighbors complain that their own household help are agitating for pay comparable to his,[52] she can be quick to pull rank if she feels as though Tony has overstepped his bounds.[53] An early episode establishes the class tension between Tony and Angela, but also Tony's status as a rights-governed citizen, when Tony attempts to prove to the other housekeepers in the neighborhood that he and Angela have a close friendly relationship that goes deeper than employer/employee by painting her car red rather than her choice, beige.[54] When Tony once again insists on his title as "housekeeper" rather than "maid," the other housekeepers in the neighborhood tell him that Angela thinks of him as the latter.

When Angela confronts Tony after seeing her car, the camera frames them in a series of medium two-shots, keeping both of them in each shot as the camera cuts in a shot-reverse shot pattern. The consistent framing of both of them in an editing pattern which would normally exclude one or the other emphasizes the closeness of their relationship but also the impending fight. When Tony offers to pay to have the car repainted, the camera cuts to a medium close-up of Angela as she tells him it will cost $1500. The cut to the closer shot underscores the shift to a much more serious situation, and after Tony makes another joke in the reverse shot, the camera cuts back to Angela, now outraged, who begins to put Tony in his place. The camera cuts to a jarringly tight close-up of Tony who begins to protest, but Angela interrupts him and the camera cuts to a medium shot of her. The tight close-up on Tony juxtaposed with the longer shot of Angela leads the viewer to identify strongly with Tony, who the viewer knows will be deeply hurt by Angela's speech. While the earlier editing pattern of the equal shot-reverse shot structure leads the viewer to see both sides of the story, the unequal framing of Tony and Angela privileges Tony's feelings and makes Angela's diatribe seem incredibly harsh. Angela moves toward the kitchen door in medium shot and tells Tony, "I don't pay you to make decisions around here, I pay you to do the damn floors. You are just the maid around here and don't you forget it!" After she delivers this line, she leaves the kitchen and the camera cuts back to another tight close-up of Tony, who stands shocked, his mouth agape as the frame fades to black. Though Tony does not get the last word with Angela in this scene, he gets the last word with the viewer, as there is no comparable shot of Angela feeling remorse for her statement, and the viewer stays in the kitchen with Tony.

In response to Angela's stinging outburst, Tony uses a strategy similar to Benson's in "One Strike, You're Out," self-consciously playing the role of a maid (or butler), dressed in a butler's uniform as opposed to his usual casual wear. He rearranges the entire family routine in order to live up to Angela's avowed expectations of him to be merely the help. He refers to Angela as "Mrs. Bower," "ma'am," or "madam," calls Jonathan "master Jonathan," and refers to himself and Samantha as "the hired help." He sets a formal dinner table for only Angela and Jonathan, and when he reveals the menu (prime rib, Yorkshire pudding, baby peas), Jonathan asks why he cannot have the franks and beans that Tony and Samantha are having. Tony replies, "Your station in life, sir." Finally Angela gives in at the end of the episode, telling Tony that if she really wanted a maid, she never would have hired a "headstrong, opinionated, pain in the neck" like him. This admission is particularly telling—Tony's insubordination marks him as not-a-maid, but it also marks him as a rights-governed citizen, and paradoxically, a *more* valuable domestic laborer who can participate as a fully engaged member of the family.

This episode, like many in the series, is highly ambivalent in its melding of class and gender politics. As Angela asserts to Mona, Tony indeed had "no right" to go against her wishes in painting her car. Mona tries to put it in perspective for Angela, agreeing that Tony was wrong, but reminding Angela that Tony is "a human being" and that her car is just "a hunk of metal." The gendered nature of Tony's move over Angela's head is clear when he tells the man who picks up Angela's car to be painted that he is "the man of the house." Thus, the episode implies, by virtue of his gender and his position as household manager, Tony is authorized to make decisions for Angela. In the end, Tony appears to be right, as Angela decides to leave her car red and Tony tries to get her to admit that she

Figure 23. Tony plays butler to prove a point to Angela on *Who's the Boss?*

really likes it. Here Tony remains a rights-governed citizen—though Mona and Angela both agree that he had no "right" to paint the car red, in fact he was "right" in choosing the color Angela really wanted but was perhaps too conservative to ask for. As Brown claims, women under liberalism "are without the mark of subjective sovereignty, the capacity to desire or choose."[55] Tony's class and the tension it creates within the household and in his relationship with Angela is never fully resolved within the series. Episodes frequently revolve around economic or social problems, yet Tony always maintains his pride, a characteristic all the other characters openly admire.[56] He also takes great pride in his work in the home, maintaining a kitchen so spotless that when Angela's client uses her kitchen for a commercial, the director complains that it lacks realism.[57]

Who's the Boss? explicitly places value on domestic labor in the episode "Housekeepers Unite," where Tony goes on strike with other housekeepers in the neighborhood who seek a rate of pay commensurate with his. Tony's role in leading and organizing the strike in solidarity with his fellow workers is especially important given the historical difficulties in organizing domestic laborers. As Cox points out, "Domestic workers are a notoriously difficult group to organize because of their isolation in separate houses. This presents practical problems because domestic workers do not necessarily know each other or meet up as a group, and they may not have the same time off or be able to travel far to meetings. Working inside a family home can also mean that domestic workers identify with their employers and overlook their own rights."[58]

When it comes to light that Tony is "the highest paid housekeeper on the eastern seaboard," the housekeepers' coffee klatch turns into a moment of union organizing, as the other neighborhood housekeepers prepare to demand Tony's rate of pay along with comparable health insurance. The other housekeepers, all women, demand "equal pay for equal work," highlighting the fact that a man's labor in the home is better paid than a woman's. Tony initially sees no reason to strike, as he is satisfied with his working conditions, but Angela insists that he support the other workers. The housekeepers' demands are quickly met, and for a moment, Tony is no longer the highest paid housekeeper. But Angela gives him a raise so that he can maintain his title, a move further showing the higher value placed on men's labor. Indeed, Tony's method of household management seems exceptional in its melding of emotional and physical labor that is so sincere that it earns him a position as a permanent family member, regardless of his continuing status as a paid laborer.

"I Sort of Take Care of Them": Emotional Labor on *Charles in Charge*

Just as Tony occupies a privileged position in Angela's house, Charles's position in the Powell family (for whom he works in the second through fifth seasons), would be a dream come true for a live-in domestic laborer. On the one hand, his wages appear to be low, based on his obsession with going over the contents of his bank account.[59] On the other hand, Charles has privileges in the Powell household that most domestic laborers do not. As Bridget Anderson shows, "Whatever hours a live-in nanny and housekeeper is supposed to work, there is virtually no time when she can comfortably refuse to 'help' her employer with a household task."[60] Yet Charles has the luxury of refusing work for a multitude of reasons—too much homework, family obligations, even (regularly) dates— and he never faces disciplinary action or the termination of his employment for his refusals, just a few jokes at his expense. In the season two episode "Weekend Weary," when Charles's best friend, Buddy (Willie Aames), tells Mr. Powell (James T. Callahan, the children's grandfather and Mrs. Powell's father-in-law), that Mrs. Powell (Sandra Kerns) gave Charles the weekend off, Mr. Powell retorts, "Vacations are for people who work!"[61] Whereas most domestic laborers are not typically allowed to host guests, Buddy is a fixture of the Powell residence, even spending Christmas with them.[62] In contradistinction to Benson, who rarely leaves the governor's mansion, Charles has a new female conquest in nearly every episode, and he regularly enjoys nights out of the house in addition to his college classes. Despite the fact that Charles "lives downstairs," as the program's theme song relentlessly points out at the beginning of every episode, Charles takes on the role of head of household. He delegates the hard labor (in the episode "The Organization Man" he tells Buddy, "An organized executive knows how to delegate authority.[63] I'll get someone else to do it") to other members of the family, while he takes on the emotional labor of raising the children. This primary focus on child-rearing is common to men who were performing more domestic labor in the 1980s. As Hochschild's research shows, "Of all the time men spend working at home, more of it goes to child-care. That is, working wives spend relatively more time 'mothering the house'; husbands spend more time 'mothering' the children. Since most parents prefer to tend to their children than clean house, men do more of what they'd rather do."[64]

Charles in Charge makes it clear that Charles enjoys helping the children with their problems—he professionalizes this service to a greater extent in the episode "Dear Charles," where he takes a temporary job as an advice columnist.[65] With Mrs. Powell's long work hours and Mr. Powell's curt manner, the children gravitate toward Charles in every episode for tender loving care and thoughtful advice. In fact, this absence of parental figures during the Powell children's crucial teenage years (where crises regularly revolve around pseudosexual romantic entanglements) positions Charles's emotional labor as vitally important, lest Jamie (Nicole Eggert) act on her sexual urges,[66] Sarah (Josie Davis) lose confidence in her academic abilities,[67] or Adam (Alexander Polinsky) become a pyromaniac.[68]

Charles's household tasks rarely include cleaning or cooking, unless he is doing someone a favor, and his only consistent duty that marks him as hired help is a running joke where Mr. Powell barks at him, "Doorbell!" every time the doorbell rings. In fact, minor characters often question Charles's employment, necessitating his explanation. In the second season episode "The Naked Truth," Charles explains to a prospective date: "This is the Powell family. I sort of take care of them."[69] His hedging—that he "sort of" takes care of them—aptly describes the tenuous nature of his employment. A few episodes later, he tells Buddy's prospective date, "I do a little of everything" when she asks what he does in the house.[70] He rarely appears to be truly necessary, yet many episodes insist that the family would fall apart without him. In the season three episode "Dutiful Dreamer," Mrs. Powell loses her job, and the family finds out their house is being sold.[71] Mr. Powell informs Charles that his employment is in jeopardy due to the confluence of these events. He labels Charles's position as a "live-in babysitter" a "luxury" that the family will have to forego. However, Charles proves he is not a luxury but a necessity by the end of the episode, when he calls his former employers, the Pembrokes, whose rented house the Powells sublet, and convinces them to buy the house and rent it to the Powells themselves. In this instance, Charles truly does a "little bit of everything." He may be a luxury when it comes to babysitting duties, but he is integral in literally maintaining the home.

Still, Charles's presence seems more and more unnecessary as the series progresses and the Powell children grow up. In the last two seasons, middle daughter Sarah is about the same height as Charles and significantly taller than Buddy, and all three children are of an age where they would be more than capable of taking care of themselves (by the last season, oldest daughter Jamie is seventeen, and youngest son Adam has started high school). Because of this increasingly curious arrangement, episodes revolve around the importance of the labor Charles provides, primarily teaching the children to take care of themselves. This lesson would have been especially pertinent for families of the 1980s, where children were increasingly "unsupervised" after school. The fifth and final season premiere demonstrates Charles's utility in this regard. In "Summer Together, Fall Apart," the whole family (including Charles) comes home from a long vacation.[72] Charles raves to Buddy about what a great time they had, but each family member enters the house one by one complaining about what a horrible trip it was. When Mrs. Powell prepares to leave town for a two-week business trip, Charles and Mr. Powell argue over whose rules the kids should follow. Mrs. Powell sides with Charles, hurting Mr. Powell's feelings and causing him to "run away" from home, leaving Charles alone to deal with the kids. The kids complain to Charles that he makes too many rules, and they convince him to let each of them make one rule apiece. Adam's rule, which structures the rest of the episode, is that there should be no rules. Initially appalled by this suggestion, Charles embraces it, knowing it can only last so long. Indeed, the kids' separate prerogatives clash, and they run to Charles to settle their disagreements. To conclude the episode, Jamie begs Charles to make some rules, telling him "It's your job to bring us up right, so please do it." His hands-off approach has taught the Powell kids the need for some structure and order to avoid complete chaos.

Similarly, in the season three episode "Where the Auction Is," Charles avoids labor in order to teach the kids self-sufficiency. Early in the episode, each family member requests some sort of labor from Charles. Adam asks him to clean his room, and Charles replies, "My job does not include cleaning your room." Jamie and Sarah ask him to make onion dip for their party and he replies, "Sorry girls, I don't do windows or dips." Mr. Powell backs him up, telling Jamie and Sarah, "Charles is right, girls, onion dip is not in his job description." This response frustrates the girls, as Jamie exclaims in exasperation, "If that's true, what good is he?" before storming upstairs. Meanwhile, in order to get a date, Charles agrees to be a part of a sorority's "slave auction," and to his horror, the Powell children buy him. Jamie explains to Mr. Powell that they bought Charles because he refused to do chores for them. Hearing this, Charles is extremely hurt and asks her, "So that's why you guys bought me, huh? Because you didn't think I do enough for you?" Charles's mother, Lillian (Ellen Travolta), smooths things over, casually telling the kids about how she raised Charles to be "self-sufficient," and they realize that he was trying to do them the same favor. Though the children are seemingly grateful to Charles for his dedication to teaching them this valu-able lesson, the episode concludes with an insistence that Charles still does emotional, physical, and material labor. He satisfies the calls of each family member—helping Sarah with her algebra, gluing Adam's thermos back together, giving Jamie dating advice, and cleaning the basement for Mr. Powell.

Charles in Charge makes Charles's emotional labor all the more important in the Powell household by contrasting it with the gruff paternal authority fig-ure of Mr. Powell, a retired marine. Charles in Charge sets up this contrast early in the second season, where Charles and Mr. Powell clash over how to handle Adam's feud with a neighbor.[73] Whereas Charles encourages "diplomacy" and suggests that Adam try to reason with his rival, Mr. Powell takes Adam in the kitchen to discuss a strategy of retaliation. In the season four episode "It's a Blunderfull Life," Charles feels compelled to save the children from the poor example Mr. Powell sets for them. He begins to realize at the beginning of the episode that the children have picked up bad habits from Mr. Powell—Adam takes food to his bedroom, leaving a trail of crumbs and failing to return his plate; Jamie gives herself a manicure at the kitchen table, spilling nail polish just as Mr. Powell spills glue from his ship models; and Adam turns into a gambler, making bets on sporting events just like his grandfather. When Charles, Adam, and Mr. Powell patronize a newsstand, Charles talks Mr. Powell out of purchasing a lottery ticket, so as to discourage Adam from gambling. The newsstand cashier recognizes Charles's moral authority, asking, "What are you, a customer or a TV evangelist?" This episode is not the first instance that Charles is held up as the familial conscience. In fact, the first episode of the second season, where Charles is just getting acquainted with the Powells, establishes him in this role.[74]

After counseling Sarah about her reluctance to date in the face of pressure from Jamie, Charles confronts Jamie, telling her that Sarah is "not ready yet, and that's her decision." Feigning disgust, Jamie retorts, "Thank you, Michael Landon," an allusion to Landon's television series Highway to Heaven (NBC, 1984–1989) where he plays an angel who helps those in need. Charles's emotional labor as moral compass of the Powell family places him squarely in the position of the Progressive Era middle-class housewife, whose duty was to guard the family from sin. By this logic, the housewife's "soft" labor was considered more important than the hard labor that was often farmed out to servants. Indeed, Charles provides this labor largely in the absence of Mrs. Powell, who does not appear in many episodes. L. S. Kim suggests that Charles in Charge is one of several programs in the 1980s representing "white male servants who take over the mother's job (because there is doubt that she can do it)."[75] However, when Mrs. Powell does appear in episodes, she usually performs the menial labor that might be relegated to hired help. She cooks,[76] serves meals,[77] does heavy cleaning[78] and laundry,[79] and goes grocery shopping.[80] Charles in Charge marginalizes her "hard" domestic labor, as episodes revolve around Charles's affective labor.

While the bulk of Charles's labor in the Powell home is emotional, several episodes display his ability to juggle the myriad tasks necessary to keep the Powell house running smoothly. When Mrs. Powell and Mr. Powell leave for the day to pick up Mrs. Powell's husband, Captain Powell, in "Piece of Cake," they provide Charles with a list of duties that need to be carried out before they return home.[81] He has to be home for the plumber to fix the sink, drop off and pick up dry cleaning, take Adam to his Boy Scout meeting, and clean the house. Charles attempts to delegate tasks, asking Sarah and Jamie to clean while he goes to the grocery store, but they instead want to bake their father's favorite cake. When Charles comes home from the grocery store, he finds Jamie ransacking the front closet, producing a huge mess while she frantically searches for the music box her father gave her. While Charles starts to pick up after her, she runs out of the house in a panic. Meanwhile, Adam comes downstairs dressed in his scout uniform and announces that Charles missed the plumber, who refused to fix the sink without an adult present to pay him. Charles and Adam walk into the kitchen to find a colossal mess left by Sarah and Jamie's ill-fated cake baking, which Sarah has abandoned in order to purchase frosting ingredients. Charles sends Adam off to purchase decorations as he tries to finish the cake. To make matters worse, as Jamie comes home in search of Charles's advice on how to make her father understand that she's not a little girl any more, Sarah returns and informs Charles that Adam has been caught shoplifting and is being detained at the market. After an exhausting chain of events (including an impromptu scout meeting at the Powell residence), Charles finally delegates enough chores to allow him to sit down and counsel Jamie, a moment that the episode frames as the most important. Charles leaves the menial tasks—decorating, fixing the sink, and running to the dry cleaners—to others, while he helps Jamie conquer her emotional crisis.

Charles's skills are so in demand that during the first season, he and Buddy try to set up a business providing other "Charleses" to families in the neighborhood.[82] Every character seems to know a family that is desperate to hire someone like Charles, so Buddy suggests that they train people that they can then stamp with the "Good Charles-keeping Seal of Approval," thus marking Charles's work in the home as somehow providing for a unique or exceptional mode of family governance. When Charles and Buddy tell the Pembrokes about their business venture, Charles says, "We feel like live-in family helpers are the wave of the future." Buddy confirms, noting that the prevalence of dual-career households necessitates outside help. Charles interviews various nightmare candidates, asking each a series of questions about dealing with and disciplining children. All of the candidates fail miserably, until a lone woman, Megan (Meg Ryan), remains. She gets past the questioning, which prompts Charles to bring on "the torture test," consisting of the Pembrokes' daughter, Lila (April Lerman), taking on the persona of a "hood," whom Megan dissuades by telling

Figure 24. Charles goes over his list of tasks on *Charles in Charge*.

her that her all-black wardrobe is out of fashion, and son, Jason (Michael Pearlman), convincing her to let him try out for the basketball team against his parents' wishes. Charles disapproves of Megan's handling of the situation and provides her (and the viewer) with specific rules by which to govern her relationship with the children she looks after: rule 1: What the parents say goes; rule 2: "There are no simple decisions"; rule 3: kids catch on quickly.

While Charles is always successful in solving familial problems, he cannot solve a momentary crisis involving one child's missing money. He accuses Jason, who denies involvement, and Megan calls after Lila, whose sunglasses she recognizes as costing the same amount as the missing money. Here Megan proves the utility of feminine fashion sense in dealing with teenage girls. Her ability to quickly diffuse a dispute among children prompts Charles to name her his only graduate. This scene cuts to a medium close-up of Lila talking on the phone, telling the teenage daughter of the family Megan will work for "how to handle a live-in family helper." Charles one-ups Lila, admitting to her that he has been telling Megan how to deal with a teenage daughter, an interesting turn of events since Charles lacked the "sensibility" to deal with Lila in the prior scene. Still, this reinscribes Charles as the supreme family manager, mitigating any credibility he may have lost in the previous scene. Further, Charles's seamless disciplining and caring for the children, presented in weekly lessons for the viewer in

Figure 25. Lila plays juvenile delinquent to help Charles train a prospective protégé on *Charles in Charge*.

arranging her or his own family similarly, underscores Elayne Rapping's comment that throughout the years the sitcom's "scrubbed, well-functioning families have invaded our living rooms and challenged us to measure up. They have presented images of family unity and harmony to a nation deep in the throes of domestic chaos and trauma."[83] *Charles in Charge* indeed presents a "well-functioning" family; however, Charles is a necessary component to that function. While *Charles in Charge* certainly does not undermine the cultural valuation of the nuclear family, it does suggest that many families need extra help in order to care for children.

Jill Pembroke (Julie Cobb), the mother on the first season of *Charles in Charge*, works as a newspaper writer. Unlike Angela's primacy on *Who's the Boss?*, *Charles in Charge* never takes place at Jill's office, and her specific work concerns rarely enter the story lines, although two grandparents suggest that she should take more of an active role in raising her children.[84] While Jill dismisses these attempted interventions, she herself bows to the pressure in the episode "Jill's Decision" where she decides not to take a promotion that would require extra hours, even though she can work from home.[85] Since Jill is a minor character, *Charles in Charge* does not devote much of the episode to her dilemma, and she seems to make her decision to turn down the promotion on the same day that she gets it. Jill's decision to sacrifice career for family plays into a tendency Alan Nadel traces, wherein "most aspects of American life during the 1980s manifested a shrinking of women's power, authority, and real income. At the same time, [Susan] Faludi makes clear, a popular rhetoric emerged that suggested women were more successful and less happy *because* of their alleged advances."[86]

Jill appears to agonize over her decision; however, Charles and the children do not seem to mind at all that she spends more time working. Meanwhile, Jill's husband, Stan (James Widdoes), does not feel the same pull toward the family, and the episode never implies that he might want or need to spend more time with the children. Instead, the burden falls squarely on Charles. Through making childcare Jill's responsibility (with Charles there for help), *Charles in Charge* essentializes childcare as feminine. As Brown claims, "The *family* or *personal life* is *natural to woman* and in some formulations *divinely ordained*; it is a domain governed by needs and affective ties, hence a domain of *collectivity*."[87] The "affective ties" that govern Jill do not in any way appear to govern her husband, who is "free" to roam the public sphere unfettered, and affective ties only govern Charles to the extent that he develops a fondness for the children whom he is paid to look after.

Even though *Charles in Charge* deals less with the mother's career than does *Who's the Boss?*, the fact that the Pembroke family needs (male) domestic help sets it apart from *Who's the Boss?* in that the Pembrokes are a two-parent household. While *Who's the Boss?* could easily rationalize Tony's presence, as Angela was a divorced mother looking for both a housekeeper and a "male role model" for her son,[88] the choice of a male caregiver in *Charles in Charge* is never explicitly explained, and the Pembrokes' need for Charles makes it clear that Jill is not expected to work the double shift all on her own. Further, the ability to employ extra help in a two-parent household has important class implications. As Elizabeth Traube points out, "In the absence of public provisioning of child care, [shared parenting] is a course available only to those with flexible work schedules and/or the financial means to hire domestic help. As it is currently practiced, shared parenting is predicated on the availability of cheap, primarily female labor and represents a privatized, middle-class solution to the problem of expanding women's choices without reducing the care provided to dependents."[89] Here Traube makes clear the limitations of any liberal celebration of the politics of *Charles in Charge*—the program implies that upper middle-class women can "have it all" by simply exploiting the labor of broke college students. However, while Charles clearly labors in the home in order to make it through college, he also is quite obviously emotionally attached to the children.

Several episodes of *Charles in Charge*, *Benson*, and *Who's the Boss?* focus on Charles, Benson, or Tony turning down lucrative job offers to remain working in the home.[90] In essence, these episodes put Charles, Benson, and Tony in the (feminine) position of sacrificing career for family, with the important distinction that their labor in the family is paid. In the *Charles in Charge* episode "Pressure from Grandma," Stan's mother, Irene (Rue McClanahan), arrives and tries to push Charles out of the home and into the (public) workplace so that she can take over the role of household caretaker. Tensions between Irene and Charles began in an earlier episode, "Home for the Holidays," where she is appalled to find that the guest room (which she refers to as her room) is already occupied and that she must compete with Charles for the children's attention. She derides Stan for allowing an "outsider to raise [her] grandchildren." In "Pressure from Grandma," Irene takes matters into her own hands, luring Charles into working for her as a traveling salesman. With each subsequent trip she makes him travel a bit further, until he is so successful that she tells him he should be traveling all along the east coast, thus allowing her to move into the Pembroke home. While Charles is off selling microwave pizza at Rutgers University, Irene babysits the children, who are uncomfortable with her rules and long for Charles. Irene suggests to the family that Charles will not be around the house much in the future, and when Charles returns, Jill inquires as to why he would be more interested in selling pizza when he has a job working for her. She asks about his financial situation, and Charles discloses that he has only saved eighty dollars in the time he has lived with the Pembrokes. By contrast, he earned nine hundred dollars in one day selling pizza. As Irene pulls Charles aside to discuss his future, Jason grabs Charles's arm. The camera pans left quickly, framing Charles and Irene in long shot, but stops abruptly and cuts to a close-up of Jason as he asks, "Charles, are you leaving us?" while gazing up expectantly at Charles off-screen. The camera cuts back to Charles and Irene, framed in a medium two-shot, as Charles explains that he is not interested in working for her. When he tells her, "I've already got a job, and I like it," the camera cuts to a long shot that includes all of the members of the Pembroke family, underscoring the importance of his managerial position in the home. In the second season premiere, Buddy tries to convince Charles not to work for his new employers, and rather to get an off-campus apartment with him, by pointing out "some children are going to have to grow up without your influence." However, Charles, of course, opts to stay and influence the Powell children, performing the vital emotional labor that their mother is too busy to provide and for which their grandfather is ill-equipped.

CONCLUSION

In all likelihood, *Charles in Charge*, *Benson*, and *Who's the Boss?* did not spur a craze of male domestic laborers, a lesson Charles himself already learned in the failure of his Charles 'R' Us venture. Susan Douglas and Meredith Michaels call attention to the unlikely scenario in *The Mommy Myth*, sarcastically noting that realistic depictions of the childcare crisis in the 1980s were obscured in favor of "fantasy hunks Tony (Tony Danza) in *Who's the Boss* and Charles (Scott Baio) of *Charles in Charge* who worked in that frequently-seen line of work, the male governess."[91] Still, Mellencamp's idea of feminist fantasy is important in looking at *Charles in Charge* and *Who's the Boss?*, especially in the context of the neoconservative family politics of the 1980s. Jane Feuer captures the disparity between gender on film and on television in the 1980s, arguing, "If the emblematic films of the period represented a masculine fantasy of hard bodies and a hard political line (Jeffords 1994), television in the eighties, I will argue, was both more feminized and more ideologically complex."[92] *Who's the Boss?*, *Benson*, and *Charles in Charge* certainly project ideological confliction, arguing that domestic labor should be valued but only when performed by men. Still, these programs offer guidelines for family organization that do not require women to work the double shift—indeed, they show that work to be virtually impossible.

CHAPTER 5

DISRUPTING THE FANTASY

REAGAN ERA REALITIES AND
FEMINIST PEDAGOGIES

In contrast to the parade of white middle-class families across the dial in the 1980s, two programs that bookended the family sitcom glut—*Gimme a Break!* (NBC, 1981–1987) and *Roseanne* (ABC, 1988–1997)—emphasized class and racial difference while maintaining a focus on gendered inequality in the domestic and public spheres. Despite the prominence of yuppie culture, shored up by the mergers and acquisitions craze memorialized in *Wall Street* (director Oliver Stone, 1987), the majority of income growth in the 1980s went to the wealthiest Americans, and the gap between rich and poor widened as manufacturing jobs moved overseas.[1] In contrast to most of the sitcoms included in this book, *Roseanne*, with its focus on a white working-class family, commanded low advertising rates despite the fact that it landed in the Nielsen Top 10 for seven seasons (tying *The Cosby Show* for the number one slot in 1989): advertisers believed it did not adequately address an upscale audience.[2] With stand-up comic Roseanne Barr playing Roseanne Conner, the series was built upon a feminist heroine who was brutally honest about the everyday dissatisfactions that came with pink-collar labor, marriage, and motherhood.

While most of the caregivers on 1980s sitcoms obscured the reality of who was doing the care work in upper middle-class families by positioning (usually white) men in these roles, *Gimme a Break!* acknowledges that this work was primarily undertaken by women of color by focusing the series on Nell (Nell Carter), an African American housekeeper to white widower Carl Kanisky (Dolph Sweet) and surrogate mother to his three daughters. In L. S. Kim's examination of sitcom maids, she shows how the white middle-class woman gains leisure and in some ways escapes confinement in the home through her own subordination of an Other, often a woman of color. She notes, "With the advent of women managing servants, some women attempt to escape (or at least circumvent some of the burdens of) sexism—through class and racial privilege."[3] Though Nell's labor does not allow a white woman to enjoy a professional career, she still "replaces" a white woman's labor in the home due to the death of Margaret Kanisky that provides the rationale for the plot. Nell cares for the Kaniskys as though she were a member of the family, and they treat her as such, a dynamic that is similar to that of *Mr. Belvedere*, *Who's the Boss?*, and *Charles in Charge*. The series positions Nell and the Kanisky daughters as progressive (including many jokes at Ronald Reagan's and Republicans' expense), against the conservative old-fashioned values of Carl, and most episodes feature the intergenerational, interracial alliance of women triumphing over the out-of-touch patriarch. Despite their more overt engagements with the socioeconomic realities of the Reagan era, both *Gimme a Break!* and *Roseanne* still functioned as liberal feminist fantasies of family life, allowing their female protagonists a significant amount of power in the family and positioning them as feminist role models for a younger generation of women and for women viewers.

CHALLENGING PATRIARCHY ON *GIMME A BREAK!*

Compared to the family sitcoms that would follow later in the decade, *Gimme a Break!* appears in many ways to be firmly lodged in the 1970s, both in terms of its visual style (muted, washed-out colors, dated home décor) and subject matter (seemingly reaching for the "relevance" designation of the Norman Lear sitcoms). Perhaps due to its seeming anachronism, the series never broke into the Nielsen Top 30, and NBC regularly changed its time slot. Still, the series ran for six seasons and was sold into off-net syndication for over $100 million.[4] Widower police chief Carl is gruff, old-fashioned, and often spouts tirades against minority groups and progressive politics. His parenting style mainly consists of angry yelling and threats of corporal punishment. Tellingly, Carl is very rarely referred to by his first name—Nell calls him "Chief," as do most of the other adult characters, and his quick temper provides many of the narrative conflicts. He regularly comes home from work in a bad mood, and he belligerently shouts many of his lines. In stark contrast to the nurturing widowers on *Who's the Boss?* and *Full House*, both of whom also raised daughters, the Chief is cut from a much older tradition of TV dad. In the pilot episode alone, he slaps his oldest daughter, Katie (Kari Michaelsen), across the face for shoplifting, ordering her to move out, and grounds his middle daughter, Julie (Lauri Hendler), "until she's married" when he discovers her kissing a boy.[5]

In comparison to the upper middle-class WASPy families of most 1980s family sitcoms, the Kaniskys are Polish American, and the Chief speaks with a thick New York accent. Jennifer Fuller claims that the Kaniskys' ethnic identity "primarily *whitened* them by sharpening their distinction from Nell" rather than othering them, but I would argue that it also serves to align them with cultural conceptions of the working class.[6] Though Carl's job as police chief and the establishing shot of the large house that opens the credit sequence would suggest the Kaniskys are at least middle class economically, the series codes them as firmly working class culturally. Richard Butsch, in one of his examinations of class in sitcoms, categorizes the Kaniskys as middle class; however, his description of the common depiction of the working-class father at least partially fits the Chief. He argues that within working-class family sitcoms, "Humor was built around some variant of working-class man's stereotypic ineptitude, immaturity, stupidity, lack of good sense or emotional outburst."[7] While the Chief is not stupid or immature, his quick temper regularly gets him into trouble, and the series marks his values and opinions as narrow-minded and usually flat-out wrong. Functioning as foils to working-class male characters are "typically working-class wives and often the children [who] were portrayed as more intelligent, rational, sensible, responsible, mature than their husbands."[8] Though Nell is not the Chief's wife, she certainly fills the role left by Margaret Kanisky, especially in bailing out the Chief when he makes a mistake, another of Butsch's tropes of working-class sitcoms.

The Chief's accented speech alone seems to symbolize working-class identity—he mentions that he grew up in Glendale, California, a suburb of Los Angeles, so it's not particularly clear where he would have picked up a New York accent.[9] Whereas Clair Huxtable on The Cosby Show didn't hesitate to spend $11,000 on a painting, the Chief loses his temper when Nell reveals that the family is six dollars over their budget for the month.[10] The season one episode "Katie the Cheat" reveals that Katie would be the first in the family to attend college, and the Chief's traditional masculine bravado and former career as an amateur boxer align him with common stereotypes of the white ethnic working class. A season two episode reveals that Margaret's sister disapproved of the Kaniskys' marriage, believing the Chief to be "beneath" Margaret.[11] Katie complains to Nell that her father never cried following her mother's death, and Nell explains that this is a result of his rigorously conventional masculinity—that policemen are "not allowed to cry."[12] In the season one episode "Mom's Birthday," Nell sees the Chief coming and rushes around the living room, fluffing throw pillows on his favorite chair and setting the mail for him to read on the side table,[13] and in another she tells the girls, "You know, the last time his dinner was late, he bit the mailman."[14] The Chief's quick, irrational temper aligns him more with stereotypes of the white ethnic working class than with middle-class decorum. As Melissa Williams notes, "Class, American-style, has typically been culturally defined by the combination of material accumulation and comportment."[15] By behavior alone, Gimme a Break! represents the Chief as working class. Though Nell is by no means subservient to him (similar to other black domestic laborers on 1970s sitcoms), her efforts to keep him happy through domestic comforts reference domestic sitcoms of the 1950s, while her concern to keep him calm and avoid conflict reference the working-class sitcom.

Nell further complicates the Kaniskys' class status, given, as Kim has pointed out, how the sitcom family's paid domestic laborers conventionally work to define the family as white and middle-class. She traces representations of maids and domestic laborers from the 1950s through the 1990s, claiming that throughout those decades, the composition of the "American household has changed as has the construction of the family, but the figure of the domestic servant remains, 'serving' to uphold certain ideals (of the structure of work, the home, the family, patriarchy, middle-classness, and whiteness)."[16] This begs the question of whether or not a family could even be considered working class if they are able to employ live-in domestic help. Yet, Nell's ambiguous role in the household (she often insists that she is not a maid, but rather a friend of Margaret's) suggests an arrangement based more on emotional ties than an exchange of labor for wages, however unlikely and ridiculous this plot device may be.

Gimme a Break! makes it clear that the Chief is clinging to a bygone era, and his character is clearly inspired by *All in the Family*'s Archie Bunker (Carroll O'Connor). Nell quips that the Chief is so old-fashioned that he "still eats TV dinners in front of the radio."[17] When youngest daughter Samantha (Lara Jill Miller) comes home from school with a black eye in the pilot episode, the Chief complains to Nell, "Do you believe that? My little girl fighting for her life in that ghetto schoolyard? That damn busin'." When Nell deadpans in response, "Your fish is dead" (Nell accidentally killing the pet fish is a recurring joke), the studio audience howls, making it obvious whose side the viewer should be on. The Chief attempts to mount an absurdly feeble defense, "When I was talkin' about busin' I wasn't talkin' about black people," but Nell calls his bluff, much to the delight of the studio audience, shooting him a glare and mockingly responding, "No, no, the Australians are causing all the problems." Fuller points out that *Gimme a Break!* attempts to position Nell as not-a-mammy while simultaneously reinforcing this role. She notes one particularly telling moment in the pilot episode when the Chief takes his gun out to put it in his closet lockbox. Upon seeing the weapon, Nell jumps and cries out, "Oh please, massa, massa, please don't shoot!" Fuller explains, "Nell's hysterical response to seeing her boss hold the gun isn't supposed to read as an actual expression of fear; it is mockery. It reiterates that even though she takes care of him, she's not subservient to him. Moments like these attempted to distance her from the very stereotypes that she resembles. *Gimme a Break* strove to present a character that in all respects seems like a mammy but is not one."[18]

Indeed, the studio audience, in guiding the viewer's reading of these scenes, is almost always on Nell's side. Further underscoring her relative power and agency in the household, when the Chief makes a comment about hiring Nell in the pilot, she corrects him, saying she "volunteered," promising his late wife that she would make sure he "didn't do anything stupid," another reference to working-class sitcom tropes. However, Fuller points out that this dynamic ends up aligning Nell even more closely with the mammy figure, as "iconic film mammies also chose their roles; this was powerful evidence of their loyalty to white women and children."[19]

The series continually tries to diffuse Nell's resemblance of the mammy stereotype by directly addressing it with a comedic tone. In a season two episode, when Nell is serving breakfast to the family, Samantha asks her to define "cliché," a word she just read in the newspaper. Nell replies, "That's a black woman serving pancakes to a white kid."[20] *Gimme a Break!* acknowledges that its premise is cliché, seemingly to signal that it is in on its own joke, and thus is ironically referencing a cliché rather than simply *being* cliché, a tightrope the series continually walks. In season two's "The Custody Suit," the girls' Aunt Blanche (Gretchen Wyler) comes to visit and suggests that the Chief "send Nell down to get my luggage." Nell responds in an exaggerated Southern accent, "Oh, Miss Blanche I would just love to tote your barge and lift your bale!"[21] Similarly, the series often referred to *Gone With the Wind*—in one episode Nell sits next to a *Gone With the Wind* poster Julie has hanging on her bedroom wall,[22] and when the Chief discusses his will with Nell and reveals that she would inherit his house, she exclaims, "Oh, Miss Scarlett, you mean you're leaving me Tara!?"[23] These moments, which reinforce that the series is self-conscious about viewers perceiving Nell as a mammy, work to shore up the mammy image itself—with a nod and wink, the series tells the viewer it's "okay" that Nell is a mammy, because she understands the racialized history of that role and can ridicule it.

Fuller discusses the many ways *Gimme a Break!* attempted to mitigate, contain, and address criticism of Nell's representation, shifting the character's role in the household over the program's six seasons. She claims, "Nell was accused of being shockingly out-of-date when *Gimme a Break* began, and although the series made major changes, it couldn't keep pace with the new expectations brought on by *The Cosby Show*. Therefore, Nell was passé when the series ended, as well."[24] Yet in constantly undermining the powerful white patriarch, Nell provides much of the comedic pleasure for women viewers of *Gimme a Break!*. The Chief yells and attempts to assert his dominance, but Nell always succeeds in taking him down a few pegs. In a season one episode, the Chief threatens to beat Katie with his belt, menacingly chasing her around her bedroom. Katie runs downstairs screaming for Nell's assistance, ultimately hiding behind her. Nell handily diffuses the situation:

NELL: You lay one hand on this child and tomorrow's headline will read "beautiful woman wastes crazy man!"
CHIEF: Stand aside! I'm still head of this household, king of this castle!
NELL: Well your majesty, your pants are falling down.

This sort of exchange is typical—the Chief directly asserts his dominance, and Nell immediately undermines it. Much of the conflict in the program comes

Figure 26. Nell serves pancakes to Samantha on *Gimme a Break!*.

from the clash between Nell and the Chief, often in the same manner as the exchange above—the Chief overreacts, Nell undercuts him. Nell usually wins, as the Chief modifies his position or relinquishes it entirely. Fuller shows how *Gimme a Break!* labored to maintain an asexual antagonism between the two main characters, since "Nell fulfills the Kaniskys' need for a new mother, but she can't be the new wife. The show attempts to resolve this contradiction by putting Nell and Carl in an antagonistic relationship. But this isn't enough, as romantic narratives have cultivated the expectation that sexual tension underlies the bickering between male and female lead characters, and that the duo will eventually attempt a romantic relationship."[25] Indeed, the premise of *Gimme a Break!* is similar to that of *Who's the Boss?*, where the cross-class attraction between Angela and Tony finally came to fruition in the seventh season. Fuller argues that *Gimme a Break!* utilizes Nell's overweight body to connote a lack of sexual appeal for the Chief and thus avoids raising the specter of interracial sex.

Nell is not alone in raising opposition against the Chief—the Kanisky daughters usually join her, leaving the Chief to single-handedly defend his outmoded ideas and arguments and desperately cling to his dominance in the household. Fittingly, in a season one episode, Nell calls him "a one-man Moral Majority."[26] In the fourth season, when Katie moves into an apartment, one by one the rest of the family, including Grandpa Kanisky (John Hoyt), move in with her to get away from the Chief.[27] Nell appears to function as a surrogate for Margaret, who held significantly more liberal views than the Chief. In the season one episode "The Emergency," Katie ends up in the hospital due to complications with her IUD.[28] Nell is understanding but anticipates that the Chief will be livid to learn his daughter is sexually active, and unsurprisingly, he is, attempting to shame Katie by asking, "What would your mother think?" To his shock, she reveals that her mother knew about the IUD, and, the episode implies, she helped her daughter acquire it. While the Chief may like to believe that his wife would have been on his side, the episode suggests that Margaret and Nell had much more similar views than Margaret and the Chief.

As Fuller has suggested, Nell's position in the Kanisky family calls upon a long history of images of black domestic servants. Nell's relationship with the Kanisky girls in particular is reminiscent of a set of early silent films where white women and their black maids work together to trick white men into kissing the maids rather than the white women. Jacqueline Stewart argues that in these films "transgressive maids . . . perform and are performed upon in ways that suggest that African Americans, like white women, are falling out of the personal and social control of white men and, therefore pose threats to traditional gender and racial hierarchies."[29] Seventy years later, Nell and the Kanisky girls attempt to undermine and overthrow the patriarchal authority represented by the Chief. Of course, the Chief's job as chief of police has broad implications for the racial dynamics of the household, as his daughters taunt him by asking, "Why don't you just get the rubber hose?" when he threatens them with corporal punishment, referencing the police's (and thus the Chief's) active role in maintaining white supremacy.[30] In a season three episode, Nell tells Samantha about civil rights demonstrations, prompting Samantha to organize a sit-in to save a historic building. When Samantha practices civil disobedience, locking arms with her fellow protesters, her sisters, and Nell, the Chief arrests every member of his family and makes the news as a "hick chief."[31] However, with everyone united against the Chief, including the mayor who insists he let the protestors go, the episode points to the potential efficacy of collective action in the face of white patriarchal power.

Gimme a Break! often evades dealing with issues of race directly by instead having Nell and the Kanisky girls unite against the Chief's old-fashioned views on a broad array of subjects that only occasionally include race, but more often have to do with gender and sexuality. In the season one finale, Katie's pregnant friend Valerie (Helen Hunt) is staying with the Kaniskys.[32] The Chief is outraged that Valerie does not plan to marry her boyfriend and tells Nell that he doesn't want Valerie in his house. Nell informs him, "Well, I got news for you. We told her she could stay." Irate, the Chief shouts, "Absolutely not! No chance! No way, no how!" Without pause, Nell rebuts, "Thank you for your vote—you lose, four to one." As in most episodes, the Chief has expressed a traditional, conservative

Figure 27. The Chief locks up his entire family and their supporters on *Gimme a Break!*

view in a surly fashion, and his attempt at asserting power in the family is swiftly undermined and outnumbered by Nell and his daughters. Surprisingly, however, this season ends by affirming the Chief's firmly held beliefs—in a dizzyingly quick and unlikely change of heart, Valerie decides she not only wants to marry her boyfriend but that she must marry him before the baby is born. Of course, she goes into labor minutes after making this decision, and she and her boyfriend manage to be pronounced husband and wife just as she delivers her baby.

This ending, a rare win for the Chief and his conservative values, is quickly undercut in the fifth episode of the next season when Valerie (now played by Bonnie Urseth) shows up at the Kanisky house and announces that her husband walked out on her and the baby, demonstrating the unsurprising outcomes of the Chief's rigid views.[33] Reinforcing his conservative ideas of gender and the family, the Chief is flustered and embarrassed when he finds Valerie breastfeeding in the living room. He apologizes, telling her he didn't realize she was "B-R-E-A-S-T-feeding" and asks if she would feel "more comfortable doin' that where it's dark." Bemused by the Chief's seeming inability to speak the word "breast," Nell suggests, "Why don't we just blindfold the baby?" Valerie reveals that she is considering giving her baby up for adoption, but Nell and the Kanisky girls rally to support her as a newly single mother, underscoring their liberal views of family and belief in the power of female community. The Chief tries to convince

Nell that Valerie should go through with the adoption, arguing, "Every day down at the station house I see kids who are the product of broken homes like that, and they're usually being finger-printed and booked." In contrast to many 1980s sitcoms, which showed that "broken homes" could in fact be perfectly functional, happy families, here the Chief insists that a traditional nuclear family is the only surefire way to avoid juvenile delinquency.

Gimme a Break! continually plays the Chief's conservative identity and anti-quated ideas for laughs. In the first season, the Chief kills a robber who is holding up a drug store and is riddled with guilt.[34] He goes to a Catholic church in the hopes of confessing, but he finds only a young priest (Jay Johnson) when he asks for the more senior Father Donovan. The scene revolves around the Chief feeling uncomfortable with the "hip" priest, as the priest awkwardly calls the Chief, several decades his senior, "my son," and the Chief calls the priest "Father." The priest offers the Chief a seat in the rec room and the Chief reacts incredulously:

CHIEF: Don't you have to go into—to one of those little dark booths?
PRIEST: Oh, not really, that's uh, sort of like fish on Friday and uh, Saint, uh, Mr. Christopher. It's, uh, it's optional now.
CHIEF: I see.
PRIEST: A lot of people find that a small, informal room is nice place to rap.
CHIEF: Well, I'm not here to rap—I want to confess.

The scene emphasizes the Chief's unease with changing institutions—even in a church, he is out of place, and doesn't know how to behave or interact with the young priest. Here *Gimme a Break!* establishes that the Chief is more traditional and rigid than the Catholic Church, the symbolic epitome of tradition and rigidity.

The Kanisky girls, as guided by Nell, and presumably their mother, operate under more progressive gender roles. Katie is a (responsible) sexually active teen-ager, Julie is smart and ambitious, and Samantha is a tomboy. Katie regularly attempts to help Julie achieve a higher social standing, as in the season one epi-sode "Julie's First Love," where Julie has trouble finding a date to the prom. The episode begins with Julie on the phone with a boy, who rejects her offer to attend the prom as her date. Julie slams down the phone and cries, "I hate this!" while crossing the boy's name off a list—suggesting he was not her first call. Katie tries to be encouraging, citing the advertising industry's adoption of feminist ideals:

KATIE: Julie, it's the 1980s! It's okay for a girl to call a guy for a date. In fact, [in a breathy tone] "it's downright upright."
JULIE: Katie, don't compare me to that stupid woman on the commercial. [In a mocking tone] "Hi Doug? This is Stephanie. How about coming up to my place for some expensive sherry?" . . . Might be worth a try.

Figure 28. The Chief finds himself at odds with a young priest on *Gimme a Break!*.

Here Julie and Katie reference the late 1970s and early 1980s advertising campaign for Harvey's Bristol Cream, which featured women "inviting themselves over" to men's apartments with the pretense of giving them a bottle of sherry. A 1978 television spot features a woman calling a man to ask if she can stop by with a gift, then directly addressing camera, telling the viewer, "A few years ago, I wouldn't have dreamed of inviting myself over to Michael's place. People would have said it wasn't respectable. But times have changed." A 1980 ad follows the same general format, but following her call, the woman primps in the mirror while her voice-over tells the viewer, "That was a first. But today it's perfectly acceptable to invite myself over. In fact, giving Harvey's Bristol Cream makes it downright upright." The commercial ends with the man and woman cuddled up by the fire while a male voice-over states, "Times may change, but quality never does."

By drawing on this ad campaign, *Gimme a Break!* establishes the Kanisky girls as influenced by popular (commodified) feminism. The ad's insistence that "times have changed" is consistent with *Gimme a Break!*'s representation of the Chief, who surely would have been one of those who would not have found the pitchwoman's assertive actions "respectable." Julie's initial mockery of the ad suggests she sees through the calculated commercial appeal to feminism, while her quick capitulation that the tactic "might be worth a try" hints that these images, though commodified and clearly capitalizing on liberal feminism, still have an impact on how women see themselves and how they organize their behavior. The episode later emphasizes that the Chief is "behind the times" in more ways than one. Julie eventually secures a prom date with a boy she meets in a video-game arcade. However, after the Chief calls her a "tramp" and grounds her, Julie runs out of the house and disappears. The Chief eventually finds her back at the arcade and attempts to bond with her by playing one of the video games. Julie is skeptical of his gaming abilities, but he assures her that he used to "live in penny arcades." Julie scoffs, "*Penny* arcades? That must have been a *long* time ago." Undeterred, the Chief awkwardly inserts a quarter into the machine and tries to play it as though it were a pinball machine. Confused, he asks Julie, "Where are the pretty girls whose buns used to light up when you made a double score?" When Julie explains that it's a computer game that involves spaceships, the Chief is disappointed, lamenting, "No buns?" Julie confirms, "No buns." Julie's mastery of new technology, one that has changed with the times to exclude overtly sexist imagery, seems to convince the Chief to revoke her punishment, and the episode ends with Julie introducing the Chief to her prom date, who is an arcade technician, and thus just as "up with the times" as the men in the Harvey's Bristol Cream ad. Even so, this episode does not really bring the Chief up to the present day—indeed, his and Julie's compromise is that he will drive them to the prom in his squad car, thus wrapping her progressive dating rituals in a patriarchal bow.

The fact that the Chief can openly lust after "pretty girls whose buns light up" shortly after calling his daughter a tramp highlights his blatant hypocrisy when it comes to sexual mores. In a two-part episode in the second season, the Chief discovers that his only female police officer, Mary Beth (Maggie Cooper), has posed nude in a porn magazine.[35] When his daughters express interest in seeing the centerfold, he declares, "I don't want you girls looking at naked women!" Sarcastically responding to his outrage, Julie declares, "Thank goodness, I'll never have to take another shower!" Nell encourages the Chief to "keep an open mind" about the incident, but when the Chief calls Mary Beth into his office, he fires her, explaining, "What you did was wrong. It was stupid, and it was morally disgusting." Asserting her intention to appeal, that she will not accept the termination "lying down," the Chief predictably sexually harasses her, quipping, "Why not? It seems to be your favorite position." Despite his protestations that the pornographic images of Mary Beth are "morally disgusting," the Chief's qualm does not seem to be that she chose to pose nude—after all, he had already established his delight in the sexual objectification of women on his childhood pinball machines. Rather, his problem seems to stem more from the fact that there's a woman working in his police department in the first place. The episode codes the police station as a male-dominated space; it is solely populated by male officers until Mary Beth enters, wearing a police uniform that nonsensically includes a long skirt rather than pants, emphasizing her difference from the norm. Imme-

diately upon her entrance, the other officers sexually harass her, further marking her lack of belonging, and suggesting (from the Chief's perspective) that a
woman in the office is a distraction from business as usual. By firing Mary Beth,
the Chief gets his all-male workplace back, but once again, the episode represents him as hopelessly out of touch as he encounters a backlash that he did not
seem to anticipate.

Back at the Kanisky home, Nell, Katie, and Julie toast "to Mary Beth," after
they have gone door-to-door collecting signatures in support of Mary Beth along
with Grandpa Kanisky, establishing that the Chief's elderly father is more
forward-thinking than he is. Further underscoring the Chief's belief that women
belong in the home and not in the police station, he tries unsuccessfully to get
Nell and then successively each of his daughters to fix him breakfast (Nell offers
him a box of stale cereal). When the Chief arrives at the station, he's greeted by
a small contingent of middle-aged women protesters, and one of his officers reads
through a stack of telegrams the station has received from feminist celebrities
like Jane Fonda ("She hates your guts!") and Gloria Steinem ("She thinks you're
an oink-oink"). Shortly thereafter, a television news reporter arrives, prefacing
his live segment with "we're here in the Glenlawn police station talking to Chief
Carl Kanisky, who's been accused of being a redneck, racist, chauvinist bigot."
Here as in many episodes, the Chief resembles Ronald Reagan in his tendency
to act as though the 1960s and 1970s never happened, or as though the U.S. would
be best served by turning back the clock. As Daniel Marcus observes, "In his
public demeanor, professions of conservative personal values, and cultural tastes,
Reagan embodied a belief in and yearning for a nation undisturbed by the social
controversies and political traumas of post-1963 America."[36]

However, while Reagan tried to draw on a nostalgic, white-washed, *Father
Knows Best*-style image of 1950s America, the Chief represents the seamy under-
belly of this image—as the news reporter puts it, a "redneck, racist, chauvinist
bigot." Melissa Williams claims, "Reagan's genius lay in presenting a masculine-
yet-benign, populist image of himself and his vision of American national identity," and by contrast, the Chief's masculinity seems to be malignant.[37] The
punishments he metes out to his daughters are often vicious and cruel—in one
extended scene, he mimes a violent assault on Samantha's imaginary friend as
she sobs and begs him to stop.[38] As in other episodes where the Chief threatens
to strike his daughters with his belt, Samantha races to Nell for comfort and
protection, and Nell refuses to let the Chief into her room to see Samantha. Nell
manages to diffuse the situation by understanding the root of Samantha's bond
with her imaginary friend—the maternal, soft skill of listening was all that was
required, but the Chief is sorely lacking in this department. The fact that Nell
repeatedly needs to shield the Kanisky girls from their father both reinforces his
role as malignant patriarch while shoring up the intergenerational, interracial
alliance of women that can challenge him. Once Nell has successfully encouraged

Samantha to give up her imaginary friend and look outward for companion-
ship, the Chief pokes his head into Nell's room, and asks, "Will somebody
please fill me in, what's goin' on now?" With Nell's support, Samantha replies,
"Nothing—you know, just woman talk." Clearly uncomfortable, the Chief stands
frozen in the doorway and begins to slowly back away as the studio audience
chuckles. He finally mutters, "Well, don't stay up too late, huh?" and closes the
door. Samantha looks at Nell and declares, "That'll get him every time!" suggesting that their emotionally grounded, gendered alliance can effectively undermine the Chief's patriarchal power in the household.

Perhaps because the Chief rarely serves as a point of identification on *Gimme
a Break!*, the series regularly pokes fun at Reagan. In the episode where he fires
Mary Beth, the Chief complains to her, "When people see a police officer naked
in a magazine, how do you suppose they can respect the police department?"
She replies, "Well, Chief, if they can respect a president who makes movies with
monkeys, they can respect anybody!" Nell regularly makes fun of Republicans
(observing Katie's lame dance moves, she quips, "You been hanging out with
Republicans?"[39]), and both the president and first lady serve as the butt of jokes
in a wide range of situations—in "Sam Faces Death," the family watches a news-
cast that mentions the Reagans' "month-long working vacation in Tahiti,"[40] and
in "Take My Baby, Please," Valerie laments her lack of polish in job interviews
by claiming, "I get this vacant stare and all I can do is smile and nod my head,"
to which Nell replies, "It worked for Nancy Reagan."[41] These jokes at the Reagans'
expense are especially significant given that the early seasons of *Gimme a Break!*
coincided with Reagan's early years in office, when his popularity rating was
the highest. From the beginning, the series issues an indirect cautionary tale,
suggesting through the figure of the Chief that Reagan's nostalgic yearning for
the past was not as innocent as he often made it out to be. The Chief's open hostility toward feminism and a range of progressive causes paints a much more
frank picture of the implications of Reagan's nostalgic posturing. Marcus claims,
"Reagan offered a past that was stable, comforting, and complimentary—which,
for his supporters, seemed more important than whether it was true or not."[42]
The Chief destabilizes this image of the past, representing it as retrograde rather
than nostalgic. Indeed, Marcus suggests, "Given the failure of the Democrats to
put forward their own vision of the past effectively, the realm of popular culture
constituted the strongest response to conservative attempts to define the Fifties
and the Sixties. Films, television series, songs, and novels kept alive alternative
sets of memories and historical understandings, preventing conservatives from
monopolizing social and national memories of the recent past."[43] Unlike
Reagan, or even Alex P. Keaton, whose incarnation of Reagan's policies as a slick
yuppie-in-training was mostly innocuous, the Chief represents the id of Reagan's
ideology—*Gimme a Break!* critiques Reagan's gender politics (along with his

racial and sexual politics), and almost never represents the Chief as a point of identification for the viewer.

Michael Schaller points out the contradictions at the heart of gender politics in the 1980s, claiming,

> At one level, the nation appeared increasingly tolerant of nontraditional life-styles. Out of choice or necessity, well over half of all single and married women, including those with young children, now worked outside the home in a variety of professions. Sexuality in general was depicted much more openly in the arts and entertainment, and homosexuality was widely acknowledged, if not fully accepted, as part of the human experience. At the same time, religious conservatives and other members of the New Right in and out of the Republican Party denounced gays, abortion, gender equality, pornography, and a host of other "sins" as the progeny of "secular humanism." Reagan and the religious right celebrated what they called the "traditional family," consisting of a bread-winning husband and a wife who served as mother and homemaker.[44]

Gimme a Break! plays out these very contradictions. As Fuller shows, the program regularly features frank sexual humor, commonly through Nell, and while the Chief usually disapproves of more relaxed sexual mores, he often at least comes to understand and accept different views. In one episode, the Chief tells a homophobic joke while on a stakeout at a laundromat, only to learn that Jerry (Eugene Roche), the detective to whom he is telling the joke, is gay.[45] The Chief devolves into a paranoid rant as he speculates on which other officers could be gay due to various personality or behavioral traits, until Jerry suggests it could be "an older guy, keeps to himself, not very happy, you never see him out with a woman." The Chief eagerly presses him for a name, and Jerry leans toward him and says, "Kanisky. Carl Kanisky." Reinforcing his homophobia, the Chief replies, "You're lucky I don't hit men of the opposite sex." After admitting that he is "prejudiced, bigoted, and old-fashioned," the Chief protests that he has an open mind, but that "being gay can lead to a lot of trouble," and launches into a long story to explain the root of his homophobia. The camera slowly zooms in from a medium shot to a medium close-up to underscore the Chief's increasingly emotional state as he relays that his beloved elementary school teacher was busted in a gay bar and later died, and that his uncle refused to allow him to attend the funeral.

In an attempt to be sympathetic, Jerry praises the Chief for being more open minded than his uncle, but the Chief blows up in defense of his uncle, proclaiming, "Everything I learned I learned from my uncle Joey! It's because of him that I didn't grow up to be, to be, to be one of you!" As he makes this statement, he backs further away from Jerry, growing increasingly agitated, and his stammering suggests that Jerry is, in fact, right—that the Chief does have more capacity for understanding different sexualities than his uncle did. Overcome with emotion, the Chief locks himself in the bathroom. Alone in the stakeout room, Jerry turns his attention back to monitoring the laundromat, only to find a robbery in progress. He tries to alert the Chief to no avail, then draws his gun and runs to apprehend the robber. The Chief emerges from the bathroom in time to hear gunshots over the police radio. The scene ends with an ominous close-up of Jerry's binoculars sitting on top of the radio, an image that dissolves into an interior long shot of the darkened Kanisky living room. The Chief enters through the front door, pours himself a drink, and Nell emerges from her bedroom to join him. The Chief reveals to Nell that Jerry was shot (but will survive) while he was locked in the bathroom and that Jerry is "one hell of a guy." When Nell replies, "It takes one to know one," the Chief takes a long glance at her as the studio audience laughs. He turns back to his drink and responds in a halting fashion, interrupted by more laughter, "I wish you . . . hadn't put it . . . exactly like . . . that." Nell leans toward him and asks, "What?" ending the episode on an uncertain note. Throughout the episode, *Gimme a Break!* has it both ways—the topic of homosexuality is openly introduced through Jerry (and implicitly through the undercover officer who's dressed as a woman and the butt of many jokes), while the Chief's disapproval of homosexuality pays lip service to conservative values. However, because the Chief has been marked throughout the series as a point of disidentification, it's clear that the viewer is meant to sympathize with Jerry in opposition to the Chief.

Gimme a Break! consistently critiques the Chief's dismissal of progressive gender politics—he is always outnumbered by the alliance of Nell and his daughters, and his views are routinely condemned by the series' story lines. Very rarely is the viewer encouraged to take his side in a disagreement; it's usually assumed that he will eventually come to understand Nell's position, however begrudgingly. As Fuller observes, Nell's "saucy comebacks" bring blackness into the Kanisky home and usually get the last laugh in any conflict with the Chief.[46] By framing the family dynamics from the very beginning with Nell's claim that her goal is to help the Chief avoid doing anything stupid, the series sets up Nell as the voice of reason, mitigating the potential damage the Chief could do in raising his daughters.

While Nell is clearly superior to the Chief in the domestic realm, *Gimme a Break!* further suggests that the she is superior to him when it comes to his own job. In "The Robbery," the Chief and his daughters return home from a ceremony honoring him as "Law Enforcement Officer of the Year" only to find a burglary in progress.[47] The Chief encourages the girls to follow the burglars' directions, which results in the four of them being tied up on the couch. Meanwhile, Nell comes home just as Samantha has let it slip that her father is chief of police, a revelation that prompts the burglars to agree that they have "no choice" but to kill the family. As one of the burglars instructs the other to turn on the television to drown out the noise of impending gun shots, the camera slowly pans across the couch for maximum dramatic effect, as the Chief and the girls sit silently, paralyzed with fear. The episode then cuts to Nell, tellingly seated in the Chief's usual chair, who breaks the silence with an inspired plan:

NELL: Chief, did they get the *jewels*?

CHIEF: Jewels?

NELL: Yeah, Margaret's diamond ring and *twenty dollar* gold pieces?

BURGLAR TO NELL: What are you talking about?

CHIEF: Yeah, what *are* you talking about?

Even with Nell's obviously coded emphasis, the Chief has no idea that she has come up with a scheme to save them, until she explains that he keeps the valuables in a locked box in the closet, revealing to the Chief, the girls, and the viewer her plan to turn the Chief's gun on the burglars. The fact that the Chief is so slow to pick up on Nell's signals further calls into question his title as "Law Enforcement Officer of the Year." Proving herself more prepared to handle law enforcement than the Chief, Nell handily turns the tables on the burglars, allowing the Chief to get the burglars' gun and setting the girls free.

When two officers arrive at the scene, the Chief, understanding that Nell's heroics have undermined his authority, takes one officer aside and says, "Try and keep this one under your hat, will ya?" The officer informs him, "It's a little too late for that, Chief" as a television news crew rushes in through the open front door. A reporter quickly greets the Chief and then stands in front of him facing a camera, introducing his live segment by claiming the Chief "single-handedly apprehended two armed men who were burglarizing his home." The Chief initially plays along, but, just as she undermined the Chief in front of the burglars, Samantha interrupts the interview and offers, "While Katie, Julie, and my dad were all tied up, Nell tricked the burglars and got my dad's gun." After a beat, the reporter clarifies, "You mean, the chief of police was tied up in his own home?" Adding insult to injury, Samantha adds, "Yeah, but he's not just chief of police. He's law enforcement officer of the year." Nell grabs Samantha and attempts damage control, telling the reporter that Samantha is distraught from the incident and "doesn't know what she's saying." The reporter goes back to the Chief and asks, "Can you show our viewers the exact spot where they tied you up while the rest of your family was helpless?" Nell interjects and explains to the reporter, "Part of the Chief's brilliant plan was to let them tie him up." Nell directly addresses the news camera (and thus the fictional and actual viewer), "He saved my life. The man is my hero, he's a saint. The man should be head of the FBI." The Chief stops Nell, saying that he is unashamed of the chain of events and explains, "This woman risked her life to save us. She did a brave and wonderful thing, and we'll always be grateful."

Though the Chief positions Nell as self-sacrificing (and thus aligns her with the mammy stereotype, willing to die to protect the white family), the robbery scene itself suggests that Nell is just as concerned with self-preservation. When she gets the burglars to drop their gun, the first thing she says is, "Now, which one of you called me 'tubby'?" Though comedic, this question implies that her first priority is comeuppance for the personal insult the burglars lobbed at her and that securing the family's safety is secondary. Nell doesn't take her eyes off the burglars, as Samantha leaps up and hugs her. The episode's repeated emphasis on the Chief's status as "Law Enforcement Officer of the Year" suggests Nell is superior to him in every facet of his life and further underscores the continual erosion of his masculine dominance both in the home and in society.

The Chief's tenuous hold on patriarchy comes to an abrupt end; Dolph Sweet was diagnosed with cancer during the fourth season and died shortly before the season finale aired. In the fifth season premiere, Nell is reverent of the Chief, refusing to let any member of the family touch his bedroom, even forcing Julie, newly married, to stay in her cramped bedroom with her husband Jonathan (Jonathan Silverman).[48] In "Katie's Korner," the remaining men of the household prove to lack the Chief's virility: Jonathan is unable to fix the garbage disposal and has to enlist the bumbling Officer Simpson (Howard Morton) to help him, while all Grandpa Kanisky wants to do is take a bath and listen to Bette Midler.[49] As a result of the Chief's absence, the fifth and sixth seasons of *Gimme a Break!* focus more on Nell and a rotating cast of characters. In the sixth season premiere, Samantha leaves for college in New Jersey, and Julie, her husband, and baby (named Nell) move to San Jose.[50] With Katie having moved to San Francisco the previous season, Nell is left as the only original cast member, and the program's direction shifts considerably as she moves to New York to live with her friend Addy (Telma Hopkins) and raise foster sons Joey (Joey Lawrence) and Matthew (Matthew Lawrence), with the help of Grandpa Kanisky and Nell's mother Maybelle (Rosetta LeNoire), who subsequently both move to New York.[51]

No longer tethered to the Kanisky home, Nell and Addy share an apartment in Manhattan, and Nell secures a job reading manuscripts for a publishing company. Her new life is marked by a new opening credit sequence that clearly references *Kate & Allie*, with Nell and Addy gallivanting around the city, relaxing in Central Park, and in the final shot, buying a hot dog from a street vendor and feeding it to each other as if they were a married couple sharing wedding cake. In the end, Nell lives the feminist fantasy on offer from most of the decade's family sitcoms, a fantasy the series had previously denied her. She has escaped domestic drudgery, she has a fulfilling professional career, and she is supported by an extended family network that helps raise her two foster children.

ROSEANNE: A WORKING-CLASS FEMINIST MOUTHS OFF

Premiering one day before the first anniversary of Black Monday, the Wall Street crash of 1987, *Roseanne* depicted a family struggling to maintain a working-class standard of living at the end of Reagan's second term. Marcus notes that following the crash and the uncovering of insider trading, public opinion shifted against Reagan's economic policies, as it became increasingly clear that they "mainly benefited small groups of corrupt corporate elites, while middle-class incomes stagnated and homelessness spread among the poor."[52] Indeed, as Schaller points out, "One of the most troubling economic trends of this period was the sharp increase in the number of people who worked full-time but could not lift themselves and their families out of poverty."[53] Whereas *Gimme a Break!* primarily used speech codes and reactionary politics to represent the Chief as working class, *Roseanne* centered both its characters and its episodic narratives on the everyday socioeconomic challenges of a working-class family. As Melissa Williams claims, *Roseanne* "touched on a reality that plagued many Americans in the 1980s: the growing disparity between rich and poor and the lack of respect for American workers that characterized an increasingly corporatized and post-Fordist economic culture."[54] Episodes frequently depict Roseanne and her husband, Dan (John Goodman), navigating precarious employment situations and struggling to make ends meet. In the second episode of the series, Roseanne reveals her approach to paying household bills: "You pay the ones marked 'final notice' and throw the rest away."[55] While *Gimme a Break!* codes the Kaniskys (and especially the Chief) as *culturally* working class, *Roseanne* makes it clear that the Conners are also *economically* working class.

During the first season, Dan has difficulty maintaining consistent work as a contractor, losing multiple bids and failing to bring in a regular paycheck. Roseanne works on an assembly line at a plastics factory, and episodes often feature scenes where she and her pink-collar colleagues discuss their poor working conditions on their lunch break. Both Dan and Roseanne undergo multiple job changes and periods of unemployment throughout the series, in stark contrast to most other sitcoms where the characters have *careers*. When Angela Bower loses her job as an advertising executive on *Who's the Boss?*, she starts her own advertising agency. Elyse Keaton on *Family Ties* moves from working as a freelance architect to working in an architecture firm, and Maggie Seaver on *Growing Pains* leaves her job as a newspaper reporter to become a television reporter. By contrast, after Roseanne quits her job at the plastics factory at the end of the first season, she holds a wide variety of entry-level, unskilled, pink-collar positions in food service, clerical work, telemarketing, a beauty salon, and so on.

As detailed in chapters two and three, many 1980s sitcoms featured parents working from home, seamlessly shifting between work and family. At the beginning of *Roseanne*'s second season, Roseanne sells magazines over the phone from her kitchen while her family makes little effort to curtail their loud arguments out of respect for her work. Upon hanging up the phone, Roseanne comments, "You know what I like about this job, Dan? Nothing."[56] A later episode that takes place on tax day reveals that Roseanne's earnings from this thankless job are so low that she doesn't even need to file a 1099 form.[57] Roseanne is the perfect example of Rena Bartos's demographic category of the "just-a-job" working woman, who Bartos noted made up the largest portion of the female population.[58] She holds a series of jobs in order to make money to support her family, but she doesn't define herself primarily (or even partially) through her occupation, and she finds both the work itself and the working conditions largely dissatisfying. A season three episode in which Roseanne meets with the principal of daughter Becky's (Lecy Goranson) school makes her sense of identity explicit: when the principal attempts to sympathize with Roseanne, telling her "I know how hard it is to juggle a career and children," she interrupts, "Hey, uh, my children *are* my career, okay? You must be talking about my job, which you're making me late for."[59]

The world of work for most women on 1980s sitcoms is fairly glamorous, though as chapter two shows, these programs do not ignore the significant difficulties professional women encounter in the workplace. On the level of mise-en-scène, however, Clair Huxtable, Elyse Keaton, Maggie Seaver, and Angela Bower all enjoy an array of luxuries, epitomized by their fashionable wardrobes and spacious, tastefully decorated homes. Each of these programs featured episodes built around these women's career successes and milestones—satisfied clients, industry awards, promotions, and so on. By contrast, Roseanne's wardrobe is usually casual (jeans and billowy button-down shirts or oversized t-shirts), her style epitomized by a large white t-shirt featuring the graphic image of a chicken and egg she wore in many episodes as a running joke.[60] The Conner home is of modest size, decorated with souvenir Elvis plates and a print of dogs shooting pool. Up until season five when Roseanne, her sister, Jackie (Laurie Metcalf), and their friend Nancy (Sandra Bernhard) decide to open a restaurant, episodes that focus on Roseanne's jobs rarely celebrate her success, instead emphasizing her family as the center of her life and the primary source of her identity. Roseanne explains her desire to run her own business to incredulous daughter Darlene (Sara Gilbert), "I would like to have something to show for my life besides stretch marks."[61]

The comparison between representations of the "career woman" and the "just-a-job working woman" would have been quite clear to viewers in the 1980s, as ABC originally scheduled *Roseanne* on Tuesday nights, following *Who's the Boss?*. Thus viewers would move from watching Angela Bower, who drove a Jaguar and was greeted after work by her handsome male housekeeper who often presented her with a glass of champagne or a martini, to Roseanne Conner, who came home from work to a messy house with screaming kids and immediately began cooking dinner, often before she even removed her coat. During a season two episode, Roseanne came home from her fast-food job, started dinner, and then headed back out to her second job as a bartender.[62] Dan made the comparison explicit in the season three premiere, in which Roseanne suspected she might be pregnant.[63] Protesting the possibility of adding a fourth child in their late thirties, Dan exclaims, "We ain't yuppies! I mean, it ain't hip for us to be havin' babies now. We had 'em when we were young and stupid like we were supposed to!"

Williams notes that *Roseanne* is part of a broader trend in the late 1980s and 1990s, the "slob-com," wherein "characters very deliberately violate the 'norms' of middle-class manners on their programs; frequently, these characters are visually and narratively coded as working-class, and content often pushes the boundaries of topics such as sexuality, marriage, work ethic, and public behavior."[64] Counting Fox's *Married . . . with Children* (1987–1997) and *The Simpsons* (1989—) as part of this trend, she suggests that the slob-com sought to attract viewers who were growing weary of the glossy lives of upper middle-class families broadcast across the networks. So-called slob-coms effectively undermined the fantasy families that most other sitcoms offered, providing an over-the-top, sarcastic take on domestic life that simultaneously appealed to realism. *Roseanne's* mise-en-scène bears this out, as the Conner home is usually messy, cluttered, and chaotic. Judine Mayerle describes the great care that went into the set design, including the purchasing of furniture from the Sears catalog.[65] One of the stock closing credit sequences during the first season featured the camera moving 360 degrees around the kitchen table, mirroring the opening credit sequence, only this time, the Conners are absent, having left the table littered with a random assortment of items including half-eaten food, dirty dishes, nail polish bottles, newspapers, and toys. The shot fades to black when youngest child, DJ (Michael Fishman), enters the room and reaches up to grab a crumbled piece of cookie off the table. This scene in particular contrasts the tidy kitchens of sitcoms like *Who's the Boss?* (where Angela once discovered Tony vigorously scrubbing a bar of soap[66]) and *Full House* (where Danny's obsessive neatness was a running joke).

Further disrupting television images of the typical, upper middle-class television family, both Roseanne and Dan often shout at each other and the children with bitingly sarcastic dialogue. Mayerle argues that by 1988, cable's steadily growing penetration rate ensured that the network audience would be primed for *Roseanne's* edgier comedy, thanks to the popularity of stand-up comedy specials (including those which helped Barr land her sitcom) and cable's racier fare.[67] As Williams shows, the Conners' everyday behavior flies in the face of middle-class decorum, a dynamic the series highlights not only through comical interactions between the Conners and various middle-class characters but also through eldest daughter Becky's disapproval of and embarrassment by her parents' behavior. When the whole family goes to a bowling alley where Becky's new boyfriend works, she begs her parents to pretend as though they don't know her, as Roseanne picks her nose and Dan performs his best imitation of trailer park stereotypes to taunt her.[68] For Kathleen Rowe, Barr's body itself violates cultural norms. She maintains, "It is [Barr's] *fatness*, however, and the *looseness* or lack of personal restraint her fatness implies, that most powerfully define her and convey her opposition to middle-class and feminine standards of decorum and beauty."[69] Julie Bettie stresses that Roseanne's and Dan's bodies function to other them, as "in the U.S., where weight is inversely correlated with socioeconomic status, fat, itself, becomes associated with 'lowbrow' status."[70] Patricia Mellencamp argues against assigning too much importance to Roseanne's body, however, due to television's privileging of the aural over the visual. She suggests, "The joke is Roseanne's ultimate weapon, a verbal assault which includes her intonation and grammar . . . . For Roseanne, jokes deem her clever, wise, and always the winner, since no one one-ups her remarks."[71]

Williams explains a central conflict at the heart of *Roseanne*'s production— that executive producer Marcy Carsey conceived of the program as making a generalized feminist statement, while star and eventual executive producer Barr "wanted desperately to speak for herself as a working-class feminist, and she knew *exactly* what she wanted to say: 'It's about housework being a political thing. It's about never being included in the gross national product, it's about the segregation and apartheid of women's work, and women's energy.'"[72] From the beginning of the series, conflicts about domestic labor structure Roseanne and Dan's relationship. The pilot episode's narrative tension revolves around how Roseanne and Dan are going to divide familial tasks in the late afternoon and early evening.[73] After Roseanne has left work an hour early in order to meet with Darlene's teacher and shop for Becky's school supplies, she comes home to discover that Dan has not completed the only chore she could convince him to take on: unclogging the sink. As she begins to do the work herself while admonishing Dan, he predictably protests, "Hey, I do plenty around here!" When Roseanne asks him for examples, Dan stares blankly for a beat, before coming up with "cleaning the gutters." Unimpressed, Roseanne asks for another example, which Dan fails to supply. The episode foregrounds Roseanne's perspective, following her to work at the factory where she has to beg her boss to let her leave early, to Darlene's school to meet with her teacher, who asks to reschedule when Roseanne arrives late, and back home, where Roseanne has to make dinner for the kids. Despite Dan's feeble protests that he chips in at home, the episode provides no evidence to support his claim, further validating Roseanne's perspective and aligning the viewer with her. Indeed, in a season five episode wherein DJ gets in trouble at school, Roseanne has to tell Dan the name and location of the school, and when he arrives the staff notes that they had assumed Roseanne was widowed.[74]

An episode tellingly titled "Saturday" opens with a long shot of Roseanne lugging a laundry basket across the kitchen and offscreen into the laundry room.[75] She reemerges and (judging by her rubber gloves) resumes cleaning the stove burners, already in the midst of a full day of domestic chores, on what might

Figure 29. Roseanne spends her Saturday performing domestic tasks on *Roseanne*.

conventionally be considered a "day off" for many workers. Dan enters the kitchen asking for more rags to work on his truck and receives a phone call from his friend, Dwight (William Sadler), who plans to come over and help him. Establishing their labor as at least partially, if not entirely leisure, Dan tells Dwight, "We've got plenty of beer." When Roseanne makes fun of Dwight, Dan jokingly suggests that she could join them in working on the truck. Roseanne responds that she should do just that to ensure they actually complete the work, as he and Dwight "never finish nothing but a six-pack." Roseanne bets Dan that he will not be able to fix the truck by the end of the afternoon, a bet Dan confidently accepts. Foreshadowing Dan's loss, Dwight enters the kitchen to fetch another six-pack from the fridge as Roseanne fixes lunch for DJ. The episode repeatedly contrasts Roseanne's domestic labor with Dan's domestic leisure, and the fact that Dan cannot complete a single task given the entire day and two friends to help further points to the gendered differences in household labor even on days of "rest." In one season two episode, Roseanne refers to their house as "this prison without bars, this den of inequality."[76]

Dan does manage to pull his weight on occasion, and he does not conform to the common sitcom role of the bumbling father—both he and Roseanne give as good as they get, and their deadpan banter indicates their intimacy and compatibility. As Rowe puts it, "Roseanne often asserts her authority in the household by teasing Dan, but the show does not compromise his essential dignity."[77]

During the first season, Roseanne's colleagues at the plastics factory regularly comment on what a good husband Dan is, and in one episode where their boss, Booker (George Clooney), announces mandatory overtime, Dan quickly picks up the slack around the house.[78] When Roseanne comes home to chaos and wants to take a bath, she discovers that DJ has splattered paint all over the bathroom. As Roseanne announces she has to get out of the house, Dan encourages her to leave and promises to take care of everything. Roseanne goes to a diner for coffee and commiserates with a waitress, who tells Roseanne that she's widowed and dreads returning to her empty, quiet home. A medium close-up of Roseanne gazing down contemplatively dissolves into a medium long shot of Dan on his hands and knees in their living room, scrubbing paint out of the carpet and singing Tammy Wynette's "Sometimes It's Hard to be a Woman." Upon returning home, Roseanne exclaims that the house looks "immaculate," and she and Dan collapse on the couch, admiring the painting DJ made of their family, complete with bright yellow sun and flowers, prompting Dan to observe, "It's kinda nice he can see somethin' pretty in all this mess."

Whereas many 1980s sitcoms present fantasies where domesticated dads like Cliff Huxtable and Steven Keaton do their fair share of household labor without complaint (and often without being asked by their wives to do so), *Roseanne* provides a different sort of fantasy, where the beleaguered, overworked wife can openly express hostility toward and disappointment with her husband and children, and where that hostility is represented as justified, without marking her as a "bad mom." Most of the decade's programming allowed for arguably escapist fantasies of harmonious family life, but *Roseanne*'s fantasy allowed its female protagonist the power to speak to her family in ways that many women probably only wished they could. Bettie notes that one woman she interviewed at one of Barr's book signing events "liked the show because 'it's about the shit that happens to women at work. You wish you could be so quick and witty, say those things like she does.'"[79] Contrasting Roseanne's "proletarian" feminism to Murphy Brown's "bourgeois" version, Bettie avers, "The show routinely provides a fantasy response to working-class women's attempts to sustain self-esteem in a world where they have little control."[80]

At the same time, it seems likely that many of Roseanne's challenges to authority and hostile retorts to ungrateful family members would be just as attractive to the bourgeois Murphy Brown feminists, who would have been even more beholden than Roseanne to the bourgeois norms of motherhood and femininity that would frown on this behavior. As Mellencamp puts it, Roseanne "is never silenced, and often she is not nice—capital offenses for women."[81] Just as the Chief in *Gimme a Break!* represents the id of Reagan's supposedly nonthreatening, paternal masculinity, Roseanne undoubtedly represents the id of not only working-class women, but women across the socioeconomic spectrum who were frustrated both by their husbands' and children's reticence to take on more of the daily care work and by the everyday sexism they experienced in the work-place and in the public sphere in general. Although Barr wanted the program to specifically be a working-class feminist mouthpiece, it is easy to recognize why Marcy Carsey believed it would speak to middle-class and upper middle-class women as well. After all, as Roseanne tells her father-in-law in a season one episode, "When I speak, I'm speaking for all of womankind."[82]

In the season one finale, Roseanne's co-workers encourage her to confront the new boss, Mr. Faber (notably played by future Republican senator and presidential candidate Fred Thompson), on their behalf, as he has raised their daily quotas beyond what anyone can reasonably accomplish.[83] Throughout the episode, Mr. Faber talks down to Roseanne—recognizing the powerful influence she holds over the other women, he demeans her by calling her "honey," "doll," "sweetheart," and so on. When Roseanne appeases her colleagues and asks Mr. Faber to lower their quotas, he agrees, on the condition that she act deferential toward him in public and "respect [his] authority." Roseanne begrudgingly assents and spends the next scene holding her tongue and following Mr. Faber's orders, only to go home and vent her frustrations to Dan, who suggests that she quit. Mr. Faber shortly ends up intensifying his power trip, announcing that he is raising the quotas back to an unattainable number. When Roseanne confronts him, he reveals that their deal was just a test to see if he could "break" her—and he believes he did just that. Intent on proving him wrong, Roseanne walks off the job, and one by one, her co-workers follow her. Victorious, Roseanne turns back to Mr. Faber and says, "I guess we're not going to make our quota today, honeybunch." In the episode's final scene, the women sit together at a bar, and Jackie raises her bottle of beer and declares, "It's high time that we thank the woman responsible for our emancipation, my sister, ex-Wellman employee, and a heck of a woman in her own right . . . what was your name, again?" Jackie holds her beer bottle out toward Roseanne as if it were a microphone, and Roseanne triumphantly calls out "Sally Field!" While this episode clearly deals with working-class issues with its references to *Norma Rae* (director Martin Ritt, 1979), Mr. Faber's overt sexism expands Roseanne's workplace grievances beyond a critique of capitalist exploitation alone, thus appealing to women in a variety of class positions and occupations. The fact that Mr. Faber is obviously intimidated by Roseanne and that her fellow workers look up to her and depend upon her leadership explicitly situates Roseanne as a feminist hero.

Despite Roseanne's failure to find a job she enjoys at the beginning of the second season, her friends credit her with helping them find more fulfilling employment. Vonda (Charlaine Woodard) thanks Roseanne for getting all of the women "out of that hell-hole. Quitting Wellman was the best thing you ever did."[84] After thanking Roseanne for encouraging her to quit, and thus allowing her the opportunity to sell cosmetics door-to-door, Crystal (Natalie West) hugs Roseanne and cries, "I just don't understand, what is wrong with you, Roseanne?

Why won't anyone hire you?" Roseanne gestures toward answering that question when she laments to Dan that it was a mistake to quit just because her boss gave her "a little bit of lip," suggesting that she was too quick to stand up for herself. Roseanne spoke for the other women, allowing them the freedom to pursue more meaningful employment opportunities; however, it is her very outspokenness that impedes her ability to find the same. Several of Roseanne's employers and prospective employers complain that she has a "bad attitude," which typically expresses itself as a refusal to buy into the workplace ideologies of the service economy. When Roseanne's teenage boss at a fast-food restaurant tells her "that negative attitude of yours, it's going to get you nowhere," Roseanne shoots back "this *is* nowhere."[85] Yet, Roseanne's entrepreneurial foray into the restaurant business in season five provides her with fulfillment as well as feminist community, as she goes into business with Jackie, their friend Nancy, and her mother, Beverly (Estelle Parsons).[86]

Barr's centrality to the series further marks it as feminist fantasy. Contrary to other 1980s sitcoms whose titles prioritized their male protagonists, (e.g., *Benson, Charles in Charge, The Cosby Show*), *Roseanne* carries its star's and its female protagonist's name. As Rowe points out, in the opening credit sequence, "family life is shown to be a circle which literally begins and ends on her," as the camera moves around the kitchen table, beginning and ending with Roseanne.[87] The coda to this sequence, her famous laughter, emphasized through a fade to black that isolates this aural expression of female pleasure, acts as a sound bridge between the theme song and the episode's narrative, reminding viewers that *Roseanne* depicts Roseanne's story and that she (almost) always has the last laugh—indeed, in the third and fourth seasons, her laughter accompanies an image of her raking in her winnings upon laying down a victorious poker hand before the fade to black. Despite the strong ensemble cast (Laurie Metcalf won three Emmys for her role, and John Goodman and Sara Gilbert were both nominated several times), episodes primarily focus on Roseanne's daily life at work and at home—we very rarely see Dan on any of his job sites, unless Roseanne is there too. When Roseanne is absent from a scene, dialogue often references her. The series encourages viewers to align themselves with Roseanne and to understand her perspective, thus seeing the other characters as she does.

In season two's "An Officer and a Gentleman," Roseanne visits her hospitalized father, only appearing briefly at the beginning and end of the episode.[88] Explaining that Dan is working twelve-hour days, Roseanne asks Jackie to be on "monster patrol," helping out with the kids. Both Dan and Roseanne seem to doubt Jackie's ability to handle the household responsibilities (Roseanne sends Crystal over to check on her), but to everyone's surprise, Jackie becomes something of a Stepford wife. She watches eagerly out the kitchen window for Dan to return home from work, and upon catching a glimpse of him, she flies into action, assembling his favorite meal on a plate. When Dan asks why she's still at the

Figure 30. Jackie plays happy homemaker for Dan on *Roseanne*.

house, she explains that she's "playing housewife." Entering the kitchen, Dan replies, "I don't think this room has ever been used for that before." As Jackie announces that she managed to get the week off from work, the camera cuts from the kitchen to a long shot of Dan from the living room, putting Jackie's domestic aptitude on display as he marvels at the unusually tidy space, complete with fresh flowers in a vase on the coffee table. Jackie listens attentively as Dan describes his accomplishments for the day and anticipates his every desire— serving up a second helping of potatoes and fetching applesauce just before he asks. She neither eats nor contributes anything substantial to the conversation besides offering him praise, a stark contrast to the way Roseanne would approach the evening. Heightening this comedic divergence, the next morning, Jackie wears a frilly apron and hums the *Leave It to Beaver* theme song while preparing an elaborate breakfast. The soundtrack picks up the theme song when Jackie sends the kids off to school in a parody of *Leave It to Beaver*'s opening sequence, handing each a lunch bag and waving after them from the front door.

The kids and Dan can't believe their luck as Jackie plays happy homemaker, but the episode critiques this image not only through Jackie's unnerving enthusiasm for her role, but also through uncomfortable scenes featuring Jackie flirting with Dan, made all the more unsettling thanks to the viewer's usual alignment with Roseanne. These scenes also reveal Jackie's low self-esteem, as Dan prompts her to discuss her many failed romantic relationships and chastises her for allowing men to manipulate her. She confesses her high school crush on him, but consistent with her self-effacing attitude throughout the episode, claims that he would never remember the first time they met. When Roseanne calls, Jackie prepares to leave, but Dan holds his hand over the phone and tells Jackie what he remembers about the first time he saw her. As Dan describes the moment in vivid detail, the camera zooms in from a medium long shot to a medium close-up of Jackie, her body frozen in the midst of putting on her jacket, as she stares intensely offscreen towards Dan. When he finishes, Jackie clutches her chest and sighs deeply, clearly moved by his recollection. Her reaction further suggests that Dan's act of seeing (and remembering) her validates her as a person, deepening Jackie's characterization as dependent on male approval, an obvious point of departure from Roseanne. Roseanne returns home at the end of the episode, and as the family swarms her for a group hug, the camera cuts to a medium shot of Jackie, gazing longingly at the happy family. The end credits repeat the *Leave It to Beaver* sequence, this time in black and white, emphasizing the fact that Jackie's mode of familial care is a relic of the past.

Though this conclusion pokes fun at the 1950s ideal of the traditional nuclear family as represented on sitcoms, Jackie's explicit longing for a husband and family, not to mention the series' continual positioning of her as lonely and unlucky in love (despite her protestations to the contrary), reinscribes the role of wife and mother as a desirable one. Mellencamp points out the contradiction that structures *Roseanne*, arguing, "While domesticity, romance, and femininity are critiqued, marriage, along with motherhood, is upheld."[89] The message of "An Officer and a Gentleman," thus, is not that mothering is unfulfilling work or that marriage is an oppressive institution. Rather, the message seems to be that conforming to the June Cleaver model of wife and mother only serves others, not oneself, while conforming to the Roseanne Conner model of wife and mother may grant a modicum of power and pleasure in the family and domestic sphere. While an explicitly feminist program (in one episode, Darlene remarks about Roseanne, "Oh God, she's going feminist on me"), *Roseanne*'s major departure from other family sitcoms (especially in the 1980s) was its representation of the working-class family.[90] As Sut Jhally and Justin Lewis note in their study of *The Cosby Show*, "to be an affluent, attractive professional on television is to be normal."[91] Like most of the programs in this book, *Roseanne* represents a model of feminism acted out within the conventional parameters of the nuclear family.

To further hammer home the distinction between Jackie and Roseanne (and perhaps to undercut the discomfiting sexual tension between Dan and Jackie), a few episodes after "An Officer and a Gentleman," Jackie brings her new boyfriend, Gary (Brian Kerwin), to meet the family, and Roseanne is horrified by the way Jackie fawns over him.[92] Once Jackie realizes (with Roseanne's prodding) that she has been going along with whatever Gary wants, she expresses concern to

Roseanne over how to assert herself: "I'm afraid that if I tell him all this stuff about me, then he won't like me so much, because maybe he's one of those guys who only likes women that he can control." Roseanne reasons, "Well, now, you would like to find out about that, you know, and if it is true, then you don't want him around anyway." Exemplifying Jackie's attitude toward romantic relationships and her serial dependence on men, she asks, "I don't?" and Roseanne, exasperated, shouts, "No!" and observes that Jackie has been "acting like Gidget on an aphrodisiac." Roseanne serves as a feminist relationship coach, encouraging Jackie to be more assertive and direct with Gary. These episodes establishing Jackie's tendency to play doormat with men lay the groundwork for a season five plot wherein she becomes a victim of domestic violence.[93]

In the first of a two-part episode, Darlene discovers that Jackie is covered in bruises, forcing Jackie to confess to Roseanne that her live-in boyfriend, Fisher (Matt Roth), had beaten her. Dan springs into action, assaulting Fisher and ending up in jail, while Roseanne takes Jackie to the hospital. The second episode deals with the fallout as Jackie struggles to come to terms with her relationship.[94] Roseanne gleefully prepares to move Jackie out of Fisher's apartment, as Jackie enters the Conner kitchen sullenly, looking alternately at the floor and a large moving box with apprehension. Roseanne explains, "I left a message on your scum-sucking ex-boyfriend's machine that he better not bring his bony ass over to that apartment while we're moving you out or else I'm gonna bash his skull in. Only I said it mean." Jackie proceeds to stall the process, claiming she needs to eat breakfast and that the boxes Roseanne has procured will not be sufficient for her needs. Roseanne promises to "whore [herself] in every grocery store in this town if that's what it takes," making it clear that she will not allow Jackie to avoid facing the task of leaving Fisher, a sentiment that draws cheers and applause from the studio audience. Continuing Dan's observations from season two, Roseanne exclaims, "You're all the time making excuses for people that treat you like crap! God, you are the most gutless, pathetic thing I've ever seen!" Jackie confirms this description, replying, "I know you're just saying that 'cause you're worried about me." Jackie finally acknowledges that Roseanne is right, and Roseanne confirms her role as feminist life coach, declaring, "God, you know how much time we could save if you could just keep that in your mind as a given!?"

Yet when Fisher shows up while Jackie and Roseanne pack, Jackie's nerve wavers and Roseanne attempts to take matters into her own hands, threatening Fisher and telling Jackie not to talk to him. After protesting that she can think for herself, Jackie undermines this false confidence by sitting on the floor with her back to Fisher and Roseanne, who continue to argue over her. When Fisher unwittingly reveals to Roseanne that his abuse of Jackie was serial, not the one-time incident that Jackie had made it out to be, Roseanne asks Jackie to confirm Fisher's account, and Jackie remains silent, avoiding eye contact with either of them. Perhaps sensing that Jackie needs to leave the relationship on her own accord, Roseanne walks out of the apartment, telling Jackie, "I'm gonna go down-stairs and sit in my car. When you figure out what it is you're gonna do, you let me know." Assuming that he can manipulate Jackie in the absence of Roseanne, Fisher suggests he and Jackie can work things out, "We just need to be alone." Jackie replies, "Yeah, we do. 'Cause, I don't want Roseanne thinking that she's the reason I'm leaving, and I don't want you thinking that either." She opens the door to leave, only to find Roseanne standing in the hallway waiting for her. While Jackie manages to assert herself in this moment, Roseanne warns Fisher against any future attempts at preying on Jackie's weakness, threatening, "If you ever come near her again, you're gonna have to deal with me. And I am *way* more dangerous than Dan. I got a loose meat restaurant—I know what to do with the body." With this resolution, Roseanne has successfully guided Jackie to stand on her own two feet, with the reassurance that she will never stand alone.

Conclusion

Roseanne not only plays feminist mentor to onscreen characters like Jackie, Crystal, and her female co-workers, she also plays feminist mentor to viewers. Both *Roseanne* and *Gimme a Break!* consistently align the viewer with their female leads, and both series invite the viewer to delight in Nell's and Roseanne's comedic takedowns of patriarchal figures and systems. Both women talk back to men, their employers, and their (surrogate) children, and unlike most 1980s sitcoms, both series give these characters plenty to talk back about—constant overt sexism, racism, classism, unequal distribution of household labor, bratty kids. In contrast to the sitcoms that represented men taking on equitable loads of domestic and care work, *Roseanne* and *Gimme a Break!* reflected the reality that most of this labor was still performed by women. At the same time, both series also provide feminist fantasies of collectivity: Nell and the Kanisky girls work together to fight against the Chief's patriarchal authority, Roseanne leads Jackie and her female co-workers to escape oppressive working conditions and abusive personal relationships. Despite each series' flirtations with realism, they maintained the comforting generic reassurances of the family sitcom and deliv-ered feminist fantasies of collective action and support in the face of patriarchal oppression.

CONCLUSION

By and large, the family sitcom was responsible for the ratings success of first NBC, and subsequently ABC, in the 1980s and into the 1990s. CBS lagged behind, only fielding one successful, long-running family sitcom, *Kate & Allie*. Despite scheduling *Kate & Allie* on the same night as *Cagney & Lacey* (1982–1988), a move senior programs vice president Harvey Shephard labeled, "Gloria Steinem's fantasy come true," CBS was steadily losing young women and urban viewers.[1] NBC won the ratings war for much of the decade thanks in no small part to the dominance of *The Cosby Show*. Though largely overshadowed by NBC's runaway success, ABC built an impressive roster of family comedies that continued into the 1990s. *Roseanne*, which NBC executive Brandon Tartikoff famously passed on, came out swinging in 1988, building on the strength of its lead-in *Who's the Boss?*, and beating *Cosby* in the ratings from 1990–1992.

Despite the dramatic rise in number and longevity of family sitcoms on network television in the 1980s, the seeds for the genre's decline were, from the beginning, sown in its familial structure: Ella Taylor notes that in an attempt to reconstitute a mass audience in the late-network era, family sitcoms developed separate but intertwining storylines for characters that represented different target demographics (notably, women eighteen to forty-nine, teens twelve to seventeen and kids two to eleven).[2] As these programs aged, so did their child actors. Many of the series struggled in their later seasons to find rationales for their college-aged "kid" characters to be either living with their parents or at least spending a significant amount of time in the family home. Jennifer Gillan has suggested that sitcoms featuring strategic age differences in their child actors allow actors to "age in" to teenage roles as their older TV siblings "age out," citing programs like *My Three Sons* (ABC, 1960–1965, CBS, 1965–1972), *The Brady Bunch* (ABC, 1969–1974) and *The Partridge Family* (ABC, 1970–1974) as early adopters of this strategy.[3] Several 1980s series added younger kids as their original cast grew up: Elyse on *Family Ties* has a baby in season three, Maggie on *Growing Pains* has a baby in season four, *The Cosby Show* adds a stepdaughter for Denise in season six, Uncle Jesse and his wife Becky have twins in the fifth season of *Full House*, Tony and Angela become foster parents in the seventh season of *Who's the Boss?*, and Nell becomes a foster parent in the third season of *Gimme a Break!*. The addition of the younger children often helped keep the older kids involved in family life—for example, although Alex Keaton began attending college in the third season of *Family Ties*, the series' addition of baby brother Andrew in that same season kept him around, as he attempted to take the child under his neoconservative wing, protecting him from the liberal influences of the rest of the family.

Long-running 1980s family sitcoms, originally targeted to upscale, professional women, ended up helping to precipitate a shift toward addressing teen (and younger) audiences more explicitly. Later seasons focused more on the characters played by teen idols, like Kirk Cameron and Leonardo DiCaprio in *Growing Pains*, Michael J. Fox and Justine Bateman in *Family Ties*, Ricky Schroder in *Silver Spoons*, and Alyssa Milano in *Who's the Boss?*, all of whom paved the way for tween heartthrob Jonathan Taylor Thomas (nicknamed JTT) to take center stage in the 1990s family sitcom holdout *Home Improvement* (ABC, 1991–1999). As Thomas Doherty has pointed out, television and radio are the perfect media for teen idols, allowing young stars maximum visibility and access to teen and tween audiences, visibility that is magnified even further when these series are sold into syndication and stripped five days a week.[4]

In brokering syndication deals, television production companies often used teen stars as guarantees of success in the after-school hours for independent stations. As these shows started to focus more on teen-oriented themes like underage drinking, drugs, sex, and academic dishonesty, the handling of these issues remained suitable for younger viewers—the episodes were about teens but appropriate for and arguably pitched toward a slightly younger group that would later be labeled tweens. Gillan notes about ABC's 1960s programming, "While any actual teen might find the dilemmas of a television teen at odds with real experience, a tween or even a kid might be attracted to the representative fun and independent teen lifestyle that they imagine they will experience in the future."[5] Prior to widespread recognition of the "tween" as a profitable marketing demographic and audience group, ABC launched its "family-friendly" kid and teen-oriented sitcom block TGIF in 1989.

The programs ABC scheduled for its TGIF block, especially *Full House, Family Matters* (ABC, 1989–1997, CBS, 1997–1998), *Boy Meets World* (ABC, 1993–2000), and *Step by Step* (ABC, 1991–1997, CBS, 1997–1998) used this "family-friendly" narrative dynamic to target young teens and tweens. As Ted Harbert, then executive vice president of ABC Entertainment explained, "As soon as they can get out of the house, teens leave on Friday nights. You're left with parents and their kids, and that was the original concept behind the Friday-night comedies that became TGIF."[6] Since older teens would be unlikely to be home watching TV on a Friday night, TGIF provided their younger siblings with sanitized images of what their future Fridays away from the TV screen might look like. An article in *Broadcasting & Cable* describes Bill Bickley and Michael Warren, producers of TGIF shows *Family Matters, Step by Step,* and *Hangin' with Mr. Cooper* (ABC, 1992–1997) as attracting "kids first—and their parents as a consequence."[7] The article frames Bickley and Warren as silent ratings assassins, a force to be reckoned with, explaining, "If they aren't household names, it may be because none of their shows has provoked a vice president or featured nudity . . . or used adult language, but the pair quietly have grown to be a major force for ABC and Warner Bros. Television . . . . Although the TGIF shows are hardly the darlings of critics, it's reaching the proper demographics—not generating glowing reviews—that brings home the syndication bacon."[8]

Setting the stage for TGIF's approach to "teen issues," Kirk Cameron delivered an impassioned antidrug plea in a 1987 episode of *Growing Pains,* coincidentally titled "Thank God It's Friday."[9] Like many episodes of *Growing Pains,* it offers a metacommentary on the prominent place of television in family life. The episode opens with then-youngest child Ben informing his father Jason that Friday is the best TV night of the week, setting in motion the B-plot, wherein Ben, his sister Carol, their parents, and a neighbor girl will spend their Friday evening eating microwave dinners in front of the television, providing a premonition of TGIF's imagined audience. The A-plot concerns Mike and his friends Eddie (K. C. Martel) and Boner (Andrew Koenig) attending a college party where seemingly everyone has their own personal stash of cocaine. While Mike, clearly horrified, attempts to convince his friends (and the viewer) to stay off drugs and leave the party, *Growing Pains* simultaneously blames television for making cocaine attractive to teens in the first place. Back at the Seaver home, mother Maggie tries to pull the family away from their Friday night show of choice, which is not named but is clearly a reference to *Miami Vice* (NBC, 1984–1989). Maggie brings dessert into the living room and finds Ben transfixed by the unfolding narrative. When Maggie asks what she missed, Ben exclaims, "Plenty! The Colombian cartel has these mules runnin' a half-ton of uncut snow through the Miami pipeline. We're talkin' a street value of sixteen million big ones here!" The camera cuts to Carol, considering his estimate. She then responds, "Sounds low to me," at which point the camera cuts to a medium two-shot of Maggie and Jason, both shocked at their children's apparent knowledge of the street value of cocaine, as Maggie interjects, "I've got a great idea, why don't we watch a Disney movie on tape?" Over the sounds of machine gun fire coming from the television, Maggie suggests *Cinderella.*

Her suggestion is met with consternation from Carol and Ben, both clearly too old for Disney, implying the need for a middle ground between adult programming and children's programming, a middle ground, the episode implies, that *Growing Pains* provides. In fact, TGIF was launched as a counter-programming strategy, as ABC recognized that the other networks were targeting the sort of adult audience that *Miami Vice* sought with dramas on Friday night.[10] By approaching the "adult" subject matter of drugs in a family-friendly way, *Growing Pains* positions itself as appropriate for prime-time broadcasting as well as for after school syndication. Mirroring the address of an *Afterschool Special*, the episode ends back at the party with Mike and his friends for a public service announcement. These PSAs were central to *Growing Pains*'s syndication strategy—*Broadcasting* magazine noted in 1989 that Warner Bros. Domestic Television intended to use them to convince viewers that *Growing Pains* was not "just another lightweight sitcom" by adding some dramatic depth to Cameron's popular character.[11] At the same time, the article points out that Jim Moloshok, senior vice president of Warner Bros. Domestic Television Distribution, was reticent to allow Cameron's teen idol status to position *Growing Pains* as a teen series. Moloshok carefully hedges, "'Michael is considered by some to be the core of the show'. . . . But the company believes the show will succeed because it has 'broad family appeal.'"[12] Indeed, the ultrasincere, preachy tone Cameron adopts in his PSA is unlikely to persuade actual teen viewers and seems pitched more toward younger viewers and their parents.

By the mid-to-late 1980s, many of ABC's family sitcoms were marketed through their teen idols and their teen-oriented story lines, such as in one 1986 promo, where Alyssa Milano and Kirk Cameron hang out after school and share milk and cookies. ABC has long solicited a tween audience. Gillan traces this approach back to ABC's broadcasting of Disney programming in the 1950s as well as to *The Adventures of Ozzie & Harriet* (ABC, 1952–1966), which used teen idol Ricky Nelson to lure in younger viewers. Gillan labels ABC's strategy a "narrowcast inflection," wherein certain characters and story lines appeal to younger viewers, while the series itself maintains broad appeal.[13] At the same time, Amanda Keeler shows that ABC was already experimenting with narrowcasting in the 1970s with its series of *Afterschool Specials*, named for their late afternoon timeslot and thus expressly marketed to kids and teens coming home from school.[14] *Growing Pains*'s PSA campaign fits neatly with ABC's kid- and teen-oriented programming, making it particularly appropriate for late afternoon and early fringe syndication.

While ABC led the way in appealing to tweens even before the launch of TGIF, NBC was also conscious of teen idol power. *Family Ties* was originally conceived with the parents as the main focus of the show, but Michael J. Fox proved so popular as Alex P. Keaton that NBC programming head Brandon Tartikoff asked creator Gary David Goldberg to make his role the center of the show.[15] The marketing of *Family Ties* for syndication focuses on its appeal to numerous demographics, with a two-page ad in *Variety* proclaiming, "Each member of the family is a strong character, a point of identity for key demographic audience segments. Still, the family is the comedic unit. Situations of uncommon humor and universal familiarity bind the Keatons together for appeal to men, women, teens and children. In a market of increasing fragmentation, *Family Ties* brings people together."[16] Despite this claim, the image foregrounds the teens, with Justine Bateman in the center, gazing directly at the reader as if into a mirror, surrounded by cosmetics, while Fox poses with shaving cream and a razor, emphasizing his adolescent masculinity. As Gael Sweeney claims, "Even the hint of an exploitable teen idol is enough to change the entire direction of the series. 'Ozzie and Harriet' and 'Family Ties' foregrounded their young male idols while pushing the balance of the characters into oblivion."[17]

NBC further experimented with using teen-centric programming to attract tweens and younger kids with its Saturday morning programming, premiering teen sitcom *Saved by the Bell* (1989–1993) the same year that ABC launched TGIF. With its Saturday morning time slot, *Saved by the Bell* was even more explicitly targeted to tweens and kids than TGIF, taking over the daypart traditionally associated with cartoons, as Brandon Tartikoff was concerned that the network was not reaching the older segment of the kids demographic.[18] *Saved by the Bell* executive producer Peter Engel recalls NBC's research team telling him, "You've hit an underserved, underreported audience . . . mainly kids between twelve and seventeen."[19] *Saved by the Bell* was so successful during its time slot, the network eventually branded Saturday morning TNBC (Teen NBC) with a series of *Saved by the Bell*-inspired sitcoms like *California Dreams* (1992–1997), *Hang Time* (1995–2000), and *Saved by the Bell: The New Class* (1993–2000). Just as with family sitcoms, *Saved by the Bell* was sold into syndication, and its audience grew in the after-school hours. Indicative of both the series' popularity and the television industry's shift toward narrowcasting, a spin-off, *Saved by the Bell: The College Years*, followed several of the series' core cast members to college and aired on NBC in prime time during the 1993–1994 season.

In 1986, *Variety* noted the importance of "kid appeal" for syndication, claiming that although CBS's *Kate & Allie* was a hit in prime time, its failure to attract kids and teens would hurt its syndication prospects.[20] Despite the fact that *Kate & Allie* had two teenage girls in its primary cast, *Webster* (ABC, 1983–1987, first-run syndication, 1987–1989), which had no teenagers whatsoever, was dominating the syndication market. Paramount TV president Robert Reiss claimed that *Webster* "has wide appeal among kids, teens and young adults."[21] An ad for *Webster* in *Variety* similarly notes, "He's #1 with Teens and Kids too, the secondary audience necessary for any early fringe or access win."[22] *Webster* ran on ABC on Friday nights, helping to set the stage for TGIF. Though not a teen, Webster (Emmanuel Lewis), similar to Ricky on *Silver Spoons*, lived a charmed life with wealthy, clueless parents, and prefigured later teen-centric sitcoms like *Boy Meets World* in the character's marginalization of the adults. Originally conceived as a vehicle for married co-stars Alex Karras and Susan Clark, legend has it that ABC's programming head was desperate to cast Emmanuel Lewis after seeing him in a Burger King commercial and reoriented the entire series with Lewis at the center, naming it *Webster* to underscore that focus (much to the dismay of his adult co-stars).

Webster was so successful in syndication that following its cancellation by ABC, it continued for two additional seasons in first-run syndication. Similarly, though CBS cancelled the Scott Baio vehicle *Charles in Charge* after one season, it ran for four seasons in first-run syndication with a revamped teen-centric premise and co-starring Nicole Eggert, fresh off a recurring role as Samantha's snobby best friend Marcy on *Who's the Boss?*. While women eighteen to forty-nine were the original target market for the 1980s family sitcom, at least from the perspective of the networks who wanted to guarantee this demographic to advertisers, from the production companies' perspective, kid- and teen-appeal were equally if not more important. The syndication market promised long-term profit opportunities, and, as Derek Kompare shows, the dearth of successful network sitcoms in the early 1980s left syndicators eager for content.[23]

Taking a page from the syndication success of sitcoms with "narrowcast inflections" targeting tweens, Warner Bros. Domestic Television Distribution president Dick Robertson told *Broadcasting & Cable*, "If it works on Fox or TGIF, it will work in syndication. The older [skewing] shows cannot work; they haven't worked in eight years. They cannot work because the audience responsible for their success during their network run is different from that watching them in syndication."[24] Seeds of the end of TGIF were sown in 1997, when *Family Matters* and *Step by Step* both moved to CBS. ABC Entertainment president Jamie Tarses claimed that those shows were both failing, that "the only strength that those two shows had were in kids and teens. Obviously we want kids and teens, but we also want young adults. So we'll be fine."[25] But by 2000, ABC's attempt to skew older backfired, when *Broadcasting & Cable* reported that thanks to their cancellation of the TGIF block and their scheduling game show *Who Wants to Be a Millionaire?* four nights a week in prime time, ABC's median age shot up from 41.6 years to 46.2 years in thirteen months—seemingly in seeking young adults, the network overshot and skewed older.[26] Michael Warren, co-creator of *Family Matters*, blamed TGIF's decline on a cultural shift toward multiple television set households, observing, "Mom and dad started saying, 'We don't want to watch *Family Matters*. If you guys want to watch those, you can go to your room and watch your own TV.' And when the kids went in the other room, they didn't watch those shows. They watched *Friends*."[27]

Indeed, although ABC's focus on family-friendly programming propelled it ahead of ratings stalwart NBC in the late 1980s and early 1990s, NBC wrested control back by largely abandoning family appeal. Perhaps inspired by their success with *Saved by the Bell* and *Cosby* spin-off *A Different World* (1987–1993), both of which focused on a group of friends (albeit in high school and college, respectively) rather than a nuclear family, NBC ushered in a shift in the sitcom form. A twist on the workplace family, and similar to the network's 1980s hit *Cheers,* NBC's 1990s sitcoms (especially those that aired during the Thursday night "Must See TV" lineup) revolved around a friend-family, assembling a group of young adult professionals who regularly gather in a particular location like a coffee shop or a bar. By the mid-1990s, as Ron Becker shows, "The networks targeted young adult sensibilities much more aggressively, greenlighting shows that ran the risk of alienating younger and older audiences."[28] Becker dubs the most sought after demographic of this period the "Slumpy"—socially liberal, urban-minded professional. And for the Slumpies, the family sitcom would be utterly passé—as Becker points out, networks conceived of this demographic group as "'hip,' 'sophisticated,' urban-minded, white, and college-educated 18-to-49 year olds (perhaps even 18-to-34) with liberal attitudes, disposable income, and a distinctively edgy and ironic sensibility."[29] Thus it makes sense that within this milieu (and despite its working-class family setting) *Roseanne* maintained a solid position in the Nielsen ratings well into the 1990s, finishing its run in 1997.

Family sitcoms began to disappear from network schedules in the early to mid-1990s, boasting few hits in the Nielsen Top 10 after 1994. As Fox siphoned off viewers with the "edgier" families of *Married . . . with Children* (1987–1997) and *The Simpsons* (1989–), and the conception of the family audience splintered in favor of niche demographics, network family sitcoms in the 1990s centered around established stars and actors (Will Smith in *The Fresh Prince of Bel-Air* [NBC, 1990–1996], Fran Drescher in *The Nanny* [CBS, 1993–1999], John Lithgow in *3rd Rock from the Sun* [NBC, 1996–2001]), and teen idols (Jonathan Taylor Thomas in *Home Improvement*, Joey Lawrence in *Blossom* [ABC, 1991–1995], Rider Strong in *Boy Meets World*). While many of these programs contain similar emphases on domestic labor and childcare, they represent a departure from the liberal feminist fantasies of their 1980s counterparts. *The Fresh Prince of Bel-Air* and *The Nanny* represent excessively wealthy families, *3rd Rock from the Sun* veers into more of science-fiction fantasy realm, *Blossom* and *Family Matters* derive most of their comedy from their dim-witted doofus characters (Joey and Six [Jenna von Oy] in the former and Steve Urkel [Jaleel White] in the latter), and *Boy Meets World* relegates the parents to the periphery, staging much of the action outside of the family home. Despite the shift in prime-time programming, family sitcoms remained a staple of afternoon syndicated programming, continuing to bring their lessons of family governance to a younger generation of children after school.

Arlie Hochschild highlights the fact that these model fantasies of family life were ritualistically embedded in the daily routines of many of the dual-career households she studied. She observes, "After dinner, some families would sit together, mute but cozy, watching sitcoms in which *television* mothers, fathers, and children talked energetically to one another."[30]

Certainly the majority of the prime-time television audience did not resemble the largely white, upper middle-class happy families they saw on their screens. But the programs repeatedly played out everyday situations of domestic strife, parenting dilemmas, and work-related stress, with resolutions that offered up models of family governance and fantasies of reformed masculinity that would reinvigorate the "stalled revolution."

ACKNOWLEDGMENTS

While in many ways a lifelong project, the research for this book began in earnest during my graduate studies at the University of Minnesota. My dissertation advisor, Laurie Ouellette, was instrumental in shepherding this project from beginning to end, and I also must thank my dissertation committee members: Elaine Tyler May, Anna McCarthy, Gilbert Rodman, and Mary Vavrus. Elaine and Lary May's dissertation writing group gave extensive feedback on early versions of several chapters. Despite my longtime enthusiasm for television, I only discovered it as an object of scholarly inquiry thanks to my incredible undergraduate education in the Film and Digital Media department at the University of California-Santa Cruz. Shelley Stamp was and continues to be a model scholar-teacher-mentor, and I am grateful for her longstanding support. Amelie Hastie, L. S. Kim, Peter Limbrick, Megan Mercurio, Edward O'Neill, Irene Gustafson, and Margaret DeRosia were all inspiring teachers and fueled my desire to continue my studies in graduate school. At the University of Iowa, I was fortunate to study with Paula Amad, Corey Creekmur, Rosalind Galt, and Lauren Rabinovitz, all of whom helped shape my approach to television and film studies.

Miranda Banks, Suzanne Leonard, and Mary Vavrus generously provided indispensable advice and guidance through the process of turning the dissertation into a book. In the last ten years, I have presented material from this project at various meetings of the Society for Cinema and Media Studies and Console-ing Passions, and have received helpful feedback and support from a number of scholars and friends. In particular, I would like to thank Elizabeth Ault, Shelley Cobb, Neil Ewen, Bambi Haggins, Hannah Hamad, Caley Horan, Eun Joo Kim, Amanda Klein, Elana Levine, Joanne Morreale, Elizabeth Nathanson, Diane Negra, Devon Powers, Joe Tompkins, Julie Wilson, and Emily Chivers Yochim. Special thanks to Erin Meyers, who took up the slack on a side project while I completed the manuscript.

I am lucky to be a member of the Media and Communication Studies department at Ursinus College, among smart, supportive colleagues. Lynne Edwards, Jennifer Fleeger, Colleen Grzywacz, Tony Nadler, and Louise Woodstock make coming to work fun. Special thanks to Sheryl Goodman, who has generously mentored me from the moment I moved into my office, and whose support and guidance mean the world to me. Talia Argondezzi organized a summer writing group that dramatically increased my productivity and enabled me to deliver the manuscript on time. I would also like to thank Deborah Barkun, Julin Everett, Anna Maria Hong, Annie Karreth, and Johannes Karreth.

Rutgers University Press has been a pleasure to work with from start to finish. Lisa Banning was enthusiastic and supportive of the project from the beginning and has been immensely helpful every step of the way. The two anonymous reviewers improved the manuscript with thoughtful, detailed feedback. Thanks to the production staff, Vincent Nordhaus, Angela Piliouras, and Catherine Mallon for their exceptional attention to detail.

Finally, I would like to thank my family and friends for their ongoing support, patience, and interest in my work. My parents, Ann and Richard Leppert, encouraged and supported me every step of the way. Even though they tried to limit the amount of time I spent watching television as a child, they never for a moment smirked at the idea of my career path. I have benefited greatly from being a second-generation academic, and I cannot thank them enough. I owe much of my enthusiasm for 1980s popular culture to my older brother, Adam Leppert, who introduced me to a steady diet of age-inappropriate media throughout my childhood. I am delighted that my nephew, Callum, now shares my enthusiasm for *Full House,* and I hope he teaches his sister Audrey to appreciate it as well, without driving Adam and Annabelle Sherry crazy. My in-laws, Kathy and Richard Nadler and Scott and Becky Blakley, have always been understanding and accommodating when I needed time to work during family visits. Caroline Rummel and Ann Vardeman kept me sane and provided much needed distractions from the beginning of my dissertation research to the copyediting of the final manuscript. I found plenty of inspiration for writing and revising while walking my dog, Juliette, and the miraculous reunion of Guns N' Roses gave me an unexpected boost in the final push. Most importantly, I thank my husband, Tony Nadler. His unflagging support and enthusiasm for my work has propelled me for years, and his intellectual curiosity never ceases to inspire me.

NOTES

INTRODUCTION

1. Susan Faludi, *Backlash: The Undeclared War against American Women* (New York: Crown, 1991), 67.

2. Frederick R. Strobel, *Upward Dreams, Downward Mobility: The Economic Decline of the American Middle Class* (Lanham, MD: Rowman and Littlefield, 1993).

3. Faludi, *Backlash*.

4. See, for example, Judith Mayne, "*L.A. Law* and Prime-Time Feminism," in *Framed: Lesbians, Feminists, and Media Culture* (Minneapolis: University of Minnesota Press, 2000); Tania Modleski, *Feminism without Women: Culture and Criticism in a "Post-feminist" Age* (New York: Routledge, 1991); Elspeth Probyn, "New Traditionalism and Post-Feminism: TV Does the Home," in *Feminist Television Criticism: A Reader*, eds. Charlotte Brunsdon, Julie D'Acci, and Lynn Spigel (Oxford: Oxford University Press, 1997), 126–137.

5. For example, *The Mary Tyler Moore Show* (CBS, 1970–1977), *The Bob Newhart Show* (CBS, 1972–1978), *Taxi* (ABC, 1978–1982; NBC, 1982–1983), *WKRP in Cincinnati* (CBS, 1978–1982), *M*A*S*H* (CBS, 1972–1983).

6. Family sitcoms peaked at 78% of all sitcoms in 1985, compared to 18% ten years earlier.

7. Probyn, "New Traditionalism," 126–137; Sasha Torres, "Melodrama, Masculinity, and the Family: *thirtysomething* as Therapy," *Camera Obscura* 19 (1989): 86–107.

8. Bonnie J. Dow, *Prime-Time Feminism: Television, Media Culture, and the Women's Movement since 1970* (Philadelphia: University of Pennsylvania Press, 1996); John Fiske, *Media Matters: Race and Gender in U.S. Politics* (Minneapolis: University of Minnesota Press, 1996); Herman Gray, *Watching Race: Television and the Struggle for Blackness* (Minneapolis: University of Minnesota Press, 1995); Darrell Y. Hamamoto, *Nervous Laughter: Television Situation Comedy and Liberal Democratic Ideology* (New York: Praeger, 1989); L. S. Kim, "Maid in Color: The Figure of the Racialized Domestic in American Television" (PhD diss., University of California, Los Angeles, 1997).

9. Dow, *Prime-Time Feminism*.

10. Michel Foucault, "Governmentality," in *The Essential Foucault*, eds. Paul Rabinow and Nikolas Rose (New York: The New Press, 2003).

11. Nikolas Rose, *Governing the Soul: The Shaping of the Private Self*, 2nd ed. (London: Free Association Press, 1999).

12. Thomas Lemke, "'The Birth of Bio-politics': Michel Foucault's Lecture at the Collège de France on Neo-liberal Governmentality," *Economy and Society* 30 (May 2001): 191.

13. Jacques Donzelot, *The Policing of Families*, trans. Robert Hurley (New York: Pantheon, 1979).

14. Stephanie Coontz, *The Way We Never Were: American Families and the Nostalgia Trap* (New York: Basic Books, 1992), 23.

15. Mary Beth Haralovich, "Sit-coms and Suburbs: Positioning the 1950s Homemaker," in *Private Screenings: Television and the Female Consumer*, eds. Lynn Spigel and Denise Mann (Minneapolis: University of Minnesota Press, 1992); Nina C. Leibman, *Living Room Lectures: The Fifties Family in Film and Television* (Austin: University of Texas Press, 1995); George Lipsitz, "The Meaning of Memory: Family, Class, and Ethnicity in Early Network Television Programs," in *Private Screenings: Television and the Female Consumer*, eds. Lynn Spigel and Denise Mann (Minneapolis: University of Minnesota Press, 1992).

16. Lara Descartes and Conrad P. Kottak, *Media and Middle Class Moms: Images and Realities of Work and Family* (New York: Routledge, 2009), 42.

17. Ibid., 17.

18. Ibid., 114.

19. Judith Light, interview by Adrienne Faillace, *Emmy TV Legends*, Archive of American Television, Apr. 30, 2015.

CHAPTER 1 — SELLING MS. CONSUMER

1. For a detailed overview of the development of this demographic during the late 1970s and 1980s, see Julie D'Acci, *Defining Women: Television and the Case of Cagney & Lacey* (Chapel Hill: University of North Carolina Press, 1994), 63–104.

2. Bob Knight, "Networks Search for New Series Trend: CBS Chases ABC While NBC Dreams of Olympics," *Variety*, Jan. 9, 1980, 224.

3. "ABC Looks Ahead to Midseason with Crop of Comedies, *Variety*, Aug. 20, 1980, 50+; "ABC Puts on a Comic Face," *Variety*, May 12, 1982, 452+; "CBS Takes Light-Hearted Approach to '82–83 Sked," *Variety*, May 12, 1982, 451+; "Four Sitcom Pilots Ordered by CBS," *Variety*, Feb. 6, 1980, 95; Dave Kaufman, "New CBS Pilots Heavy on Comedy; Shoot 11 Dramas," *Variety*, Mar. 3, 1982, 70; Bob Knight, "New ABC-TV Schedule Accents Comedy: Web Promises Stronger Pix," *Variety*, Apr. 30, 1980, 151; Bob Knight, "Season, at Long Last, Is in High Gear: Sked Stability May Be Elusive," *Variety*, Oct. 29, 1980, 37+; "MGM Pilots: Lots of Comedy," *Variety*, Apr. 6, 1983, 39+.

4. "Comedy in the Fall for NBC Primetime," *Variety*, May 7, 1980, 577; Dave Kaufman, "NBC to Accent Comedy Series for Midseason," *Variety*, Sept. 8, 1982, 93+; Bob Knight, "NBC Pilot Crop Leans to Comedy," *Variety*, Mar. 24, 1982, 262+; Bob Knight, "NBC Sked: It's Tartikoff's Baby," *Variety*, May 5, 1982, 113+; Bob Knight, "Silverman Builds Stairs Out of Cellar: Sitcom Strategy Is Still the Key," *Variety*, Mar. 5, 1980, 55+; Bob Knight, "Tartikoff Endures at NBC to Cope with 82–83 Sked; Sees 7–9 Hours of Change," *Variety*, Apr. 14, 1982, 34+.

5. Quoted in John Dempsey, "'We're Optimistic,' NBC Sez in Planning for Its Affil Meet," *Variety*, May 14, 1980, 118.

6. "TV Comedy Smells, Says Lear; Ratings War Hurts Viewers," *Variety*, Apr. 30, 1980, 150.

7. Bob Knight, "Webs Off on a Fool's Errand?," *Variety*, May 12, 1982, 451.

8. Mary C. Gilly and Thomas E. Barry, "Segmenting the Women's Market: A Comparison of Work-Related Segmentation Schemes," *Current Issues and Research in Advertising* 9 (1986): 151.

9. Rena Bartos, *The Moving Target: What Every Marketer Should Know About Women* (New York: Free Press, 1982). Bartos' other oft-cited publications include: "Beyond the Cookie Cutters," *Marketing and Media Decisions* (1981): 54–59; "The Moving Target: The Impact of Women's Employment on Consumer Behavior," *Journal of Marketing* (July 1977): 31–37; "What Every Marketer Should Know about Women," *Harvard Business Review* 56 (May-June 1978): 73–85.

10. See for example, Thomas E. Barry, Mary C. Gilly, and Lindley E. Doran, "Advertising to Women with Difference Career Orientations," *Journal of Advertising Research* 25 (Apr./May 1985): 26–35; Gilly and Barry, "Segmenting the Women's Market," 149–170; Ved Prakash, "Segmentation of Women's Market Based on Personal Values and the Means-End Chain Model: A Framework for Advertising Strategy," *Advances in Consumer Research* 13 (1986): 215–220; Sandra Salmans, "Banishing Clichés in Advertising to Women," *New York Times*, July 18, 1982; Charles M. Schaninger and Chris T. Allen, "Wife's Occupational Status as a Consumer Behavior Construct," *Journal of Consumer Research* 8 (Sept. 1981): 189–196; Valarie A. Zeithaml, "The New Demographics and Market Fragmentation," *Journal of Marketing* 49 (Summer 1985): 64–75.

11. Barry et al., "Advertising to Women," 26.

12. "Women Like 'Liberated' Blurbs," *Variety*, May 27, 1981, 40.

13. D'Acci, *Defining Women*, 69. Original emphasis.

14. Sut Jhally and Justin Lewis, *Enlightened Racism: The Cosby Show, Audiences, and the Myth of the American Dream* (Boulder, CO: Westview, 1992), 76.

15. "Womens' [sic] Roles on TV & Radio Getting Better," *Variety*, Jan. 9, 1985, 100+.

16. This term is usually attributed to Christine Frederick and her book *Selling Mrs. Consumer* (New York: The Business Bourse, 1929).

17. Bartos, *The Moving Target*, 162.

18. He cites Beverlee B. Anderson, "Working Women vs. Non-Working Women: A Comparison of Shopping Behavior," in *1972 Combined Proceedings*, eds. Borris W. Becker and Helmut Becker (Chicago: American Marketing Association, 1972), 355–357; Suzanne H. McCall, "Meet the 'Workwife'" *Journal of Marketing* 41 (July 1977): 55–65; Mary Joyce and Joseph P. Guiltinan, "The Professional Woman: A Potential Market Segment for Retailers," *Journal of Retailing* 54 (Summer 1978): 59–70.

19. He cites Susan P. Douglas and Christine D. Urban, "Life Style Analysis to Profile Women in International Markets," *Journal of Marketing* 41 (July 1977): 46–54; Fred D. Reynolds, Melvin R. Crask, and William D. Wells, "The Modern Feminine Life Style," *Journal of Marketing* 41 (July 1977): 38–45.

20. He cites Bartos, "The Moving Target," 31–37; Bartos, "What Every Marketer," 73–85; Shreekant G. Joag, James W. Gentry, and JoAnne Mohler, "Explaining Differences in Consumption by Working and Non-Working Wives," in *Advances in Consumer Research* Vol. 12, eds. Elizabeth Hirschman and Morris Holbrook (Provo, UT: Association for

Consumer Research, 1985), 582–585; Schaninger and Allen, "Wife's Occupational Status," 189–196.

21. McCall, "Meet the 'Workwife,'" 55–65, Douglas and Urban, "Life Style Analysis," 46–54, Reynolds et al., "The Modern Feminine Life Style," 38–45; Bartos "The Moving Target, 31–37, William Lazer and John E. Smallwood, "The Changing Demographics of Women," *Journal of Marketing* 41 (July 1977): 14–22; Marianne A. Ferber and Helen M. Lowry, "Woman's Place: National Differences in the Occupational Mosaic," *Journal of Marketing* 41 (July 1977): 23–30; Dan H. Robertson and Donald W. Hackett, "Saleswomen: Perceptions, Problems and Prospects," *Journal of Marketing* 41 (July 1977): 66–71; William J. Lundstrom and Donald Sciglimpaglia, "Sex Role Portrayals in Advertising," *Journal of Marketing* 41 (July 1977): 72–79.

22. Barbara Hackman Franklin, "Guest Editorial," *Journal of Marketing* 41 (July 1977):10.

23. Bartos, *The Moving Target*, 244–245.

24. Franklin, "Guest Editorial," 11.

25. McCall, "Meet the 'Workwife,'" 55.

26. Ibid., 62.

27. Ibid., 56.

28. Zeithaml, "The New Demographics," 64–75; McCall, "Meet the 'Workwife,'" 55–65; Prakash, "Segmentation of Women's Market," 215–220.

29. Ruth La Ferla, "Flaunting Success," *New York Times*, Sept. 25, 1988.

30. Salmans, "Banishing Clichés."

31. Bartos, *The Moving Target*, 14.

32. Ibid., 16.

33. McCall, "Meet the 'Workwife,'" 55.

34. Bartos, *The Moving Target*, 145.

35. Ibid., 37.

36. Gilly and Barry, "Segmenting the Women's Market," 163.

37. Bartos, *The Moving Target*, 272.

38. Ibid., 251.

39. Ibid., 234.

40. John Dempsey, "Rating Drop Worries Networks: Clearances Off, Cable Indies Show Big Gains," *Variety*, July 2, 1980, 1+.

41. Jack Loftus, "No Rush To Buy Fall TV Season: Wait for Web Moves to Juice Up Skeds," *Variety*, Oct. 29, 1980, 1+.

42. Jack Loftus, "Record Upfront Primes 4th Qtr. Sales: TV Webs Pocket a Cool $700-Mil," *Variety*, Nov. 3, 1982, 64.

43. Quoted in "Buyers Handicap the Season: 'Gloria,' 'Newhart' To Survive; Web Shares Continue to Slide," *Variety*, Sept. 29, 1982, 90.

44. Gary David Goldberg, *Sit, Ubu, Sit: How I Went from Brooklyn to Hollywood with the Same Woman, the Same Dog, and a Lot Less Hair* (New York: Three Rivers Press, 2008), 36.

45. Jack Loftus, "CBS Yields to Agency Demands, Makes Demographic Guarantees," *Variety*, July 27, 1983, 43+.

46. "Society's Flux Forces ABC into Research Expansion," *Variety*, Oct. 21, 1981, 60+.

47. Ken Auletta, *Three Blind Mice: How the TV Networks Lost Their Way* (New York: Vintage Books, 1992), 495.

48. Ibid., 511.

49. "Web Prime Spots Get $1.5-Billion; ABC Rate Down," *Variety*, July 30, 1980, 1+.

50. Lauren Rabinovitz, "Sitcoms and Single Moms: Representations of Feminism on American TV," *Cinema Journal* 29 (Fall 1989): 7.

51. "Agencies Predict NBC to Stay on Top," *Broadcasting*, Aug. 11, 1986, 48+; "CBS Breaks ABC's Hold on Women," *Variety*, Feb. 11, 1981, 89.

52. Marvin S. Mord, "Webs Look at New Demos: Research on TV Values," *Variety*, Jan. 13, 1982, 170.

53. Bob Knight, "2d Season Chemistry," *Variety*, Feb. 1, 1984, 42.

54. Bob Knight, "Year of the Sitcom for TV Nets: 'Cosby' Sets Precedent, ABC Hits on Tuesday," *Variety*, Dec. 4, 1985, 1+.

55. "Embassy to Bid 'Who's the Boss?,'" *Variety*, Dec. 17, 1986, 39+; Morry Roth, "'Cosby' Pulls $22-Mil in Chicago; Expected to Reap $500-Mil Total," *Variety*, Nov. 19, 1986, 35+; "'Growing Pains' Draws 18 Deals," *Variety*, July 30, 1986, 41+; "Embassy TV Gets a $1-Bil Chuckle from Its Sitcoms," *Variety*, Jan. 1, 1986, 29+; "'Spoons' & 'Facts' Boost Embassy's TV Sales Record," *Variety*, Nov. 20, 1985, 47; John Dempsey, "'Spoons' Serves Up Lotsa Silver to Embassy for Syndie Sales," *Variety*, Sept. 18, 1985, 45+; "Syndie Fever Hot for 'Webster' As Par Claims 1st-Round Records," *Variety*, Aug. 7, 1985, 42+; "Failed Sitcoms Out of Mothballs to Help Feed Those Needy Indies," *Variety*, Jan. 23, 1985, 51+; John Dempsey, "Syndies Reviving Axed Sitcoms: Stations Try to Limit Runaway Prices," *Variety*, Dec. 12, 1984, 1+; "'Ties' Knots $75-Mil," *Variety*, Sept. 19, 1984, 47; "Par TV Uncorks 'Family Ties' as High-Priced Cheers' Combo," *Variety*, Aug. 22, 1984, 85; "Syndie Loves Off-Net Sitcoms; Looks Like Embassy Got Things Rolling as 'Facts' Tops $111-Mil," *Variety*, Jul. 4, 1984, 49+; John Dempsey, "TV Stations Going Bananas in Off-Net Program Bidding; 'Cheers' Chug-a-Lugs a Record," *Variety*, Jun. 27, 1984, 1+; "MCA Strikes It Rich: 'Gimme A Break' Could Hit $100-Mil Mark; 'Knight Rider,' 'Simon,' 'A-Team' in Wings," *Variety*, Jun. 13, 1984, 41+.

56. Dempsey, "Syndies Reviving Axed Sitcoms," 1+; John Dempsey, "Sitcoms & Courtrooms Liven Up NATPE: Lotsa Wheeling & Dealing in New Orleans," *Variety*, Jan. 22, 1986, 33+; "MCA and Tribune to Resurrect 'Charles in Charge' for Syndie," *Variety*, Mar. 26, 1986, 48; John Lippman, "Sitcom Spurt Clogs Syndie Mart: Some 45 New Entries Reverse the Trend," *Variety*, May 21, 1986, 1+; "Embassy Adds 'Silver' Lining," *Variety*, May 28, 1986, 38; John Dempsey, "Fox TV Fare, Sitcoms in Spotlight at Indie Stations' L.A. Convention," *Variety*, Jan. 7, 1987, 39+.

57. Ken Auletta, *Three Blind Mice*, 354.

58. Ibid., 534.

59. Judith Stacey, *Brave New Families: Stories of Domestic Upheaval in Late-Twentieth-Century America* (Berkeley: University of California Press, 1998), 17.

60. Prakash, "Segmentation of Women's Market," 216.

61. Auletta, *Three Blind Mice*, 114.

62. Michele Hilmes, "Where Everybody Knows Your Name: *Cheers* and the Mediation of Cultures," in *The Sitcom Reader*, ed. Joanne Morreale (Syracuse: Syracuse University Press, 2003), 218.

63. Bartos, *The Moving Target*, 249.

64. "The X Team," *Silver Spoons*, Season One (NBC, Apr. 30, 1983).

65. "How Ugly Is He?," *The Cosby Show*, Season One (NBC, Nov. 15, 1984).

66. "Full House," *The Cosby Show*, Season Two (NBC, Feb. 27, 1985).

67. "How Do You Get to Carnegie Hall?" *The Cosby Show*, Season Five (NBC, Nov. 24, 1988).

68. "Mrs. Huxtable Goes to Kindergarten," *The Cosby Show*, Season Five (NBC, Jan. 26, 1989).

69. "This Year's Model," *Family Ties*, Season Two (NBC, Oct. 26, 1983).

70. Bartos, *The Moving Target*, 262.

71. "The Seavers vs. the Cleavers," *Growing Pains*, Season One (ABC, Jan. 28 1986).

72. "Jason's Rib," *Growing Pains*, Season Two (ABC, Dec. 9, 1986).

73. Bob Knight, "Women Stir Comatose ABC-TV: Third-Place Network Perks Up with Improved Femme Demos," *Variety*, June 18, 1986, 47+.

74. "Thank God It's Friday," *Growing Pains*, Season Two (ABC, Feb. 10, 1987).

75. They could have easily gotten this trick from *Silver Spoons*, where Ricky uses it in "A Little Magic," *Silver Spoons*, Season One (NBC, Dec. 4, 1982).

76. "My Brother, Myself," *Growing Pains*, Season Two (ABC, Feb. 24, 1987).

77. Brandon Tartikoff and Charles Leerhsen, *The Last Great Ride* (New York: Turtle Bay Books, 1992), 164.

78. Ken Auletta, *Three Blind Mice*, 452.

CHAPTER 2 — "I CAN'T HELP FEELING MATERNAL—I'M A FATHER!"

1. Gary David Goldberg, *Sit, Ubu, Sit: How I Went from Brooklyn to Hollywood with the Same Woman, the Same Dog, and a Lot Less Hair* (New York: Three Rivers Press, 2008), 43.

2. Nikolas Rose, *Governing the Soul: The Shaping of the Private Self*, 2nd ed. (London: Free Association Press, 1999), 213.

3. Bridget Kies, "Television's 'Mr. Moms': Idealizing the New Man in 1980s Domestic Sitcoms," *Feminist Media Histories* 4 (Winter 2018): 142–170, 147.

4. Judith C. Daniluk and Al Herman, "Children: Yes or No, A Decision-Making Program for Women," *Personnel and Guidance Journal* 62 (Dec. 1983): 240–243; Marolyn Parker, Steven Peltier, and Patricia Wolleat, "Understanding Dual Career Couples," *Personnel and Guidance Journal* 60 (Sept. 1981): 14–18; Janet Dreyfus Gray, "Counseling Women Who Want Both a Profession and a Family," *Personnel and Guidance Journal* 59 (Sept. 1980): 43–46; Jacqueline B. Stanfield, "Research on Wife/Mother Role Strain in Dual Career Families: Its Present State Has Laid an Adequate Basis for Representative Empirical Studies," *American Journal of Economics and Sociology* 22 (July 1985): 355–363; Nancy M. Rudd and Patrick C. McKenry, "Family Influences on the Job Satisfaction of Employed Mothers," *Psychology of Women Quarterly* 10 (1986): 363–372; Kathleen V. Hoover-Dempsey, Jeanne M. Plas, and Barbara Strudler Wallston, "Tears and Weeping among Professional Women: In Search of New Understanding," *Psychology of Women Quarterly* 10 (1986): 19–34; Janet Dreyfus Gray, "The Married Professional Woman: An Examination of Her Role Conflicts and Coping Strategies," *Psychology of Women Quarterly* 7 (Spring 1983): 235–243.

5. Parker et al., "Understanding Dual Career Couples," 15.

6. "Pilot," *Family Ties*, Season One (NBC, Sept. 22, 1982).

7. Goldberg, *Sit, Ubu, Sit*, 82.

8. "Margin of Error," *Family Ties*, Season One (NBC, Feb. 9, 1983).

9. "Suzanne Takes You Down," *Family Ties*, Season One (NBC, Mar. 16, 1983).

10. "Elyse D'Arc," *Family Ties*, Season One (NBC, Apr. 11, 1983).

11. "Working at It," *Family Ties*, Season Two (NBC, May 10, 1984).

12. "Not an Affair to Remember," *Family Ties*, Season Two (NBC, Nov. 2, 1983); "Lady Sings the Blues," *Family Ties*, Season Two (NBC, Feb. 23, 1984); "Diary of a Young Girl," *Family Ties*, Season Two (NBC, May 3, 1984).

13. Rudd and McKenry, "Family Influences," 363–372; Rosemary J. Key and Margaret Mietus Sanik, "Children's Contributions to Household Work in One- and Two-Parent Families," in *Proceedings of the Southeastern Family Economics/Home Management Conference* (New Orleans: Louisiana State University, 1985): 48–51.

14. "Love Thy Neighbor," *Family Ties*, Season Three (NBC, Oct. 11, 1984).

15. "Sweet Lorraine," *Family Ties*, Season Two (NBC, Nov. 16, 1983).

16. "Oh Donna," *Family Ties*, Season Three (NBC, Jan. 3, 1985).

17. "Keaton 'n Son," *Family Ties*, Season Three (NBC, Oct. 18, 1984).

18. "Mr. Wrong," *Family Ties*, Season Four (NBC, Oct. 17, 1985).

19. "The Real Thing (Part 2)," *Family Ties*, Season Four (NBC, Oct. 3, 1985).

20. Steven Dougherty, "For New Mom Meredith Baxter Birney There's Nothing Like a Baby Boom to Strengthen *Family Ties*," *People*, Feb. 4, 1985, 88–90.

21. "Birth of a Keaton, Part 1," *Family Ties*, Season Three (NBC, Jan. 24, 1985) and "Birth of a Keaton, Part 2," *Family Ties*, Season Three (NBC, Jan. 31, 1985).

22. Meredith Baxter Birney doesn't appear in the following episodes: "Love Thy Neighbor," "Keaton 'n Son," "Hot Line Fever," *Family Ties*, Season Three (NBC, Nov. 1, 1984); "4 RMS OCN VU," *Family Ties*, Season Three (NBC, Nov. 8, 1984); "Help Wanted," *Family Ties*, Season Three (NBC, Dec. 6, 1984); "Karen II, Alex 0," *Family Ties*, Season Three (NBC, Dec. 13, 1984); "Auntie Up," *Family Ties*, Season Three (NBC, Jan. 10, 1985). She appears only minimally in "Best Man," *Family Ties*, Season Three (NBC, Nov. 15, 1984); "Don't Kiss Me, I'm Only the Messenger," *Family Ties*, Season Three (NBC, Nov. 29, 1984); "Philadelphia Story," *Family Ties*, Season Three (NBC, Jan. 17, 1985).

23. "Cry Baby," *Family Ties*, Season Three (NBC, Feb. 7, 1985).

24. Goldberg, *Sit, Ubu, Sit*, 87.

25. "Bringing Up Baby," *Family Ties*, Season Three (NBC, Feb. 21, 1985).

26. "Remembrance of Things Past (Part 1)," *Family Ties*, Season Three (NBC, Mar. 28, 1985); "Remembrance of Things Past (Part 2)," *Family Ties*, Season Three (NBC, Mar. 28, 1985).

27. Steven compares Alex to his father in "Pilot."

28. "Nothing But a Man," *Family Ties*, Season Four (NBC, Jan. 2, 1986).

29. Alex's influence over Andrew is a continuing problem, to the point where during the fifth season, a two-part clip show episode attempts to reeducate Andrew, detailing Alex's problematic gender politics. "Battle of the Sexes (Part 1)," *Family Ties*, Season Five (NBC, Feb. 19, 1987); "Battle of the Sexes (Part 2)," *Family Ties*, Season Five (NBC, Feb. 19, 1987).

30. Additionally, in a prior argument with Alex, he claimed: "I am the man, but I'm not number one, and neither is your mother. You can be the man without feeling you're superior to the woman." "The Graduate," *Family Ties*, Season Two (NBC, Mar. 15, 1984).

31. Felice N. Schwartz, "Management Women and the New Facts of Life," *Harvard Business Review*, Jan.–Feb. 1989, 65–76; Susan Butruille, Eleanor Haller, Lynn Lannon, and Joan Sourenian, "Women in the Workplace," *Training & Development Journal*, Nov. 1989, 21–30.

32. Judith Stacey, *In the Name of the Family: Rethinking Family Values in the Postmodern Age* (Boston: Beacon Press, 1996), 34.

33. "Pilot"; "The Fugitive Part 1," *Family Ties*, Season One (NBC, Jan. 19, 1983); "I Gotta Be Ming," *Family Ties*, Season One (NBC, Feb. 23, 1983); "Batter Up," *Family Ties*, Season Two (NBC, Nov. 30, 1983); "Lady Sings the Blues"; "Fabric Smarts," *Family Ties*, Season Three (NBC, Oct. 25, 1984); "Don't Kiss Me, I'm Only the Messenger"; "Designated Hitter," *Family Ties*, Season Four (NBC, Oct. 24, 1985); "Mr. Right," *Family Ties*, Season Four (NBC, Nov. 21, 1985); "You've Got a Friend," *Family Ties*, Season Four (NBC, Dec. 19, 1985); "Teacher's Pet," *Family Ties*, Season Four (NBC, Mar. 2, 1986); "My Buddy," *Family Ties*, Season Four (NBC, Mar. 6, 1986); "Be True to Your Preschool," *Family Ties*, Season Five (NBC, Sept. 25, 1986); "My Back Pages," *Family Ties*, Season Five (NBC, Oct. 16, 1986); "The Big Fix," *Family Ties*, Season Five (NBC, Nov. 17, 1986); "My Brother's Keeper," *Family Ties*, Season Five (NBC, Nov. 20, 1986); "Paper Lion," *Family Ties*, Season Five (NBC, Dec. 11, 1986); "My Mother, My Friend," *Family Ties*, Season Five (NBC, Dec. 18, 1986); "Keaton vs. Keaton," *Family Ties*, Season Five (NBC, Mar. 5, 1987); "The Freshman and the Senior," *Family Ties*, Season Five (NBC, Mar. 26, 1987); "The Visit," *Family Ties*, Season Five (NBC, May 7, 1987).

34. "Death of a Grocer," *Family Ties*, Season One (NBC, Dec. 1, 1982); "Sherry Baby," *Family Ties*, Season One (NBC, Jan. 12, 1983); "The Fugitive Part 1"; "Elyse D'Arc"; "This Year's Model"; "Working at It"; "Fabric Smarts"; "Oh Donna"; "My Buddy"; "My Brother's Keeper."

35. "Keaton 'n Son."

36. "Speed Trap," *Family Ties*, Season Two (NBC, Nov. 9, 1983); "Once in Love with Elyse," *Family Ties*, Season Four (NBC, May 1, 1986); "The Graduate."

37. "Big Brother Is Watching," *Family Ties*, Season One (NBC, Nov. 17 1982); "This Year's Model"; "Mrs. Wrong (Part 1)," *Family Ties*, Season Five (NBC, Nov. 6, 1986); "High School Confidential," *Family Ties*, Season Five (NBC, Dec. 4, 1986); "Oh, Brother (Part 1)," *Family Ties*, Season Five (NBC, Jan. 8, 1987).

38. Review of *Growing Pains*, *Variety*, Oct. 2, 1985, 123.

39. "Pilot," *Growing Pains*, Season One (ABC, Sept. 24, 1985); "Springsteen," *Growing Pains*, Season One (ABC, Oct. 1, 1985); "Jealousy," *Growing Pains*, Season One (ABC, Oct. 8, 1985).

40. "The Career Decision," *Growing Pains*, Season One (ABC, May 6, 1986).

41. While Maggie's workplace isn't as overtly gendered as Elyse's on *Family Ties*, Maggie implicitly appreciates her female boss when she is courted for a more prestigious job by a powerful man who tries to seduce her in "Confidentially Yours," *Growing Pains*, Season Two (ABC, May 11, 1987).

42. "The Anniversary That Never Was," *Growing Pains*, Season One (ABC, Mar. 4, 1986).

43. "Superdad!," *Growing Pains*, Season One (ABC, Oct. 29, 1985).

44. "Choices," *Growing Pains*, Season Two (ABC, Jan. 13, 1987).

45. "Higher Education," *Growing Pains*, Season Two (ABC, Jan. 20, 1987).

46. "Some Enchanted Evening," *Growing Pains*, Season Two (ABC, Jan. 27, 1987).

47. "Jimmy Durante Died for Your Sins," *Growing Pains*, Season Two (ABC, Mar. 3, 1987).

48. "Be a Man," *Growing Pains*, Season One (ABC, Mar. 11, 1986).

49. "First Blood," *Growing Pains*, Season One (ABC, Jan. 14, 1986).

50. "Long Day's Journey into Night," *Growing Pains*, Season Two (ABC, Oct. 28, 1986).

51. Alda also serves as a masculine ideal on *Family Ties*. When Jennifer has a falling out with a close male friend, Elyse extols his virtues, leading Jennifer to retort sarcastically, "He's not Alan Alda." "I Know Jennifer's Boyfriend," *Family Ties*, Season One (NBC, Oct. 6, 1982).

52. Sut Jhally and Justin Lewis, *Enlightened Racism: The* Cosby Show, *Audiences, and the Myth of the American Dream* (Boulder, CO: Westview, 1992), 41.

53. Ibid., 42; Ibid., 110.

54. Beretta E. Smith-Shomade, *Shaded Lives: African-American Women and Television* (New Brunswick, NJ: Rutgers University Press, 2002), 34.

55. John D. H. Downing, "'The Cosby Show' and American Racial Discourse," in *Discourse and Discrimination*, eds. Geneva Smitherman-Donaldson and Teun A. van Dijk (Detroit: Wayne State University Press, 1988), 54. Original emphasis.

56. Ibid., 28.

57. Ibid.

58. "Vanessa's Bad Grade," *The Cosby Show*, Season Two (NBC, Jan. 16, 1986).

59. "Cliff Babysits," *The Cosby Show*, Season Five (NBC, Jan. 12, 1989).

60. Robin R. Means Coleman, *African American Viewers and the Black Situation Comedy: Situating Racial Humor* (New York: Garland Publishing, 2000), 197.

61. "Clair's Case," *The Cosby Show*, Season One (NBC, Feb. 21, 1985).

62. "Slumber Party," *The Cosby Show*, Season One (NBC, Mar. 28, 1985).

63. "First Day of School," *The Cosby Show*, Season Two (NBC, Sept. 26, 1985).

64. "The Andalusian Flu," *The Cosby Show*, Season Three (NBC, Apr. 2, 1987).

65. "A Girl and Her Dog," *The Cosby Show*, Season Three (NBC, Dec. 4, 1986).

66. "Cliff in Charge," *The Cosby Show*, Season Three (NBC, Dec. 18, 1986).

67. "Calling Dr. Huxtable," *The Cosby Show*, Season Three (NBC, Feb. 12, 1987).

68. "Rudy Spends the Night," *The Cosby Show*, Season Three (NBC, Jan. 15, 1987).

69. Bambi L. Haggins, "There's No Place Like Home: The American Dream, African-American Identity, and the Situation Comedy," *The Velvet Light Trap* 43 (Spring 1999): 23–36.

70. Downing, "The Cosby Show," 60.

71. Jhally and Lewis, *Enlightened Racism*, 5.

72. "Father's Day," *The Cosby Show*, Season One (NBC, Dec. 20, 1984).

73. "Cliff in Love," *The Cosby Show*, Season Two (NBC, Oct. 17, 1985).

74. "The Auction," *The Cosby Show*, Season Two (NBC, Jan. 16, 1986).

75. "Cliff Babysits."

76. "It Comes and It Goes," *The Cosby Show*, Season Five (NBC, March 9, 1989).

77. Bartos, *The Moving Target*, 271.

78. "How Ugly is He?" *The Cosby Show*, Season One, (NBC, Nov. 22, 1984).

79. Jhally and Lewis, *Enlightened Racism*, 41.

80. Ibid., 39.

81. "Rudy's Sick," *The Cosby Show*, Season One (NBC, Dec. 20, 1984).

82. "The Juicer," *The Cosby Show*, Season Two (NBC, Oct. 3, 1985).

83. "Theogate," *The Cosby Show*, Season Four (NBC, Oct. 1, 1987).

84. "Pilot," *Silver Spoons*, Season One (NBC, Sept. 25, 1982).

85. Edward and Kate get married in "Marry Me, Marry Me: Part 2," *Silver Spoons*, Season Three (NBC, Feb. 10, 1985).

86. "A Little Magic," *Silver Spoons*, Season One (NBC, Dec. 4, 1982).

87. "The Empire Strikes Out," *Silver Spoons*, Season One (NBC, Feb. 26, 1983).

88. "Who's the Boss?," *Silver Spoons*, Season Five (First-run syndication, Sept. 15, 1986).

89. "Boys Will Be Boys," *Silver Spoons*, Season One (NBC, Oct. 2, 1982).

90. "Grandfather Stratton," *Silver Spoons*, Season One (NBC, Oct. 9, 1982).

91. "Honor Thy Father," *Silver Spoons*, Season One (NBC, Nov. 20, 1982).

92. For example, "Father Nature," *Silver Spoons*, Season One (NBC, Nov. 27, 1982); "The Empire Strikes Out."

93. Ricky and/or Edward cry in "Pilot," "Boys Will Be Boys"; "Evelyn Returns," *Silver Spoons*, Season One (NBC, Oct. 30, 1982); "I'm Just Wild about Harry," *Silver Spoons*, Season One (NBC, Nov. 13, 1982); "Three's a Crowd," *Silver Spoons*, Season One (NBC, Feb. 19, 1983).

94. "Evelyn Returns."

95. "Won't You Go Home, Bob Danish?," *Silver Spoons*, Season One (NBC, Mar. 5. 1983).

96. "Me and Mr. T," *Silver Spoons*, Season One (NBC, Oct. 16, 1982).

97. Lynne Segal, *Slow Motion: Changing Masculinities, Changing Men* (New Brunswick: Rutgers University Press, 1990), 51.

98. Estella Tincknell, *Mediating the Family: Gender, Culture and Representation* (London: Hodder Arnold, 2005), 65.

99. Kies, "Television's 'Mr. Moms,'" 160.

100. Mary Douglas Vavrus, "Domesticating Patriarchy: Hegemonic Masculinity and Television's 'Mr. Mom,'" *Critical Studies in Media Communication* 19, no. 3 (Sept. 2002): 353.

101. Ibid., 361.

102. Sonya Michel, *Children's Interests/Mothers' Rights: The Shaping of America's Child Care Policy* (New Haven, CT: Yale University Press, 1999), 3.

103. Joan Williams, *Unbending Gender: Why Family and Work Conflict and What to Do about It* (Oxford: Oxford University Press, 2000).

104. Nancy L. Marshall and Rosalind C. Barnett, "Work-Family Strains and Gains among Two-Earner Couples," *Journal of Community Psychology* 21 (Jan. 1993): 64–78, 75.

CHAPTER 3 — SOLVING THE DAY-CARE CRISIS, ONE EPISODE AT A TIME

1. Geraldine Carro, "Who's Minding the Children?" *Ladies' Home Journal,* Jan. 1982, 69–71, 103–104; Steve Forbes, "Who Will Care for the Children?" *Forbes,* July 25, 1988, 29; Connaught Marshner, "Is Day Care Good for Kids?" *National Review,* May 19, 1989, 46; "Who's Watching the Kids?" *New York Times,* July 12, 1985.

2. Marshner, "Is Day Care Good for Kids?" 46.

3. For an analysis of the day-care center sexual abuse scandals see Chapter 3 of Susan J. Douglas and Meredith W. Michaels, *The Mommy Myth: The Idealization of Motherhood and How It Has Undermined All Women* (New York: Free Press, 2004); A. E. Hardie, "Fire Points Up Dilemma Over Child Care Choices," *New York Times,* Nov. 29, 1986; Wendell Rawls, Jr., "Four Children and an Adult Die in Atlanta after Boiler Explodes at Day-Care Nursery," *New York Times,* Oct. 14, 1980.

4. Milton Friedman, "Day Care: The Problem," *National Review,* July 8, 1988, 14; Connaught Marshner, "Socialized Motherhood: as Easy as ABC," *National Review* May 19, 1989, 44–47.

5. Cited in James Zampetti, "Building ABCs for an On-Site Childcare Center," *Management Review,* Mar. 1991, 54.

6. Jaclyn Fierman, "Child Care: What Works—and Doesn't," *Fortune*, Nov. 21, 1988, 163.

7. Nadine Brozan, "The Toll of Losing Day Care Is Studied," *New York Times*, June 17, 1982; "Child Care Grows as a Benefit," *BusinessWeek*, Dec. 21, 1981, 60-61, 63; Jaclyn Fierman, "Nursery Rhyme, Day Care Reason," *New York Times*, July 29, 1982; "Who'll Mind America's Children?," *New York Times*, Mar. 29, 1984.

8. "The Day-Care Problem Won't Go Away," *New York Times*, Sept. 8, 1984; Georgia Dullea, "Ranks of American Nannies Are Growing," *New York Times*, Jan. 18, 1985; David Gumpert, "10 Hot Businesses to Start in the '90s," *Working Woman*, June 1991, 55-56; Jacqueline Shaheen, "Another College Will Offer a Course on How to Be a Nanny," *New York Times*, Aug. 24, 1986; Darrel Patrick Wash and Liesel E. Brand, "Child Day Care Services: An Industry at a Crossroads," *Monthly Labor Review*, Dec. 1990, 17-24; Phillip H. Wiggins, "Child Day Care Profits Mount," *New York Times*, Mar. 3, 1987.

9. Sonya Michel, *Children's Interests/Mothers' Rights: The Shaping of America's Child Care Policy* (New Haven, CT: Yale University Press, 1999), 256.

10. Fierman, "Child Care," 176.

11. "Tips on Finding Day Care," *New York Times*, Sept. 3, 1984.

12. Fern Schumer Chapman, "Executive Guilt: Who's Taking Care of the Children? And How Will Kids Raised by Nannies and in Day Care Centers Turn Out?," *Fortune*, Feb. 16, 1987, 30-37.

13. Claudia Wallis, "The Child-Care Dilemma: Millions of US Families Face a Wrenching Question: Who's Minding the Kids?" *Time*, June 22, 1987, 54.

14. Michel Foucault, "The Subject and Power," in *The Essential Foucault*, eds. Paul Rabinow and Nikolas Rose (New York: New Press, 2003), 138.

15. Aaron Bernstein, "Business Starts Tailoring Itself to Suit Working Women," *BusinessWeek*, Oct. 6, 1986, 50-54; "A Boost for Day Care," *New York Times*, Dec. 19, 1981; "Child Care Grows as a Benefit," 63; Julie A. Cohen, "Keeping Kids at Work," *Management Review*, Jan. 1991, 26-28; "The Day-Care Problem Won't Go Away"; Karen De Witt, "TV Stations Join Forces to Provide Day Care," *New York Times*, Jan. 12, 1980; Susan B. Garland, "America's Child-Care Crisis: The First Tiny Steps toward Solutions," *BusinessWeek*, July 10, 1989, 64, 68; Marjorie Hunter, "Senate Day Care at Hand," *New York Times*, Dec. 9, 1983; "Job and Family: The Walls Come Down," *US News and World Report*, June 16, 1980, 57-58; Charlotte Libov, "Day Care in Workplace to Be Tried in Stamford," *New York Times*, Nov. 23, 1986; "Pooling Day-Care Information," *New York Times*, Feb. 13, 1984; "Providing Help and Referrals," *New York Times*, Jan. 5, 1987; Suzanne Schiffman, "Making It Easier to Be a Working Parent," *New York Times*, Nov. 24, 1980; "Some Fresh Approaches," *Management Review*, Mar. 1985, 8-9; "Who's Taking Care of the Kids?," *New York Times*, Sept. 6, 1983.

16. Carro, "Who's Minding the Children?"; Lynn Langway, "The Superwoman Squeeze," *Newsweek*, May 19, 1980, 72-79; Alfonso A. Narvaez, "The Housekeeper outside the Law: Suburbanites Turn to Illegal Aliens," *New York Times*, Feb. 9, 1980.

17. Friedman is cited or quoted in Andree Brooks, "Corporate Ambivalence on Day Care," *New York Times*, July 21, 1983; Bradley Hitchings, "Today's Choices in Child Care," *BusinessWeek*, Apr. 1, 1985, 104-108; Stephen Koepp, "Make Room for Baby: Corporate Nannies Watch Youngsters for Parents on the Job," *Time*, Sept. 3, 1984, 61; Tessa Melvin, "Day-Care Options Explored," *New York Times*, Nov. 4, 1984; Irene Pave, "The Insurance Crisis That Could Cripple Day Care," *BusinessWeek*, June 17, 1985, 114-115.

18. John P. Fernandez, *Child Care and Corporate Productivity: Resolving Family/Work Conflicts* (Lexington, MA: Lexington Books, 1985), cited in Chapman, "Executive Guilt," 31.

19. Robert J. Trotter, "Project Day-Care," *Psychology Today*, Dec. 1987, 32.

20. Quoted in Nadine Brozan, "Mapping Future of Child Care," *New York Times*, Oct. 5, 1987.

21. T. Berry Brazelton, "What You Should Look for in Infant Day Care," *Redbook*, Feb. 1982, 56; Connaught Marshner, "Is Day Care Good for Kids?," *National Review*, May 19, 1989, 46; Claudia Wallis, "Is Day Care Bad for Babies? Hard Facts Are Beginning to Clarify a Politicized Debate," *Time*, June 22, 1987, 63; Russell Watson, "What Price Day Care?," *Newsweek*, Sept. 10, 1984, 14–21.

22. Michel Foucault, "Governmentality," in *The Essential Foucault*, ed. Paul Rabinow and Nikolas Rose (New York: New Press, 2003), 241.

23. Wendy Brown, "Neoliberalism and the End of Liberal Democracy," in *Edgework: Critical Essays on Knowledge and Politics* (Princeton, NJ: Princeton University Press, 2005), 42.

24. Nadine Brozan, "Day Care in a Family Setting," *New York Times*, May 3, 1982.

25. "ABC-TV Demos Appear Improving Despite Household Ratings Slump," *Variety*, Oct. 22, 1986, 450, 478.

26. Andree Brooks, "Fluid Work Hours Urged for Day Care," *New York Times*, June 9, 1984; Janice Castro, "Home Is Where the Heart Is: Companies Try Harder to Meet the Personal Needs of Workers," *Time*, Oct. 3, 1988, 46–53; "Women's Roles vs. Social Norms," *New York Times*, Dec. 30, 1986.

27. In addition to those studied here, see *Who's the Boss?* (ABC, 1984–1992), *Charles in Charge* (CBS, 1984–1985; first-run syndication 1987–1990), *Silver Spoons* (NBC, 1982–1986), and *Growing Pains* (ABC, 1985–1992).

28. Quoted in Hitchings, "Today's Choices," 104.

29. Wallis, "Child Care Dilemma," 54.

30. Ellen Galinsky and Deborah Phillips, "The Day-Care Debate," *Parents*, Nov. 1988, 112–115; Langway, "Superwoman Squeeze," 72–79; Wallis, "Is Day Care Bad for Babies?," 63; Russell Watson, "Five Steps to Good Day Care," *Newsweek*, Sept. 10, 1984, 21.

31. "Stranger in the Night," *Mr. Belvedere*, Season One (ABC, Mar. 15, 1985).

32. Trotter, "Project Day-Care," 32.

33. "Heather's Tutor," *Mr. Belvedere*, Season Two (ABC, Feb. 21, 1986).

34. "Kevin's Date," *Mr. Belvedere*, Season Three (ABC, Oct. 24, 1986).

35. "Reunion," *Mr. Belvedere*, Season Three (ABC, Nov. 21, 1986).

36. Foucault, "Governmentality," 235–236.

37. "Strike," *Mr. Belvedere*, Season Two (ABC, Nov. 15, 1985).

38. Narvaez, "Housekeeper outside the Law."

39. Ibid.

40. Wallis, "Child Care Dilemma," 58.

41. "Deportation: Part 1," *Mr. Belvedere*, Season Three (ABC, Nov. 7, 1986); "Deportation: Part 2," *Mr. Belvedere*, Season Three (ABC, Nov. 14, 1986).

42. Fierman, "Child Care," 170.

43. Forbes, "Who Will Care," 29.

44. When Kate asks Allie about her ideal career, Allie replies, "I'd like to be supported," in "The Family Business," *Kate & Allie*, Season One (CBS, Apr. 23, 1984).

45. Elizabeth Erlich, "Child Care: The Private Sector Can't Do It Alone," *BusinessWeek*, Oct. 6, 1986, 52.

46. Watson, "What Price," 14–15.

47. Episodes frequently include jokes about Kate's inability to cook, and she very rarely does domestic work.

48. "The Very Loud Family," *Kate & Allie*, Season One (CBS, Mar. 26, 1984).

49. "High Anxiety," *Kate & Allie*, Season Three (CBS, Feb. 17, 1986).

50. Allie works at a movie theater in "Allie on Strike," *Kate & Allie*, Season Four (CBS, Apr. 6, 1987), and at a museum gift shop in "Kate Quits," *Kate & Allie*, Season Four (CBS, May 4, 1987).

51. "Odd Boy Out," *Kate & Allie*, Season One (CBS, Apr. 16, 1984).

52. Brozan, "Day Care in a Family Setting."

53. "Allie on Strike," *Kate & Allie*, Season Four (CBS, Apr. 6, 1987).

54. Geneva Overholser, "Working Women's Unworkable World," *New York Times*, Mar. 28, 1987.

55. Quoted in Wallis, "Child-Care Dilemma," 58.

56. Brooks, "Fluid Work Hours Urged," 48.

57. Quoted in "Women's Roles vs. Social Norms."

58. Castro, "Home Is Where the Heart Is," 48, 53.

59. "Whose Night Is It Anyway?," *My Two Dads*, Season One (NBC, Nov. 1, 1987).

60. Nikolas Rose, "Governing 'Advanced' Liberal Democracies," in *Foucault and Political Reason: Liberalism, Neo-Liberalism, and Rationalities of Government*, ed. Andrew Barry, Thomas Osborne, and Nikolas Rose (Chicago: University of Chicago Press, 1996), 59.

61. "Quality Time," *My Two Dads*, Season One (NBC, Dec. 6, 1987).

62. "Blast From the Past," *My Two Dads*, Season Two (NBC, Jan. 11, 1989).

63. "The Man in the Pink Slip," *My Two Dads*, Season Two (NBC, Feb. 8, 1989).

64. "Story with a Twist," *My Two Dads*, Season Two (NBC, Feb. 22, 1989) and "Playing with Fire," *My Two Dads*, Season Two (NBC, Mar. 1, 1989).

65. "Getting Smart," *My Two Dads*, Season Two (NBC, Jul. 29, 1989).

66. "Story with a Twist."

67. Majia Holmer Nadesan, *Governmentality, Biopower, and Everyday Life* (New York: Routledge, 2008), 33.

68. "The Family in Question," *My Two Dads*, Season One (NBC, May 9, 1988).

69. "Child Care Grows as a Benefit," 60.

70. Watson, "What Price," 20.

71. Forbes, "Who Will Care," 29.

72. In the episode "Fuller House," *Full House*, Season Four (ABC, Feb. 22, 1991), which follows the two-part episode in which Jesse and Becky get married, Michelle guilt-trips them to remain in the house, which they do for the rest of the series, even after having twins of their own.

73. "The Seven-Month Itch Part 2," *Full House*, Season One (ABC, Mar. 18, 1988).

74. "Jingle Hell," *Full House*, Season Two (ABC, Nov. 11, 1988).

75. "Working Mothers," *Full House*, Season Two (ABC, Feb. 3, 1989).

76. Jesse maintains this role when his wife goes back to work following the birth of their twins in the episode "Play It Again, Jesse," *Full House*, Season Five (ABC, Jan. 7, 1992).

77. "Danny in Charge," *Full House*, Season Four (ABC, Dec. 14, 1990).

78. "Our Very First Night," *Full House*, Season One (ABC, Sept. 25, 1987).

79. "A Pox in Our House," *Full House*, Season One (ABC, Jan. 29, 1988).

80. Chapman, "Executive Guilt," 30–37; "Jobs and Child Care Studied," *New York Times*, May 11, 1987; Wallis, "Child Care Dilemma," 54–60.

81. Nikolas Rose, *Governing the Soul: The Shaping of the Private Self*, 2nd ed. (London: Free Association Press, 1999), 213.

82. "The Return of Grandma," *Full House*, Season One (ABC, Oct. 9, 1987); "The Seven-Month Itch Part 1," *Full House*, Season One (ABC, Mar. 11, 1988); "The Seven-Month Itch Part 2"; "Slumber Party," *Full House*, Season Four (ABC, Oct. 12, 1990); "Danny in Charge"; "A House Divided," *Full House*, Season Seven (ABC, May 17, 1994).

83. Rose, "Governing 'Advanced' Liberal Democracies," 41.

84. Of course, as Joan Williams points out, childcare workers are hardly "strangers" to the children in their care. Joan Williams, *Unbending Gender: Why Family and Work Conflict and What to Do about It* (Oxford: Oxford University Press, 2000), 32; Andree Brooks, "Opening Centers in Apartments," *New York Times*, Oct. 16, 1988.

CHAPTER 4 — "YOU COULD CALL ME THE MAID—BUT I WOULDN'T"

1. Geneva Overholser, "Working Women's Unworkable World," *New York Times*, Mar. 28, 1987.

2. Lynn Langway, "The Superwoman Squeeze," *Newsweek*, May 19, 1980, 72.

3. Arlie Russell Hochschild with Anne Machung, *The Second Shift* (New York: Penguin Books: 2003), 20.

4. Susan J. Douglas and Meredith W. Michaels, *The Mommy Myth: The Idealization of Motherhood and How It Has Undermined All Women* (New York: Free Press, 2004); Bonnie J. Dow, *Prime-Time Feminism: Television, Media Culture, and the Women's Movement Since 1970* (Philadelphia: University of Pennsylvania Press, 1996); Susan Faludi, *Backlash: The Undeclared War against American Women* (New York: Crown, 1991); Philip Green, *Cracks in the Pedestal: Ideology and Gender in Hollywood* (Amherst: University of Massachusetts Press, 1998); Sarah Harwood, *Family Fictions: Representations of the Family in 1980s Hollywood Cinema* (New York: St. Martin's Press, 1997); E. Ann Kaplan, *Motherhood and Representation: The Mother in Popular Culture and Melodrama* (London: Routledge, 1992); Tania Modleski, *Feminism without Women: Culture and Criticism in a "Postfeminist" Age* (New York: Routledge, 1991); Elizabeth G. Traube, *Dreaming Identities: Class, Gender, and Generation in 1980s Hollywood Movies* (Boulder, CO: Westview, 1992); Mary Douglas Vavrus, "Domesticating Patriarchy: Hegemonic Masculinity and Television's 'Mr. Mom,'" *Critical Studies in Media Communication* 19, no. 3 (2002): 352–375.

5. Wendy Brown, *States of Injury: Power and Freedom in Late Modernity* (Princeton, NJ: Princeton University Press, 1995), 155.

6. Ibid., 161.

7. Ibid., 164.

8. Ibid., 165. Emphasis added.

9. Ella Taylor, *Prime-Time Families: Television Culture in Postwar America* (Berkeley: University of California Press, 1989), 157.

10. Brown, *States of Injury*, 162.

11. Barbara Ehrenreich and Arlie Russell Hochschild, "Introduction," in *Global Woman: Nannies, Maids, and Sex Workers in the New Economy*, eds. Barbara Ehrenreich and Arlie Russell Hochschild (New York: Holt, 2002), 4.

12. Rosie Cox, *The Servant Problem: Domestic Employment in a Global Economy* (London: I. B. Tauris, 2006), 53.

13. Patricia Mellencamp, *High Anxiety: Catastrophe, Scandal, Age, and Comedy* (Bloomington: Indiana University Press, 1992), 351.

14. Jennifer Fuller, "The Black 'Sex Goddess' in the Living Room," *Feminist Media Studies* 11, no. 3 (2011): 265–281.

15. "Benson's Groupie," *Benson*, Season Two (ABC, Dec. 19, 1980) and "Embarrassing Moments," *Benson*, Season Five (ABC, Jan. 20, 1984).

16. Taylor reveals this official title in "The Layoff," *Benson*, Season One (ABC, Oct. 25, 1979).

17. In, for example, "Conflict of Interest," *Benson*, Season One (ABC, Oct. 18, 1979) and "Don't Quote Me," *Benson*, Season One (ABC, Nov. 22, 1979).

18. "Change," *Benson*, Season One (ABC, Sep. 13, 1979).

19. Arlie Russell Hochschild, *The Time Bind: When Work Becomes Home and Home Becomes Work* (New York: Henry Holt, 1997).

20. "Kraus Affair," *Benson*, Season One (ABC, Jan. 31, 1980).

21. Barbara Ehrenreich and Deirdre English, *For Her Own Good: 150 Years of the Experts' Advice to Women* (New York: Anchor Books, 1978), 162.

22. Susan Strasser, *Never Done: A History of American Housework* (New York: Henry Holt and Company, 2000), 247.

23. Ehrenreich and English, *For Her Own Good*, 168.

24. "Trust Me," *Benson*, Season One (ABC, Sep. 20, 1979).

25. "Checkmate," *Benson*, Season One (ABC, Feb, 7, 1980).

26. "Don't Quote Me."

27. Ehrenreich and English, *For Her Own Good*, 163.

28. Strasser, *Never Done*, 249.

29. "Old Man Gatling," *Benson*, Season One (ABC, Mar. 20, 1980).

30. Ehrenreich and English, *For Her Own Good*, 179.

31. Herman Gray, "Television and the New Black Man: Black Male Images in Prime-Time Situation Comedy," *Media, Culture and Society* 8 (1986): 223–242, 233.

32. "Benson in Love," *Benson*, Season One (ABC, Oct. 4, 1979).

33. "The Apartment," *Benson*, Season Two (ABC, Jan. 23, 1981).

34. L. S. Kim, "Maid in Color: The Figure of the Racialized Domestic in American Television," (PhD diss., University of California, Los Angeles, 1997).

35. "The President's Double," *Benson*, Season One (ABC, Sep. 27, 1979); Robert Guillaume, interview by Meryl Marshall, *Emmy TV Legends*, Archive of American Television, Mar. 24, 1999.

36. "Takin' It to the Streets," *Benson*, Season One (ABC, Mar. 27, 1980).

37. "One Strike, You're Out," *Benson*, Season One (ABC, Dec. 27, 1979).

38. "Working Girls," *Who's the Boss?*, Season Five (ABC, Apr. 11, 1989).

39. Modleski, *Feminism without Women*, 85–86.

40. Kaplan, *Motherhood and Representation*, 188.

41. Faludi, *Backlash*, 155. N.B.: Angela only has one child, Jonathan.

42. "Savor the Veal (Part Three)," *Who's the Boss?*, Season Eight (ABC, Apr. 25, 1992).

43. Elspeth Probyn, "New Traditionalism and Post-Feminism: TV Does the Home," in *Feminist Television Criticism: A Reader*, eds. Charlotte Brunsdon, Julie D'Acci, and Lynn Spigel (Oxford: Oxford University Press, 1997), 126–137.

44. Jeffrey Sconce, "What If?: Charting Television's New Textual Boundaries," in *Television after TV: Essays on a Medium in Transition*, eds. Lynn Spigel and Jan Olsson (Durham, NC: Duke University Press, 2004), 95.

45. "Protecting the President," *Who's the Boss?*, Season One (Jan. 22, 1985).

46. Jim appears in "Truth in Dating," *Who's the Boss?*, Season One (ABC, Dec. 4, 1984); "Angela's Ex (2)," *Who's the Boss?*, Season One (ABC, Feb. 12, 1985); "Junior Executive," *Who's the Boss?*, Season Two (ABC, Jan. 7, 1986); "Not With My Client, You Don't," *Who's the Boss?*, Season Two (ABC, Mar. 18, 1986); "Angela Gets Fired (1)," *Who's the Boss?*, Season Three (ABC, Sept. 23, 1986); "Mona's Limo," *Who's the Boss?*, Season Three (ABC, Nov. 4, 1986).

47. "Angela Gets Fired (2)," *Who's the Boss?*, Season Three (ABC, Sept. 30, 1986). Even after Angela opens her own agency, she still occasionally has run-ins with Jim, who tries to steal her first client in "Mona's Limo."

48. Lauren Rabinovitz, "Ms.-Representation: The Politics of Feminist Sitcoms," in *Television, History, and American Culture: Feminist Critical Essays*, eds. Mary Beth Haralovich and Lauren Rabinovitz (Durham, NC: Duke University Press, 1999), 145.

49. Mellencamp, *High Anxiety*, 351.

50. "Angela's First Fight," *Who's the Boss?*, Season One (ABC, Oct. 23, 1984).

51. "Guess Who's Coming Forever?," *Who's the Boss?*, Season One (ABC, Jan. 29, 1985).

52. "Housekeepers Unite," *Who's the Boss?*, Season Four (ABC, Mar. 15, 1988).

53. In "Protecting the President," Angela literally tells Tony, "I'm pulling rank, this is your employer speaking" when he doesn't want to tell her what Jim Peterson really said about her.

54. "Paint Your Wagon," *Who's the Boss?*, Season One (ABC, Jan. 15, 1985).

55. Brown, *States of Injury*, 154.

56. The following episodes all deal explicitly with Tony's working-class background and economic status: "Truth in Dating"; "Requiem," *Who's the Boss?*, Season One (ABC, Dec. 18, 1984); "Keeping Up with Marci," *Who's the Boss?*, Season One (ABC, Apr. 9, 1985); "Ad Man Micelli," *Who's the Boss?*, Season Two (ABC, Oct. 8, 1985); "Junior Executive"; "Daddy's Little Montague Girl," *Who's the Boss?*, Season Three (ABC, Oct. 21, 1986); "Housekeepers Unite"; "Model Daughter," *Who's the Boss?*, Season Four (ABC, Mar. 22, 1988); "It's Somebody's Birthday," *Who's the Boss?*, Season Five (ABC, May 16, 1989); "A Well-Kept Housekeeper," *Who's the Boss?*, Season Eight (ABC, Nov. 2, 1991); "Grandmommie Dearest," *Who's the Boss?*, Season Eight (ABC, Nov. 23, 1991); "Tony Can You Spare a Dime?," *Who's the Boss?*, Season Eight (ABC, Jan. 4, 1992).

57. "Life's a Ditch," *Who's the Boss?*, Season Six (ABC, Sept. 26, 1989).

58. Cox, *The Servant Problem*, 126.

59. "Where the Auction Is," *Charles in Charge*, Season Three (First-run syndication, Apr. 20, 1988); "It's a Blunderfull Life," *Charles in Charge*, Season Four (First-run syndication, Aug. 22, 1989); "Let's Quake a Deal," *Charles in Charge*, Season Five (First-run syndication, May 11, 1990); "The Pickle Plot," *Charles in Charge*, Season Three (First-run syndication, Feb. 10, 1988).

60. Bridget Anderson, "Just Another Job? The Commodification of Domestic Labor," in *Global Woman: Nannies, Maids, and Sex Workers in the New Economy*, eds. Barbara Ehrenreich and Arlie Russell Hochschild (New York: Holt, 2002), 106.

61. "Weekend Weary," *Charles in Charge*, Season Two (First-run syndication, Apr. 25, 1987).

62. "Yule Laff," *Charles in Charge*, Season Three (First-run syndication, Dec. 24, 1987).

63. "The Organization Man," *Charles in Charge*, Season Four (First-run syndication, Sep. 16, 1989).

64. Hochschild, *The Second Shift*, 9.

65. "Dear Charles," *Charles in Charge*, Season Three (First-run syndication, Feb. 27, 1988).

66. "Big Bang," *Charles in Charge*, Season Four (First-run syndication, Aug. 22, 1989).

67. "The Pickle Plot."

68. "Buddy in Charge," *Charles in Charge*, Season Two (First-run syndication, Mar. 28, 1987).

69. "The Naked Truth," *Charles in Charge*, Season Two (First-run syndication, Jan. 10, 1987).

70. "Buddy in Charge."

71. "Dutiful Dreamer," *Charles in Charge*, Season Three (First-run syndication, Apr. 23, 1988).

72. "Summer Together, Fall Apart," *Charles in Charge*, Season Five (First-run syndication, Dec. 30, 1989).

73. "Feud for Thought," *Charles in Charge*, Season Two (First-run syndication, Jan. 17, 1987).

74. "Amityville," *Charles in Charge*, Season Two (First-run syndication, Jan. 3, 1987).

75. Kim, "Maid in Color," 3.

76. "Amityville," "Mama Mia!," *Charles in Charge*, Season Two (First-run syndication, Apr. 18, 1987).

77. "Buddy Comes to Dinner," *Charles in Charge*, Season Two (First-run syndication, Feb. 14, 1987); "Mama Mia!"

78. "Buddy in Charge."

79. "Yule Laff."

80. "Dear Charles."

81. "Piece of Cake," *Charles in Charge*, Season Three (First-run syndication, Jan. 2, 1988).

82. "Charles 'R' Us," *Charles in Charge*, Season One (CBS, Feb. 13, 1985).

83. Elayne Rapping, *Media-tions: Forays into the Culture and Gender Wars* (Boston: South End Press, 1994), 149.

84. "Home for the Holidays," *Charles in Charge*, Season One (CBS, Dec. 19, 1984); "Pressure from Grandma," *Charles in Charge*, Season One (CBS, Jan. 30, 1985); and "Meet Grandpa," *Charles in Charge*, Season One (CBS, Apr. 3, 1985).

85. "Jill's Decision," *Charles in Charge*, Season One (CBS, Jan. 23, 1985).

86. Alan Nadel, *Flatlining on the Field of Dreams: Cultural Narratives in the Films of President Reagan's America* (New Brunswick, NJ: Rutgers University Press, 1997), 88.

87. Brown, *States of Injury*, 147. Original emphasis.

88. In the pilot episode of *Who's the Boss?*, when Mona convinces Angela to hire Tony, Mona reminds her that Jonathan's child psychiatrist has insisted that he have a "male role model." "Pilot," *Who's the Boss?*, Season One (ABC, Sept. 20, 1984).

89. Traube, *Dreaming Identities*, 124–125.

90. "Pressure from Grandma"; "Charles 'R' Us"; "The Pickle Plot"; "Taylor's Bid," *Benson*, Season One (ABC, Dec. 13, 1979); "Angela's Ex (2)"; "Frankie and Tony are Lovers," *Who's the Boss?*, Season Four (ABC, Sept. 22, 1987); "Yellow Submarine," *Who's the Boss?*,

Season Four (ABC, Dec. 15, 1987); "Inherit the Wine," *Who's the Boss?*, Season Seven (ABC, Nov. 27, 1990); "Savor the Veal (3)."

91. Douglas and Michaels, *The Mommy Myth*, 263.

92. Jane Feuer, *Seeing through the Eighties: Television and Reaganism* (Durham, NC: Duke University Press, 1995), 2.

CHAPTER 5 — DISRUPTING THE FANTASY

1. Michael Schaller, *Right Turn: American Life in the Reagan-Bush Era 1980–1992* (New York: Oxford University Press, 2007), 120–126.

2. Matthew McAllister, *The Commercialization of American Culture* (Thousand Oaks, CA: Sage, 1996).

3. L. S. Kim, "Maid in Color: The Figure of the Racialized Domestic in American Television," (PhD diss., University of California, Los Angeles, 1997), 26.

4. "Syndie Loves Off-Net Sitcoms; Looks Like Embassy Got Things Rolling as 'Facts' Tops $111-Mil," *Variety*, Jul. 4, 1984, 49; John Dempsey, "TV Stations Going Bananas in Off-Net Program Bidding; 'Cheers' Chug-a-Lugs a Record," *Variety*, June 27, 1984, 1; "MCA Strikes It Rich: 'Gimme a Break' Could Hit $100-Mil Mark; 'Knight Rider,' 'Simon,' 'A-Team' in Wings," *Variety*, June 13, 1984, 41.

5. "Katie the Crook," *Gimme a Break!*, Season One (NBC, Oct. 29, 1981).

6. Jennifer Fuller, "The 'Black Sex Goddess' in the Living Room: Making Interracial Sex 'Laughable' on *Gimme a Break*," *Feminist Media Studies* 11 (2011): 275.

7. Richard Butsch, "A Half Century in Class and Gender in American TV Domestic Sitcoms," *Cercles* 8 (2003), 21.

8. Ibid.

9. "Julie's First Love," *Gimme a Break!*, Season One (NBC, Jan. 7, 1982).

10. "The Auction," *The Cosby Show*, Season Two (NBC, Jan. 9, 1986); "Nell's Ex," *Gimme a Break!*, Season One (NBC, Jan. 14, 1982).

11. "The Custody Suit," *Gimme a Break!*, Season Two (NBC, Feb. 10, 1983).

12. "Katie the Crook."

13. "Mom's Birthday," *Gimme a Break!*, Season One (NBC, Nov. 19, 1981).

14. "Julie's First Love."

15. Melissa Williams, "'Excuse the Mess, but We Live Here': Class, Gender, and Identity in the Post–Cold War Working-Class Family Sitcom" (Ph.D. diss., University of Minnesota, 2009), 8.

16. Kim, "Maid in Color," 3.

17. "The Emergency," *Gimme a Break!*, Season One (NBC, Feb. 4, 1982).

18. Jennifer Fuller, "*Gimme a Break!* and the Limits of the Modern Mammy," in *Watching While Black: Centering the Television of Black Audiences*, ed. Beretta E. Smith-Shomade (New Brunswick, NJ: Rutgers University Press, 2012), 105.

19. Ibid., 114.

20. "Take My Baby, Please," *Gimme a Break!*, Season Two (NBC, Oct. 30, 1982).

21. "The Custody Suit."

22. "Julie Smokes," *Gimme a Break!*, Season Two (NBC, Jan. 13, 1983).

23. "Love, Kidney," *Gimme a Break!*, Season Two (NBC, Jan. 6, 1983).

24. Fuller, "*Gimme a Break!* and the Limits of the Modern Mammy," 117.

25. Fuller, "The 'Black Sex Goddess' in the Living Room," 276.

26. "Grandma Fools Around," *Gimme a Break!*, Season One (NBC, Feb. 25, 1982).

27. "Monkey See, Monkey Do," *Gimme a Break!*, Season Four (Mar. 30, 1985).

28. "The Emergency."

29. Jacqueline Najuma Stewart, *Migrating to the Movies: Cinema and Black Urban Modernity* (Berkeley: University of California Press, 2005), 83.

30. "Katie the Crook."

31. "Samantha's Protest," *Gimme a Break!*, Season Three (NBC, Jan. 19, 1984).

32. "An Unmarried Couple," *Gimme a Break!*, Season One (NBC, Apr. 1, 1982).

33. "Take My Baby, Please."

34. "Your Prisoner Is Dead," *Gimme a Break!*, Season One (NBC, Dec. 10, 1981).

35. "The Centerfold, Part 1," *Gimme a Break!*, Season Two (NBC, Jan. 20, 1983).

36. Daniel Marcus, *Happy Days and Wonder Years: The Fifties and the Sixties in Contemporary Cultural Politics* (New Brunswick, NJ: Rutgers University Press, 2004), 61–2.

37. Williams, "Excuse the Mess," 76.

38. "Sam's Imaginary Friend," *Gimme a Break!*, Season Two (NBC, Oct. 16, 1982).

39. "Julie's Rejection," *Gimme a Break!*, Season One (NBC, Dec. 17, 1981).

40. "Sam Faces Death," *Gimme a Break!*, Season Two (NBC, Dec. 4, 1982).

41. "Take My Baby, Please."

42. Marcus, *Happy Days and Wonder Years*, 67.

43. Ibid., 92.

44. Schaller, *Right Turn*, 161.

45. "The Chief's Gay Evening," *Gimme a Break!*, Season Two (NBC, Nov. 13, 1982).

46. Fuller, "*Gimme a Break!* and the Limits of the Modern Mammy," 110.

47. "The Robbery," *Gimme a Break!*, Season One (NBC, Mar. 25, 1982).

48. "Joey's Train," *Gimme a Break!*, Season Five (Sep. 14, 1985).

49. "Katie's Korner," *Gimme a Break!*, Season Five (Apr. 5, 1986).

50. "Sam Goes to College," *Gimme a Break!*, Season Six (Sep. 24, 1986).

51. "Nell Goes Back to New York," *Gimme a Break!*, Season Six (Oct. 15, 1986).

52. Marcus, *Happy Days and Wonder Years*, 121.

53. Schaller, *Right Turn*, 125–126.

54. Williams, "Excuse the Mess," 53.

55. "We're in the Money," *Roseanne*, Season One (ABC, Oct. 25, 1988).

56. "Inherit the Wind," *Roseanne*, Season Two (ABC, Sept. 12, 1989).

57. "April Fool's Day," *Roseanne*, Season Two (ABC, Apr. 10, 1990).

58. Rena Bartos, *The Moving Target: What Every Marketer Should Know about Women* (New York: The Free Press, 1982), 112.

59. "Bird Is the Word," *Roseanne*, Season Three (ABC, Nov. 13, 1990).

60. This t-shirt was actually first worn on the series by Becky in "Sweet Dreams," *Roseanne*, Season Two (ABC, Nov. 7, 1989). Roseanne first wore it in the next episode, "We Gather Together," *Roseanne*, Season Two (ABC, Nov. 21, 1989). Many different characters wore it throughout the rest of the series' run.

61. "Looking for Loans in All the Wrong Places," *Roseanne*, Season Five (ABC, Oct. 20, 1992).

62. "Lobocop," *Roseanne*, Season Two (ABC, Dec. 5, 1989).

63. "The Test," *Roseanne*, Season Three (ABC, Sept. 18, 1990).

64. Williams, "Excuse the Mess," 88–89.

65. Judine Mayerle, "*Roseanne*—How Did You Get Inside My House?: A Case Study of a Hit Blue-Collar Situation Comedy," *Journal of Popular Culture* 24 (Spring 1991): 84.

66. "Daddy's Little Montague Girl," *Who's the Boss?*, Season Three (ABC, Oct. 21, 1986).

67. Mayerle, *"Roseanne,"* 73.

68. "Lovers' Lane," *Roseanne*, Season One (ABC, Dec. 6, 1988).

69. Kathleen Rowe, *The Unruly Woman: Gender and the Genres of Laughter* (Austin: University of Texas Press, 1995), 60.

70. Julie Bettie, "Class Dismissed?: *Roseanne* and the Changing Face of Working-Class Iconography," *Social Text* 45 (Winter 1995): 137.

71. Patricia Mellencamp, *High Anxiety: Catastrophe, Scandal, Age, and Comedy* (Bloomington: Indiana University Press, 1992), 341.

72. Williams, "Excuse the Mess," 108.

73. "Life and Stuff," *Roseanne*, Season One (ABC, Oct. 18, 1988).

74. "Crime and Punishment," *Roseanne*, Season Five (ABC, Jan. 5, 1993).

75. "Saturday," *Roseanne*, Season One (ABC, Jan. 10, 1989).

76. "Hair," *Roseanne*, Season Two (ABC, Feb. 6, 1990).

77. Rowe, *The Unruly Woman*, 79.

78. "Workin' Overtime," *Roseanne*, Season One (ABC, Mar. 14, 1989).

79. Bettie, "Class Dismissed?" 132.

80. Ibid.

81. Mellencamp, *High Anxiety*, 339.

82. "Father's Day," *Roseanne*, Season One (ABC, Feb. 7, 1989).

83. "Let's Call It Quits," *Roseanne*, Season One (ABC, May 2, 1989).

84. "Guilt by Disassociation," *Roseanne*, Season Two (ABC, Sept. 26, 1989).

85. "Chicken Hearts," *Roseanne*, Season Two (ABC, Jan. 2, 1990).

86. "Looking for Loans in All the Wrong Places."

87. Rowe, *The Unruly Woman*, 83.

88. "An Officer and a Gentleman," *Roseanne*, Season Two (ABC, Jan. 23, 1990).

89. Mellencamp, *High Anxiety*, 340.

90. "Home Ec," *Roseanne*, Season Three (ABC, Feb, 5, 1991).

91. Sut Jhally and Justin Lewis, *Enlightened Racism: The Cosby Show, Audiences, and the Myth of the American Dream* (Boulder, CO: Westview, 1992), 5.

92. "All of Me," *Roseanne*, Season Two (ABC, Feb. 20, 1990).

93. "Crime and Punishment."

94. "War and Peace," *Roseanne*, Season Five (ABC, Jan. 12, 1993).

CONCLUSION

1. "Few Rookies on CBS-TV: Program Exec Harvey Shephard Defends Decision to Add Only 3 ½-Hrs. of New Series," *Variety*, May 16, 1984: 56; Bob Knight, "Women Stir Comatose ABC-TV: Third-Place Network Perks Up with Improved Femme Demos," *Variety*, June 18, 1986, 47+.

2. Ella Taylor, *Prime-Time Families: Television Culture in Postwar America* (Berkeley: University of California Press, 1989), 157.

3. Jennifer Gillan, *Television Brandcasting: The Return of the Content-Promotion Hybrid* (New York: Routledge, 2015), 108.

4. Thomas Doherty, *Teenagers and Teenpics: The Juvenilization of American Movies in the 1950s* (Philadelphia: Temple University Press, 2002), 169.

5. Gillan, *Television Brandcasting*, 132.

6. Quoted in Dan Snierson and Marc Snetiker, "Thank Goodness! An Oral History of ABC's TGIF," *Entertainment Weekly*, July 27, 2017.

7. Steve Coe, "Bickley/Warren: ABC's Powerful TGIF Team," *Broadcasting & Cable*, Oct. 17, 1994: 30.

8. Ibid.

9. "Thank God It's Friday," *Growing Pains*, Season Two (ABC, Feb. 10, 1987).

10. Snierson and Snetiker, "Thank Goodness!"

11. "Syndication Roll-Out for 'Growing Pains' to Feature PSA Promos," *Broadcasting*, Aug. 7, 1989: 66.

12. Ibid.

13. Gillan, *Television Brandcasting*, 20.

14. Amanda Renee Keeler, "Premature Adulthood: Alcoholic Moms and Teenage Adults in the ABC Afterschool Specials," *Quarterly Review of Film and Video* 33.6 (2016): 483–500.

15. Gary David Goldberg, *Sit, Ubu, Sit: How I Went from Brooklyn to Hollywood with the Same Woman, the Same Dog, and a Lot Less Hair* (New York: Three Rivers Press, 2008), 42.

16. *Variety*, Aug. 22, 1984, 86–87.

17. Gael Sweeney, "The Face on the Lunchbox: Television's Construction of the Teen Idol," *Velvet Light Trap* 33 (Spring 1994): 49–59, 56.

18. Peter Engel, *I Was Saved by the Bell: Stories of Life, Love, and Dreams That Do Come True* (Lexington, KY: Top Hat Words, 2016), 165.

19. Ibid., 187.

20. "Lack of Kid Appeal Affecting 'Kate & Allie' Syndie Prospects," *Variety*, June 4, 1986, 40.

21. "Syndie Fever Hot For 'Webster' As Par Claims 1st-Round Records," *Variety*, Aug. 7, 1985, 42.

22. *Variety*, Jul. 31, 1985, 45–52.

23. Derek Kompare, *Rerun Nation: How Repeats Invented American Television* (New York: Routledge, 2005), 136.

24. David Tobenkin, "Warner Touts Young-Skewing Shows," *Broadcasting & Cable*, July 31, 1995: 21.

25. Lynette Rice, "Tarses, Bloomberg Present Unified Front," *Broadcasting & Cable*, July 28, 1997: 17.

26. Joe Schlosser, "Networks Write New Stories in November," *Broadcasting & Cable*, Dec. 4, 2000: 33.

27. Quoted in Snierson and Snetiker, "Thank Goodness!"

28. Ron Becker, *Gay TV and Straight America* (New Brunswick, NJ: Rutgers University Press, 2006), 93.

29. Ibid., 95.

30. Arlie Russell Hochschild, *The Time Bind: When Work Becomes Home and Home Becomes Work* (New York: Henry Holt, 1997), 209–210.

INDEX

ABOUT THE AUTHOR

Alice Leppert is an assistant professor of media and communication studies at Ursinus College. Her essays have appeared in *Television and New Media, Cinema Journal, Celebrity Studies,* and *Genders,* and in several edited collections. She serves as the book review editor for *Film Criticism.*